Library and Information Systems

From Alexandrian Heritage to Social Networking

(Essays in Honour of Prof. S. Parthasarathy)

Library and Information Systems

From Alexandrian Heritage to Social Networking

(Essays in Honour of Prof. S. Parthasarathy)

Editors

K.S. Raghavan

K.N. Prasad

Published By:

Ess Ess Publications

For

Sarada Ranganathan Endowment for Library Science

Bangalore

2009

Published by:
Ess Ess Publications
4837/24, Ansari Road,
Darya Ganj,
New Delhi-110 002.
Tel.: 23260807, 41563444
Fax: 41563334
E-mail: info@essessreference.com
www.essessreference.com

For:
Sarada Ranganathan Endowment for Library Science
702, 'Upstairs', 42nd Cross, III Block,
Rajajinagar,
Bangalore-560 010.
Tel. : 080-23305109
E-mail: srels@dataone.in

Rs.1175/-

First Published 2009

ISBN: 978-81-7000-549-0

Printed at Salasar Imaging Systems

PRINTED IN INDIA

Prof. Srirangapattanam Parthasarathy
23rd August 1917
:: NamostuTe ::

CONTENTS

Foreword

Festschrift Committee

LIBRARY AND INFORMATION SYSTEMS/SERVICES

1. Bibliotheca Alexandrina: Reborn from the Ashes of History 1
   Jacques Tocatlian
2. Information Literacy and Emerging Knowledge Economy in India 16
   S.B. Ghosh
   Anup Kumar Das
3. National Information System in Iran: Superior Strides in Building Up an Information Technology Infrastructure 45
   Abbas Gilvari
4. Moving India into the 21st Century Knowledge Economy: Outlines of a Proposal for Building a National Information Infrastructure 77
   M N Seetharaman

LIBRARY AND INFORMATION SYSTEMS/ SERVICES - SPECIAL

5. The AGRIS Search System - Some Ideas for a Semantics-and Knowledge Network-enabled Simple Search System 111
   L J Haravu
6. Elements of a Corporate Information 124

System in the Knowledge Society Era
Vivek Patkar

7. Importance of Archives and Archival Collection Development 142
A. Ratnakar

SOCIAL NETWORKING

8. Mobile Phones, Wimax, Web 2.0 and YouTube in Social Networking . 150
A. Neelameghan

9. The People's Network: What Is In It for Us? 168
K. Sankaraiah

INTELLECTUAL PROPERTY RIGHTS / RIGHT TO INFORMATION

10. Intellectual Property Rights and Library and Information Professionals 190
S. Amba

11. Right to Information Act in India 219
K.N. Prasad

HUMAN RESOURCES DEVELOPMENT

12. A Fresh Look at the Provision of Education and Training for Library and Information Professionals in India in 21st Century 233
R. Satyanarayana

13. Manpower Development for Technical Libraries: An Indian Perspective 567
A. Amudhavalli

14. Education of New Information Professionals in the Electronic / Digital Environment ... 275
S. Seetharama

BIBLIOMETRICS

15. A Quantitative Study of Software Literature in India with Comparison to World Literature 293
Bibhuti Bhusan Sahoo
I K Ravichandra Rao

OTHER ESSAYS

16. Relationships in Multi-Lingual Thesauri in Humanities: Issues and Case Study 318
A. Neelameghan
K.S. Raghavan

17. Classified Catalogue Code Today 341
B K Sen

18. Change: a Precursor of Knowledge 349
G. J. Narayana

19. Ghana Raga Pancharatna Kritis of Sri Tyagaraja: A Model of Fusion of Lyrics, Music and Rhythm: An analytical Study 371
T.N. Rajan

PROF. S. PARTHASARATHY: APPRECIATIONS AND LIFE SKETCH

20. The Assiduous *Mama* as Known to Ranganathan Yogeshwar 386
R. Yogeshwar

21. The Incomparable Prof. S. Parthasarathy 397
K.S. Deshpande

22. Our Professor, the Grandmaster of Information Science 402
B. Garudadwajan

23. S. Parthasarathy: A Tribute on his 92nd Birthday from a Friend and Former Colleague 406
P.K. Garde

24. Profile of Prof. S. Parthasarathy: Excerpts 410

from an Interview Session
Dr. Samyukta Ravi

25. Bio-Data of Prof. S. Parthasarathy 429

CONTRIBUTING AUTHORS 447

M. S. SWAMINATHAN RESEARCH FOUNDATION

M. S. Swaminathan
Chairman

FOREWORD

Prof S Parthasarathy's life and work have been sources of inspiration and guidance to numerous scholars and scientists in the field of library science, documentation and information science. He has been a true disciple of the legendary Dr S R Ranganathan. He developed the Indian National Scientific Documentation Centre (INSDOC) and converted a vision into an outstanding accomplishment in the field of scientific documentation. I have had close association with him for nearly fifty years and I have found him not only to be a great scholar but a wonderful humanist. He has contributed to the growth of library and information sciences in our country in a significant and inimitable manner. He has also played a very important role in the establishment and development of the Ranganathan Centre for Information Studies with which I had the privilege of being associated in its formative years as chairman of its Board of Trustees and now as its patron.

This Festschrift, containing articles written by eminent scholars from different parts of the world, is a fitting manner of expressing our admiration and gratitude to Prof S Parthasarathy for not only his past and present contributions but also for his continued guidance. I pray for his long, healthy, and satisfying life.

M S Swaminathan

3rd Cross Street, Taramani Institutional Area, Chennai (Madras) – 600 113, INDIA
Phone: +91-44-22541698, 22542790 Fax: + 91-44-22541319
E-mail: chairman@mssrf.res.in, swami@mssrf.res.in

PROF. S. PARTHASARATHY FESTSCHRIFT COMMITTEE

CHAIRMAN

Prof. A. Neelameghan
Hon. Visiting Professor, DRTC/ISI, Bangalore-560059.
***Contact**: 216, 16th Cross, 4th Main, Bangalore 560055;*
E-mail: anm2002@vsnl.net

MEMBERS

Prof. A.Y. Asundi
Professor (Retd.) Department of Library & Information Science, Bangalore University, Bangalore
***Contact**: 77,'Parvatinilaya' 3rd Main Road, Prashanth Nagar, Bangalore 560 079.*
Ph: 080-23287786.
E-mail: ashokasundi@rediffmail.com

Prof. K.S. Deshpande
Professor and University Librarian (Retd.), Karnatak University, Dharwad
Ph: 0836-2790763
***Contact**: Ramachandra Krupa, Mahishi Road, Malamaddi, Dharwad 580 007, INDIA.*
Ph. (0836) 790763;
E-mail: ksdeshpande@yahoo.com

Prof. S.B. Ghosh
Former Professor,
Indira Gandhi National Open University,
XY-72, Sarojini Nagar, New Delhi – 110023, India.
E-mail: sbghosh@hotmail.com

Prof. M.A. Gopinath
Professor & Head (Retd.), DRTC,
Indian Statistical Institute, Bangalore 560 059
Contact: 432,'Aprameya', 10th Cross,
18th Main, J.P. Nagar II Phase,
Bangalore 560 078.
Ph: (080)23327946.
E-mail: yadugirig@yahoo.com

Prof. B. Guha
1-1609, Chittaranjan Park, New Delhi 110019.
Ph. 26273801

Mr. L.J. Haravu
Founder-Trustee, Kesavan Institute of Information and Knowledge Management, Hyderabad.
Contact: Flat No. 207, Hiland Park, 6th Main,
6th Cross, V.V. Mohalla, Mysore 570 002.
E-mail: siddartha@newgenlib.com

Ms. Heera Kapasi
Director (Retd.), American Information Resources Center, New Delhi
Contact: B 49, Gulmohar Park,
New Delhi 110 049

Prof. P.N. Kaula
C-239, Indira Nagar, Lucknow 226 016,
Uttar Pradesh

Prof. P.B. Mangla
EB-210, Maya Enclave, New Delhi 110064.
E-mail: manglapb@yahoo.co.in

Mr. H.R. Mohan
Associate VP (Systems), The Hindu,
859 Anna Salai, Chennai 600002.
E-mail: hrmohan@vsnl.com

Dr. K.N. Prasad
Executive Officer, Sarada Ranganathan Endowment for Library Science,
702, 42nd Cross, 3rd Block, Rajajinagar,
Bangalore 560 010.
Ph: (080) 23305109;
E-mail: srels@dataone.in

Prof. K.S. Raghavan
Professor, Documentation Research and Training Centre,
Indian Statistical Institute, 8th Mile, Mysore Road,
Bangalore 560059.
E-mail: raghavan@isibang.ac.in ; ksragav@hotmail.com

Prof. T.N. Rajan
C-343, East-end Apts. Mayurvihar Ph. 1 Ext. Delhi 110 096;
Ph. (011) 22742362

Dr. A. Ratnakar
O 13, 'Niveditakunj', Sector X, R K Puram,
New Delhi 110022, India.
E-mail: aspari_r@hotmail.com

Prof. I.K. Ravichandra Rao
Professor and Head, Documentation Research
and Training Centre, Indian statistical Institute,
8th Mile, Mysore Road, Bangalore 560 059.
E-mail: ikrrao@hotmail.com

Dr. (Ms.) Renu Arora
Head, Training Division, NISCAIR, 14,
Satsang Vihar Marg, New Delhi 100 067

Mr. N.V. Sathyanarayana
Chairman and Managing Director,
Informatics (India) Pvt Ltd., No.194,
R.V. Road, Basavanagudi, Bangalore 560 004.
Ph.: 91-80-40387777
E-mail: info@informindia.co.in

Prof. R. Sathyanarayana
Professor & Head (Retd.).
Faculty of Library & Information Science,
Indira Gandhi National Open University, New Delhi

Prof. S. Seetharama
Professor & Head (Retd.), DRTC,
Indian Statistical Institute, Bangalore 560 059
Contact: 17, Vardarajulu Naidu Street
(Near Dasaprakash), Egmore, Chennai 600 008

Prof. (Mrs.) R.S.R. Varalakshmi
Professor, Dept. of Library & Information Science,
Andhra University, Waltair 530 003.
E-mail: rvsn1234@hotmail.com

Mr. R. Yogeshwar
Retired industrial consultant,
Contact : 39 rue deL'Ecole, L-9184,
Schrondweiler (Grand Duchy) Luxembourg.
E-mail: chriyog@pt.lu

The Sarada Ranganathan Endowment for Library Science (SRELS), founded by Dr. S.R. Ranganathan in 1961, is registered as a Charitable Endowment with the Government of India (1963).

The aims of the Endowment briefly are:

- To improve the library and information services in India
- To train library and information service personnel
- To promote the provision of efficient library and information service
- To apply research results to library and information studies

The objectives of the Endowment are:

Furthering the cause of library and information service

Organising seminars and workshops on recent developments in library and information science and related fields.

Organising periodically courses of lectures on recent developments in library and information science and related fields by national and international resource persons.

Supporting the publication of these lectures and of other nascent ideas in the field of library and information science.

There are three series of lectures organized under the auspices of the Endowment:

1. Sarada Ranganathan Endowment Lectures. (1965-);
2. Dr. S.R. Ranganathan Memorial Lectures. (1973-); and
3. Curzon-Seshachalam Endowment Lectures. (2001-).

The Endowment publishes a periodical entitled ***SRELS Journal of Information Management*** (formerly, ***Library Science with a slant to Documentation*** (from 1964 to 1988), and ***Library Science with a slant to Documentation and Information Studies*** (from 1988 to 1999)) and the texts of the series of lectures.

1

BIBLIOTHECA ALEXANDRINA: REBORN FROM THE ASHES OF HISTORY

Jacques Tocatlian[1]

If you happen to visit Alexandria in Egypt, you may be surprised to find on the seashore, along the row of old buildings, a bold, modern structure. This is the new library of Alexandria: the Bibliotheca Alexandrina.

As you examine it, you see a cylindrical structure, inclined towards the sea and partially submerged in a reflective pool of water. The sloping roof allows indirect daylight to enter the reading rooms. An Aswan granite wall, engraved with calligraphy, inscriptions and symbols from both past and present civilizations, is wrapped around the cylinder. Within the plaza, a large sphere houses a science museum and a planetarium. In the heart of the Library a space - 160 m. wide and 80 m. deep - creates a feeling of grandeur. The floor of this space terraces along 7 primary and 14 secondary levels, which produce an impressive flowing space of cascading books. The book

1. Director (Retd.), General Information Programme, UNESCO, Paris, France

stacks extend behind each terrace, protected from light. In the Library prevails a luminous and serene atmosphere, which incites study and reflection.

The Chairman of the Jury of the Architectural Competition, Mr. John Carl Warnecke, USA, in commenting on the design of the Library remarked that it is " in the form of a circle, which becomes its predominant symbol... it expresses a basic continuity to man's existence. The sun is a circle. The moon is often an emerging circle. The site of the Library looks out on the ancient harbor of Alexandria, which is in the form of a circle. The circular plan of the Library thus relates to all these elements. The circle is a symbol of unity and continuity that embraces the past, present and future... The cylindrical masonry form emerges from the earth like the rebirth of an earlier form."

Many have since described the circular building inclined towards the sea, partly submerged under the ground, as the image of the ancient Egyptian sun that, in contemporary terms, will illuminate the world with knowledge and culture.

History tells us that the Bibliotheca Alexandrina of ancient times gathered within its walls the largest collection of scrolls ever assembled at the time and attracted scientists, philosophers, mathematicians, historians, critics and poets from the Hellenistic world. It created a school of thought that pioneered the concept of research as a collaborative effort and developed a tradition of weighing the evidence and testing theory by means of observation and experiment.

Within the walls of the ancient library the circumference of the earth was calculated; the brain was identified as the focus of intelligence and the function of the heart was isolated; the natural sequence of disease was proclaimed; the technique of map drawing was developed;

the continents and constellations were mapped; the rules of syntax were elaborated; and geometry was systematized. In it, Archimedes displayed his genius in a whole series of mechanical inventions and Hero of Alexandria devised the first steam engine. Before Alexandria, knowledge was regional, but with the advent of the first universal library, knowledge became universal.

We have no record of the shape or structure of the ancient library, but the Greek geographer Strabo described it as part of a richly decorated complex of buildings and gardens. The Library, which was part of the museon, or temple of muses, was divided into departments, each headed by a dean. It contained ten large research halls, each devoted to a separate subject, botanical gardens, a zoo, dissecting rooms and an observatory. The whole environment was organized to facilitate discussion, research and reflection. Served by an aggressive acquisition policy, the great library was also used as a copying shop, a translation center and a publication office.

After several centuries the great Library was destroyed but strangely enough there are few facts and many contradictory theories about the causes of its disappearance, and no certainty even about the century in which its demise took place. Some historians believe that it was partly lost to fire and partly destroyed by earthquakes; others blame Julius Ceasar, fanatical Christians, ultra-religious Arabs, or Zenobia, queen of Palmyra. A well documented and comprehensive history of the library, including its destruction, can be found in Mostafa El-Abbadi's book 'The Life and Fate of the Ancient Library of Alexandria,' published by Unesco in 1990.

In September 2004, The Bibliotheca Alexandrina organized an international seminar entitled "What Happened to the Ancient Library of Alexandria?". The seminar was held within the framework of the Alexandria

Project, - a research project initiated for the study and documentation of the ancient library of Alexandria, Alexandrian scholarship, and other topics related to the history and civilization of the ancient city. A group of distinguished scholars participated in the seminar by presenting papers and studies based on historical evidence - textual and archaeological.

The revival of the Library of Alexandria, by the Egyptian government with the assistance of Unesco and the international community, is an attempt to transpose the ancient idea into modern terms and play an educational, cultural and scientific role throughout the region. The new Bibliotheca Alexandrina is a public research library integrated within a complex of specialized libraries, museums, exhibition areas, educational centers, a planetarium, a library and information school and an international conference center. As such, it is not a shelter for information, but is meant to create a hunger for knowledge. The Bibliotheca Alexandrina is to be:

- The world's window to Egypt.
- Egypt's window to the world.
- A leading institution of the digital age; and, above all,
- A center for learning, tolerance, dialogue and understanding.

The Bibliotheca Alexandrina is an Egyptian institution with an international dimension, under the auspices of an international council of patrons and directed by an international board of trustees, where local and international experts set its policies and follow its programmes.

In his address at the inauguration of the Bibliotheca Alexandrina on 16 October 2002, H.E. President Mohamed Hosni Mubarak said: "the efforts that supported the revival of the Library of Alexandria in the same place where it was first established 2300 years ago... came out of the deep understanding of the great value of the ancient Library of Alexandria and its international role, as well as the need to materialize this value in our present world, particularly within the current events and changes that the world is witnessing. This value lies in the commitment to a high level of scientific research and culture as well as the determined and persistent seeking of integration and interaction among civilizations and cultures."

In addressing some 800 personalities, including heads of states, queens, ministers, Nobel laureates, scientists, writers and artists, the President emphasized the need for dialogue and cultural interactions as the main avenues to end violence and tension - which is one of the functions of the Bibliotheca Alexandrina. He called on all nations "to continue their support to this cultural bridge linking different nations and peoples of the world. "Such objectives" added the President "will never be achieved without international support. I assure you that Egypt will continue to exert its utmost efforts in pushing the library forward in the coming years."

It is not surprising that Unesco, which was created to promote education, science, culture and the sharing of knowledge, was intimately associated with Egypt in launching and promoting this project. Some fifty years ago, the greatest archaeological campaign of all times was also initiated and achieved by Unesco, on the very same land, to save the treasures of Nubia, including Abu Simbel and Philae.

In 1986, Egypt requested the assistance of Unesco in the revival of the ancient Library of Alexandria. As the Director of the Programme dealing with information, libraries and archives in Unesco at that time, I was very fortunate to be put in charge of the Project. With the assistance of a number of international experts, we carried out the first phase of the feasibility study; a series of basic technical studies, prepared the architectural brief and organized an international architectural competition. At the same time, the Director General of Unesco, Mr. Makhtar M'Bow, launched an international appeal for support.

The project was started off in Egypt under the auspices of President Hosny Mubarak. The General Organization of the Alexandria Library (GOAL) was established in 1988 by decree under the chairmanship of Mr. Ahmed Sorour, Minister of Education. The University of Alexandria donated a site of 45000 square meters for the future Library, on the waterfront at the very location of the ancient Royal Palace, believed to be close to the probable site of the ancient Library. On 26th June 1988, President Hosny Mubarak and the new Director General of Unesco, Mr. Federico Mayor, brought further international attention to the project by laying the first stone of the Library. The project had moved fast and had caught the interest and imagination of the international community. A large number of articles began to appear in the international press, officials from various countries approached Egypt and Unesco to express their interest, and institutions began to offer their assistance. The project had gained a great worldwide momentum.

The organization of the international architectural competition further promoted the project, internationally. Over 1300 architects from 77 countries registered; 524 entries were received and submitted to the International Jury composed of seven architects and two librarians.

It is interesting to recall that the Snohetta team, which won the competition, was in itself international; its ten members who worked on this project originated from six countries. The team recognized that a great sensitivity was needed to successfully complete the project. A high degree of group interaction was maintained and a great deal of research and reading was done. A special trip was made to Alexandria to investigate before beginning the actual design of the competition entry. Their effort was later crowned with success.

This bold Norwegian design had then to be translated into a stone, steel and glass structure for which substantial funds were needed. An International Commission for the Bibliotheca Alexandrina was set up with the participation of Chiefs of States and high-level personalities. The meeting of the Commission took place in Aswan under the chairmanship of Mrs. Suzanne Mubarak from 11-12 February 1990. It was a great success from every point of view. The 18 members of the Commission signed the Aswan Declaration that endorsed the project and called for the international community to support and cooperate in the completion of the Library. The response to the appeal was immediate. A sum of US $64,000,000 was collected. The final cost of the Library was to be in the order of $ 220 millions.

In October 1990, the Government of Egypt and Unesco signed an agreement setting up the institutional framework and the organs of the Project. Unesco appointed a Project Manager in February 1992, to oversee the building construction. A legislative structure was created in Egypt, which made the Library an autonomous juridical entity tied directly to the President of the Republic. The law gives the President vast latitude in determining the manner in which the Library shall be governed. All the relevant regulations for the Library's financial and administrative affairs were specified in the Decree No. 76 for the year 2001.

Archaeological excavations on the site, which uncovered

ruins of Roman villas and beautiful mosaics, delayed the tender action concerning the first phase of construction (the foundations and ground engineering works), which was eventually launched in 1994. Nine companies had pre-qualified from among 34 groups. On 15 May of that year, the contractor selected, Rodio/Trevi (Italy) - Arab Contractor (Egypt) Joint Venture, officially began Phase I.

Three hundred and fourteen thousand cubic yards of dirt were excavated. One thousand workers toiled day and night. The construction work involved the most advanced technology available; the proximity of the sea demanded particular precautions to prevent any saline water seepage. A waterproof wall, reinforced by an anti-earthquake system, was erected. It represented the largest circular continually reinforced diaphragm wall in the world, 160 m. in diameter. Six hundred and two bell-bottom pillars were sunk 40 meters into the ground to support the weight of the building. Phase I was completed on 31 December 1995, at a cost of $59 million.

Phase II (structure, services, fit-out and external works) which followed was carried out by Balfour Beatty (UK) - Arab Contractors (Egypt) Joint Venture, at a cost of about $117 million.

Throughout the project Snohetta (Norway) - Hamza Associates (Egypt) Consortium acted as consultants. From December 1993 to August 1995 they had completed the design phase of the building, before phase I could start. Snohetta also designed the furniture that was donated by the government of Norway.

The Bibliotheca Alexandrina now consists of:

1) The Main Library, which is a universal library designed to serve researchers and the public at large.
2) The Taha Hussein Library for the blind and visually impaired.

3) The Young People's Library, conceived to orient 12 to 18 years old to all the services in the Main Library.
4) The Children's Library, geared towards children aged 6 to 12.
5) The Audiovisual, Multimedia and Music Library, which offers a selective collection of CD/DVD, audiocassettes, videotapes, records, slides and photographs.
6) The Microfilm Reading Room, which contains a manuscript collection in Arabic, Turkish and Persian.
7) The Rare Books Reading Room, which offers rare books, facsimile prints, limited collections and dedicated books.

In addition, the Bibliotheca Alexandrina includes the Science Museum, the Calligraphy Museum, the Alexandrina Museum, the Archeological Museum, the International School of Information Studies, a multipurpose room, an exhibition area and the Conservation and Restoration Laboratory. On the same site are the Planetarium and the International Conference Center that can accommodate 3000 delegates. In that sense the new Bibliotheca Alexandrina is not a simple library, but indeed the true revival of the ancient one.

The Library is wholly automated and possesses a computerized catalogue. The Library Information System was designed and installed by a French firm with the financial support of the French Government. The different departments are developing databases for the main disciplines covered. The program of the International School of Information Studies was developed and the Restoration Laboratory to preserve rare books and manuscripts was established, with assistance form the Italian Government. Library Staff were trained in the latest software and library management software in the US and Europe.

The size and content of the collection is a very important aspect, which has drawn maximum attention of the library management. Collection development - which consists of the selection, evaluation, weeding, replacement, preservation, and retention of library materials to best support the mission of the Library - is managed in a modern and pragmatic way. Today, collection development increasingly entails the provision of information through a balance of acquisition and access. Access has become central to the ongoing process of maximizing the acquisitions budget while, at the same time, increasing the availability of resources to the library's patrons. Print or multimedia resources are acquired traditionally or provided through some form of document delivery. Electronic resources are also either acquired or accessed by lease arrangement. This represents a significant shift from the historical emphasis on acquiring strong collections of print resources for long-term access and use. Less than ever can a library attempt to acquire all available materials across an extensive range of teaching and research areas, as the ancient Library of Alexandria once did. Times have changed. The Bibliotheca Alexandrina's aim is to provide essential print and multimedia resources for teaching, learning, and entertainment as well as print research materials, on a selective basis, together with licensed and purchased access to remote electronic resources for all library users.

The Collection Development Policy of the Bibliotheca Alexandrina is printed as a public document that describes existing collection strengths and future collecting activity in order to inform users, potential donors, and funding authorities of the principles that govern the selection and retention of library holdings and of the library's collecting priorities. Furthermore, it demonstrates the commitment of the Library to support the wide range of teaching, learning, and research goals for which it was founded. Because the development and management of the library's collections relies on cooperation between library personnel, academics, professionals, and the public, this policy is also a means of facilitating such cooperation both within Egypt and throughout the world.

Fulfillment of the mission depends upon the resources available, such as funds, expertise, physical space, and technology. Experience dictates that the total mission is an ideal goal, with some aspects going unmet when resources are insufficient. Funding for acquisitions is provided on a fiscal year basis, with the total amount being determined by the Chief Librarian. While a small amount is retained to meet general needs and contingencies, the bulk of the acquisitions budget is used for the purchase or licensing of library resources. Since a large proportion of the library's resources are acquired from overseas, the value of the Egyptian pound against foreign currencies at any particular time, especially the US dollar, is a significant factor in acquisitions decisions.

The Collection Development Committee, Resources and Technical Services Division of the American Library Association have developed widely accepted standards (ALA, 1979) that define levels of collection development. The Bibliotheca Alexandrina use these standards to guide their decisions.

It is important to emphasize that the Bibliotheca Alexandrina, as part of the larger global community, considers intellectual freedom to be fundamental to its mission. The administration of the Bibliotheca Alexandrina adheres to the Statement on Libraries and Intellectual Freedom of The International Federation of Library Associations and Institutions, IFLA. For instance, it supports, defends and promotes intellectual freedom as defined in the UN Declaration of Human Rights; it believes that human beings have a fundamental right to access expressions of knowledge, creative thought and intellectual activity; it believes that intellectual freedom is a core responsibility for the library and information profession.

The number of books in the Bibliotheca Alexandrina is still small, for the moment. The Library was designed to contain a maximum of 8 million books, compared with the national Library of France's 12 million and the US Library of Congress' 18 million. But, as mentioned earlier, access to a large reservoir of information is secured. Among the precious possessions, one can cite, for example, a hand-written manuscript of the historian Al-Makrizi, copies of the Holy Quran written in Ottoman-style calligraphy, a copy of the first edition of the New Testament printed by Johans Gutenberg in 1456, 'La Description de l'Egypte' organized by Napoleon during the French expedition in Egypt, and a manuscript of Sahid Muslim's Anthology of prophet Muhammad's Hadith. The Library also hosts important documents, maps, microfilms relevant to the Suez Canal, as well as electronic records of 300 rare historical photographs featuring the different phases of the Suez Canal construction. The Library also has a collection of rare coins and a gallery of historical paintings featuring the history of Alexandria. It has signed an agreement with the Egyptian Television that will provide the Library a selection of its cultural and educational programmes to gradually construct an important archival collection of audio-visual materials (4000 hours/year).

The strategies applied for building up and enriching the collections include:

- Negotiations with specialized and private libraries in Egypt;

- Contacts with monasteries and mosques concerning originals or copies of manuscripts;
- Negotiations with museums around the world to obtain texts and reports of the Pharaonic period;
- Negotiations with specialized libraries in other countries to obtain Greek classical texts translated into Arabic and rare historical documents;
- Preparation of agreements with foreign countries to establish exchange mechanisms; and
- Establishing a collection of administrative, legal and cultural archives covering the history of Egypt and, in particular, that of Alexandria.

Dr. Ismail Serageldin, Librarian of Alexandria and Director of the Bibliotheca Alexandrina, is known to be an energetic and pragmatic intellectual. He began with a strategy that impressed many observers: obtaining an exemption from civil service and from purchasing rules so that the library can hire and fire at will, pay competitive salaries and buy what it needs without interference from Government authorities and customs. He created in the Library a team spirit and a profound commitment to excellence.

In the short span of its existence, the Bibliotheca Alexandrina has developed many programmes, consolidated its institutional structure, further developed its human resources and trained its staff, sponsored activities in science, humanities and the arts, refined its mission and focus, issued several publications, and organized successful international seminars to address concerns of the world community, such as the ethics of science and technology, freedom of expression, youth employment, and the role of science in education.

The Library also counts among its achievements the founding of seven specialized research institutes, the establishment of many museums, the addition of tens of thousands of books, and the organisation of scores of concerts, exhibitions, conferences, lectures, seminars, workshops and meetings. (On an average there are in a year: close to a million visitors, over 500 events, including 140 concerts, 130 movie shows, 110 theatre presentations, 35 plastic arts exhibitions). The Annual Reports of the Library are an impressive record of achievements, to be consulted. In the words of Mrs. Suzanne Mubarak, Chair, Board of Trustees "Rarely in the history of institution-building has so much been achieved in so little time by so few. Like the Ancient Library of Alexandria, the Bibliotheca Alexandrina is becoming synonymous with diversity, culture, dialogue and learning; a place where minds meet and cultures flourish."

Aerial view of Bibliotheca Alexandrina

Dr. Jacques Tocatlian inside Bibliotheca Alexandrina

2

INFORMATION LITERACY AND EMERGING KNOWLEDGE ECONOMY IN INDIA

S.B. Ghosh*
Anup Kumar Das**

The process of liberalization and globalization of Indian economy started in 1990s that catalyzed the emergence of knowledge economy in India. Since then many Indian corporate organizations established their presence outside the country, forming an informal India Inc. in competing globally. The information infrastructure situation in India has also improved a lot since 1990s, not only in the corporate organizations that exploit knowledge resources for the profit making, but also in the public institutions that generate knowledge for the development of all aspects of society and humanity. Judicious use of information resources, available now mainly in the public institutions, especially in the higher educational and research

* Former Professor, Indira Gandhi National Open University, XY-72, Sarojini Nagar, New Delhi – 110023, India. E-mail: sbghosh@hotmail.com

** Centre for Studies in Science Policy, School of Social Sciences, Jawaharlal Nehru University, New Delhi - 110067, India. E-mail: anupdas2072@hotmail.com

institutions, should be measured in terms of information literacy of the stakeholders. Information literacy is required for effective use, consumption and assessment of information resources available in the institutions. Information literacy can also bridge the gap between digital divide that we observe in many grass-root level initiatives in India in the forms of 'common services centres', 'village knowledge centres', 'community information centres', 'e-choupals', 'gyandoot', etc. ushered in with the participation of NGOs, developmental agencies and corporate organizations. Present study explores various initiatives in India that address information literacy in maximizing utilization of knowledge resources. This study also focuses on the various initiatives undertaken by different institutions, starting from the elementary level to the higher educational level, professional societies and other organizations.

1. INTRODUCTION

Information literacy is an essential part in the lifelong learning process, which empowers individual lifelong learners to acquire their life skills, soft skills and vocational skills throughout their lifespan to take part in their social, cultural, vocational and professional life. Information literacy is considered as an intervention tool for socio-economic empowerment in a globalizing world to stay ahead in a competitive world with knowledge superiority. Information literacy is especially important in the context of changing global economy where knowledge-based economy supersedes other forms of economy such as agrarian economy and industrial economy, in terms of economic power of the nation and socio-economic empowerment of citizens. In his books, Amartya Sen [9, 10] justifies the notion of economic empowerment of people through the participation in continuing education until workforce attains certain levels of accuracy, understands job specifications and follows instructions.

In *The Third Wave* book, Alvin Toffler [12] divided history of the evolution of human society into three major eras, or waves. The first wave, from 8000 BC to 1750 AD was termed the agricultural revolution, and was based on farming as the world's primary occupation. In the second wave, from 1750 to 1955, the rise of industrial civilization and the industrial revolution marked the main occupation. The developed world was engaged in or moving toward mass production of industrial goods. The third wave, which began in the mid-1950s, is sometimes referred to as the information age and is based on the delivery of services. Important point to note from Toffler's viewpoint is that all the societies were profoundly transformed with each wave, and that the transition from one to the next was never easy.

What Toffler envisaged three decades ago, we can see it today in the proliferation of knowledge-based industries as well as service industries not only in developed countries but also in developing countries such as India, China and Brazil. Advanced countries such as USA, UK, Japan and Germany were ahead in third wave, which started after the World War II. Many knowledge-based industries emerged in these developed countries due to concerted efforts of advanced research, development and entrepreneurships. These nations nurtured talents and attracted creative and visionary people to establish knowledge-based economy. That is, the enterprises, which have superior knowledge resources, have tremendous growth opportunities in global markets and certainly have edge over others. They became the trend setters and are followed by many others. In the transition to the information/knowledge based society, two aspects are important - development of ICT infrastructure for information accessibility and information literate citizen.

If the large number of citizens becomes information literate, they will be able to utilize a considerable amount of information resources for the generation of wealth for the welfare of the society. They can be a driving force in demanding adequate information infrastructure. The information literacy can also play a major role in e-readiness of a country.

In a knowledge society, knowledge itself becomes the factor of productions, and plays a central role in driving economic and social development. In a knowledge economy, the knowledge-driven industries have much higher economic growth, both in terms of volume and revenue, than manufacturing industries and agriculture. This segment also requires intellectually motivated, creative, competitive decision makers who will enable the knowledge organizations to endeavor their goals. This workforce would use information resources, information services and information systems judiciously, rationally and adequately to pursue their professional goals, organizational goals and social goals. The utilization of information resources can be habituated and sensitized through the information literacy competency development programmes. The information literacy is required at every stage and sphere of a person's life, starting from the school education to higher education, from social life to professional life.

2. SITUATING KNOWLEDGE-BASED ECONOMY IN INDIA

In India large-scale industrial growth started few decades ago mostly after independence. India's first Prime Minister Jawaharlal Nehru had futuristic vision to build-up a self-sufficient nation. He also initiated many public institutions and research centres for making the nation superior in scientific and technological knowledge. Green revolution was a milestone in Indian R&D activities in 1980s, which made India self-reliant in food grains. In early 1990s, India had reformed her economy to the tune of globalisation and liberalization to attract foreign direct investments in India and to explore world markets of Indian products and services. Although first two waves came in India very lately, the third wave has already knocked the doors. But it is very limited to a few privileged states in India, particularly centered on metropolitan cities, which have basic infrastructure to host the knowledge-based industries. Now, the transitional Indian society produces success stories of knowledge-based industries in every corner of the country.

The knowledge-based economy is in existence in developed countries for a long time, whereas the emerging economies, some of them belong to popularly known BRICS (Brazil, Russia, India, China and South Africa) countries [14], are also very keen to establish knowledge-based economy utilizing their huge talent pools, entrepreneurial capabilities and improved infrastructure. Thus, knowledge-based economy is not a distance dream for India, like many other emerging economies. The impact of third wave in the emerging economies is expected much greater than the other two.

The Gross Domestic Product (GDP) is a measure of the value of goods and services produced in a year, contributed by all sectors of national economy viz., agriculture, industry (also known as manufacturing) and services (also known as tertiary) sectors. GDP is a strong economic indicator accepted worldwide. Table 1 shows the GDP contributions vis-à-vis labour force in different sectors in BRICS countries [2]. This Table also indicates that in most emerging nations, agriculture sector contributes least in national economy. On the other hand, amongst three sectors, services sector in India deploys least manpower (28% of total labour force) but responsible for the highest GDP contribution for the country (54.6% of total GDP). Table 1 also indicates that amongst the BRICS nations, China has largest economic growth rate (11.1%) followed by India (9.4%). This is because of China's excellence in manufacturing industries and India's excellence in services sector that is appreciated world over. Table 2 shows India's position in SAARC (South Asian Association for Regional Cooperation) countries based on GDP contributions by different sectors. This Table indicates that services sector becomes strong in major SAARC countries, viz. India, Pakistan, Maldives and Sri Lanka [2].

Table 1 : GDP Contributions vis-à-vis Labour Force in Different Sectors of BRICKS Countries

	GDP Contribution	Labour Force	GDP Growth Rate
Brazil	*Agriculture:* 5.1% *Industry:* 30.9% *Services:* 64%	*Agriculture:* 20% *Industry:* 14% *Services:* 66%	3.70%
Russia	*Agriculture:* 4.9% *Industry:* 39.3% *Services:* 55.8%	*Agriculture:* 10.8% *Industry:* 29.1% *Services:* 60.1%	6.70%
India	*Agriculture:* 17.5% *Industry:* 27.9% *Services:* 54.6%	*Agriculture:* 60% *Industry:* 12% *Services:* 28%	9.40%
China	*Agriculture:* 11.7% *Industry:* 48.9% *Services:* 39.3%	*Agriculture:* 45% *Industry:* 24% *Services:* 31%	11.10%
South Africa	*Agriculture:* 2.7% *Industry:* 30.9% *Services:* 66.4%	*Agriculture:* 30% *Industry:* 25% *Services:* 45%	5%

Source: The World Factbook 2007

Table 2: GDP Contributions vis-à-vis Labour Force in Different Sectors of SAARC Countries

	GDP Contribution	Labour Force	GDP Growth Rate
Afghanistan	*Agriculture:* 38% *Industry:* 24% *Services:* 38%	*Agriculture:* 80% *Industry:* 10% *Services:* 10%	8%
Bangladesh	*Agriculture:* 19.7% *Industry:* 28% *Services:* 52.3%	*Agriculture:* 63% *Industry:* 11% *Services:* 26%	6.40%
Bhutan	*Agriculture:* 24.7% *Industry:* 37.2% *Services:* 38.1%	*Agriculture:* 63% *Industry:* 6% *Services:* 31%	8.80%
India	*Agriculture:* 17.5% *Industry:* 27.9% *Services:* 54.6%	*Agriculture:* 60% *Industry:* 12% *Services:* 28%	9.40%
Maldives	*Agriculture:* 16% *Industry:* 7% *Services:* 77%	*Agriculture:* 22% *Industry:* 18% *Services:* 60%	18%
Nepal	*Agriculture:* 38% *Industry:* 20% *Services:* 42%	*Agriculture:* 76% *Industry:* 6% *Services:* 18%	1.90%
Pakistan	*Agriculture:* 19.4% *Industry:* 27.2% *Services:* 53.4%	*Agriculture:* 42% *Industry:* 20% *Services:* 38%	6.60%
Sri Lanka	*Agriculture:* 16.5% *Industry:* 27.1% *Services:* 56.5%	*Agriculture:* 34.3% *Industry:* 25.3% *Services:* 40.4%	7.40%

Source: The World Factbook 2007

Table 3 shows that the percentage share of GDP from service sector in India has already been doubled than industry sector, whereas agriculture sector is continuously reducing its GDP contribution in contrary

Table 3: Growth of GDP by Economic Activity in India

	Sector	GDP Growth Rate				GDP Contribution (percent)			
		2003-04	2004-05 (P)	2005-06 (Q)	2006-07 (R)	2003-04	2004-05 (P)	2005-06 (Q)	2006-07 (R)
1	Agriculture (Agriculture, Forestry & Fishing)	10	0	6	2.7	21.7	20.2	19.7	18.5
2	Industry (Manufacturing, Mining & Quarrying, Electricity, Gas & Water Supply, Construction)	7.4	9.8	9.6	10.9	25.6	26.1	26.2	26.6
3	Services (Trade, Hotels, Transport & Communication; Financing, Insurance, Real Estate & Business Services; Community, Social & Personal Services)	8.5	9.6	9.8	11	52.7	53.7	54.1	54.9
	Overall GDP Growth Rate	8.5	7.5	9	9.4	100	100	100	100

(P) Provisional, (Q) Quick Estimates (R) Revised Estimates

Source: Monthly Economic Report, November 2007

to its largest manpower engagement. The knowledge processing industries, IT and IT-enabled services industries are the jewels in the services sector where India's best talents get absorbed or reverse brain-drained occurred. Government of India provides appropriate supports to each state government for establishing knowledge-based industries by promoting software technology parks, biotechnology parks, export-processing zones, special economic zones and so on, beyond the metro cities. Thus, the largest contributor in the Indian economy is the service sector, which is growing very rapidly compared to other sectors.

The e-Readiness is another indicator that shows the ability to use Information and Communication Technologies (ICT) to develop one's economy and to foster one's welfare. Table 4 shows e-Readiness ranking of the countries in Asia and Pacific region, where India stands 10 out of 16 countries in this region and 54 out of 69 countries of the world. This ranking is based on the annual study of the *Economist Intelligence Unit* on the parameters such as connectivity and technology infrastructure, business environment, social and cultural environment, legal environment, government policy and vision, consumer and business adoption [3]. India's scores in these parameters are: connectivity and technology infrastructure 2.9 (out of 10), business environment 6.25, social and cultural environment 5.2, legal environment 5.5, government policy and vision 4.6, consumer and business adoption 4.5 and overall score 4.66 (out of 10), contrary to the region's toper Hong Kong's scores in these parameters which are: connectivity and technology infrastructure 8.5, business environment 8.62, social and cultural environment 6.8, legal environment 9.7, government policy and vision 9.1, consumer and business adoption 9.5 and overall score 8.72. Although the facts that India stands better than her neighboring countries

China, Sri Lanka and Pakistan in e-readiness ranking, and India has superior standing in IT-based industries, common citizens in India do not have sufficient access to ICT infrastructure and knowledge resources. Social equity through information literacy and lifelong learning can only be ensured when Indian society bridges the digital and knowledge divides across the lengths and breadths of the country. The *Human Development Report 2007-2008* (HDR) [13] also indicates India's poor standing in all aspects of human development. The HDR ranks India 128 out of 177 countries, based on different sets of indicators, whereas India's neighboring countries China stands 81, Sri Lanka stands 99 and Pakistan stands 136.

With the emergence of knowledge-based industries, digital and knowledge divides in India seems to be bottleneck in provisioning adequate information infrastructure and manpower supply, necessary for these industries and supporting services, although the country has made substantive progress in this area. Thus, the policy makers and social scientists are adopting various frameworks to address the digital and knowledge divides in India for achieving overall economic growth. Information and Communication Technologies (ICT) is being used worldwide as an intervention tool for socio-economic empowerment, better governance, illiteracy eradication and poverty removal. The ICT is also being used as a tool for empowering marginalized groups such as women, artisans, physically challenged and dalits (scheduled tribes). In India, ICT is also adopted at the grassroots level through various initiatives and pilot projects on experimental basis. The public-private partnerships (PPP) have been established across India, where many corporate organizations are collaborating with non-governmental organizations (NGOs) local self-help groups and local governments for various social development and social welfare programmes out of their

Table 4 : e-Readiness Ranking in Asia and Pacific Region

2007 e-Readiness Rank in Region	2005 e-Readiness Rank in Region	Country	2007 Overall e-Readiness Rank (out of 69 countries)	2007 e-Readiness score (of 10)	Human Development Index Ranking (out of 177 countries)##
1	1	Hong Kong	4	8.72	21
2	3	Singapore	6	8.6	25
3	2	Australia	9	8.46	3
4	4	New Zealand	14	8.19	19
5	5	South Korea	16	8.08	26
6	7	Taiwan	17	8.05	81
7	6	Japan	18	8.01	8
8	8	Malaysia	36	5.97	63
9	9	Thailand	49	4.91	78
10	10	India	54	4.66	128
11	11	Philippines	54	4.66	90
12	12	China	56	4.43	81
13	13	Sri Lanka	61	3.93	99
14	16	Pakistan	63	3.73	136
15	15	Vietnam	65	3.73	105
16	14	Indonesia	67	3.39	107

Sources: The 2007 e-Readiness Rankings; ## Human Development Report 2007/2008

'social outreach' and 'corporate social responsibility' mandates. Many national and international developmental and funding agencies are also collaborating with grassroots level NGOs, volunteering societies to address digital divide in India. Government of India and state governments are also taking appropriate steps in sustaining economic growth, employment generation and strengthening information infrastructure. Recently Government of India established National Knowledge Commission (NKC) to formulate national plans and policy frameworks for nurturing knowledge-based economy in India and addressing challenges of globalization.

3. NATIONAL KNOWLEDGE COMMISSION PROMOTING KNOWLEDGE-BASED ECONOMY IN INDIA

The National Knowledge Commission (NKC), a recent initiative of the Government of India, is a concerted approach in making India as a major economic power in the global scenario [6]. The NKC also provides adequate inputs for action to achieve the goal of knowledge society. NKC aims at establishing a knowledge-oriented paradigm of development and to address the digital divide in India. NKC was established in June 2005 with following objectives:

- To build excellence in the lifelong, non-formal, informal and formal educational systems to meet the knowledge challenges of the 21st century and increase India's competitive advantage in fields of knowledge.
- To promote creation of knowledge in S&T laboratories.
- To improve the management of institutions engaged in intellectual property rights.

- To promote knowledge applications in agriculture and industry.
- To promote the use of knowledge capabilities in making government an effective, transparent and accountable service provider to the citizen and promote widespread sharing of knowledge to maximize public benefit.

NKC has five distinct focus areas:

(i) Access to Knowledge : Providing access to knowledge resources through strengthening information infrastructure and networks; promoting and adopting open access literature, open learning resources, open courseware and open source software. Focal points in this focus area are literacy, language, translation, libraries, knowledge networks and knowledge portals.

(ii) Knowledge Concepts : Nurturing intellectual capabilities and enhancing professional and vocational skills of youths through a systematic approach to lifelong learning. Focal points in this focus area are school education, vocational education, higher education, medical education, legal education, management education, engineering education, open and distance education.

(iii) Knowledge Creation : Making self-sufficiency in knowledge creation; strengthening indigenous research capabilities in science, technology and medicine (STM) areas; generating knowledge for social development. Focal points in this focus area are science and technology, intellectual property rights (IPRs), innovation and entrepreneurship.

(iv) Knowledge Application : Deriving maximum benefits from intellectual assets, applying knowledge in fields such as agriculture, industry, health and education where productivity can be enhanced. Focal points in this focus area are traditional knowledge and agriculture.

(v) Knowledge Services : Making governance and government functionaries more accountable, transparent, efficient and sensitive to the causes of common men. Focal point in this focus area is e-governance.

NKC has recently come up with some bold recommendations for harnessing the potential of information literacy to promote a people-centred, plural and inclusive knowledge society in India [6]. It has recommended certain frameworks for achieving quality education for all, inculcating information literacy, through a wide-spread lifelong learning system in the country.

NKC is also advocating open courseware and open learning resources for sharing intellectual capitals of elite institutions in India to supplement lifelong learning systems in India [6]. For example, Government of India has initiated a programme called 'National Programme on Technology Enhanced Learning' (NPTEL). This is an open courseware initiative by seven Indian Institutes of Technology (IITs) and the Indian Institute of Science (IISc). The main objective of this programme is to enhance the quality of engineering education in the country by developing more than 200 curricula-based video and web courses. Premier institutions of India are participating in this innovative programme for the production and dissemination of quality courseware in the areas of engineering and technology. Already a number of open courseware is now available through its website. The video courses are at first broadcasted through the Eklavya Technology Channel – a technical education channel for television. This programme addresses harmonization of engineering curricula across the country, refreshing knowledge of technical teachers/students as well as the shortage of quality teaching faculty at the second and third tier (i.e., government-supported and self-supported) institutions. This open educational resource supplements the lifelong learning process of individuals who want to catching up and brushing up their knowledge.

NKC reports and recommendations have covered all aspects of socio-economic development that will trigger an equity-based, responsible, responsive, competent and competitive socio-economic platform to meet the challenges of globalization and to develop an inclusive, plural and people-centred knowledge-based society across the country.

4. INFORMATION LITERACY AND LIFELONG LEARNING

Information literacy is a set of learning skills which enable a lifelong learner to effectively cope with massive amounts of information, from a variety of media formats, such as, books, journals, magazines, newspapers, audiovisual sources, scholarly databases, and Internet. These skills include the ability to understand how to find the information he wants and how to determine the 'best' information for his needs. Information literacy is a tool for promoting lifelong learning. It is common to all learning environments, especially lifelong learning environment where learners become more self-directed, and assume greater control over their own learning. The Information Literacy Standards, as adopted by the national and international library associations, assume that an information literate individual is able to:

- Determine the extent of information needed;
- Access the needed information effectively and efficiently;
- Evaluate information and its sources critically;
- Incorporate selected information into one's knowledge base;
- Use information effectively to accomplish a specific purpose; and

- Understand the economic, legal, and social issues surrounding the use of information, and access and use information ethically and legally.

Information literacy of lifelong learners can enhance the capabilities of a nation for optimum utilization of knowledge resources. It can also make creation and generation of new knowledge a reality. To derive maximum benefits from intellectual assets, to enhance the productivity in different social sectors, and to make public functionaries more accountable and transparent, coherent knowledge dissemination to the society are the needs of the hours where lifelong learners have much more to contribute. Thus, information literacy component in lifelong learning system is needed to achieve these societal goals.

5. ROLE OF INFORMATION LITERACY IN KNOWLEDGE LIFE CYCLE

NKC has identified different phases of life cycle based on a person's entire life span, from the birth to post work age. He/She needs different kinds of information in different phases of life. The young persons are acquiring knowledge through secondary and higher education. Here, thc teachers and library professionals impart the information literacy competency to the learners through information literacy programmes. Information literacy is a lifelong process that starts at the youth age and may go until post work age. Information literacy also has a component of lifelong learning. The formal and informal ways of learning are circled around a person's life, where the person acquires new sets of knowledge of his/her interests, updates his/her existing knowledge on his/her profession or vocation. Information literate persons acquire knowledge; then use knowledge resources to generate wealth and welfare. In post work life, persons share wisdom and experiences with the younger generations. Here also information literacy plays its role to absorb the knowledge from experienced persons to and use the same knowledge in generating wealth and welfare of the society. This is also another cycle of knowledge creation, dissemination and utilization. Figure 2 depicts the knowledge life cycle, based on a person's entire lifespan, where information literacy is integrated in every phase of one's lifespan.

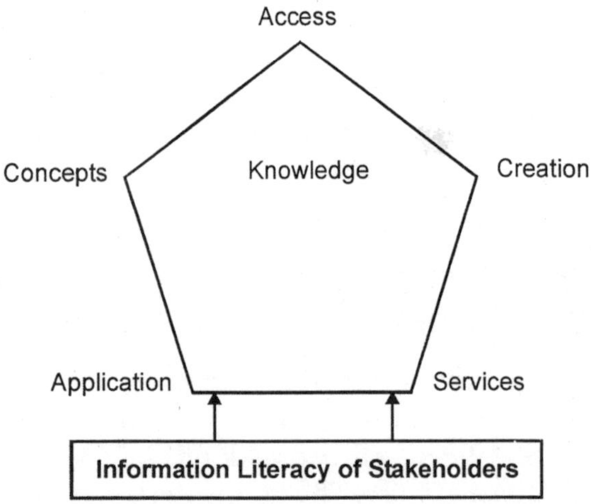

Fig. 1: Knowledge Pentagon and Information Literacy

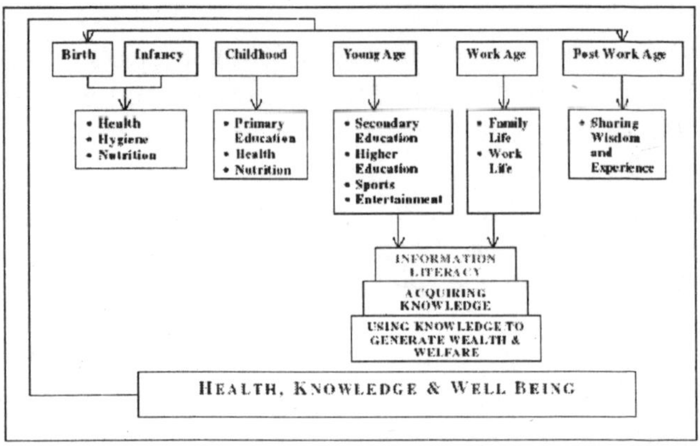

Fig. 2: Knowledge Life Cycle: Integration of Information Literacy

6. COMMUNITY INFORMATION INITIATIVES IN INDIA

Former President of India Dr. A.P.J. Abdul Kalam has coined a new term PURA (Providing Urban amenities in Rural Areas) that describes coherent knowledge and resources distribution across the country [1]. The PURA delivers three types of connectivity across the country: physical connectivity by providing roads in rural areas, electronic connectivity by providing reliable communication network and knowledge connectivity by establishing more professional institutions and vocational training centres. Schools with best infrastructure and teachers who love teaching, primary health centres, silos for storage of products and markets for promoting cottage industries and business, employment opportunities for artisans are some of the elements of PURA. PURA also helps in poverty removal. He has also envisaged establishing Village Knowledge Centres across India. To implement visions of President of India and other contemporary social reformists, Government of India and other agencies have taken up a number of programmes and initiatives across the country. Some initiatives are based on successful partnership between private bodies (such as corporate and NGOs) and public bodies (such as village Panchayats and municipalities), this may known as private public partnership (PPP), e.g., eChoupal, TARAHaat. Some initiatives provide Government to Citizens (G2C) interface to ensure better transparency in governance, e.g., Bhoomi, Gyandoot, Community Information Centres, etc. These information centres provide various kinds of community information as required by common citizens, e.g. education, health, nutrition, sanitation, agriculture, wholesale prices of agricultural products, village industries, weather, land records, utilities (such as, ration cards, driving licenses, birth certificates, death certificates, caste certificates, income certificates, etc.), and so on. Some projects have coverage in particular areas, e.g. Bhoomi (covering land records), whereas some other initiatives have coverage in an array of areas, e.g. Community Information Centres (covering education, health, utilities, etc.). Most of these initiatives are establishing information kiosks or cyber cafes at the village and the semi-urban areas, with the hardware, software, network, telephone and power supports from the respective institutions involved, and with the participations of the self-help groups or volunteers who will run the information kiosks at the doorsteps of the villagers and common citizens. VSAT terminals are also provided in few initiatives, like, Community Information Centres and eChoupal, where telephone connectivity is not adequately available. These community information initiatives deliver e-literacy programmes to the common citizens where basic skills of using computers and Internet are imparted. These initiatives also deliver information literacy training to the users of information kiosks, where learners know how to use information resources available within the respective initiative's portal, intranet and Internet, and how these information can be used in solving the problems of individuals in their vocational (e.g. agricultural know-how), personal (e.g. getting a certificate) and social (e.g. sanitation) life.

According to a study [4], only 29,820 rural libraries exist in India (supported by a government agency such as Raja Rammohan Roy Library Foundation, central government, state library authority, or local administration), in contrast to proposed 600,000 village knowledge centres. If the village knowledge centres are established, the villagers would get exposure to the information resources for decision making in their respective areas of interest such as health, land records, agriculture, village industries, etc. The community information centres in 10 states are also disseminating

Table 5: Community Information Initiatives in India

Name of the Project (with Web Address)	Coverage	Institutions Involved	Type of Participation
Common Services Centre (CSC) (www.mit.gov.in/default.aspx?id=825)	establishing 100,000 Common Services Centers in 600,000 villages of India	Department of Information Technology; Infrastructure Leasing & Financial Services Limited	G2C
Akhaya (www.akshaya.net)	1 State (Kerala)	Kerala State Information Technology Mission	G2C
Bhoomi (www.revdept-01.kar.nic.in)	1 State (Karnataka)	Revenue Department; National Informatics Centres	G2C
Community Information Centres (CIC) (www.cic.nic.in)	10 States (Arunachal Pradesh, Assam, Manipur, Meghalaya, Mizoram, Nagaland, Sikkim, Tripura, Jammu & Kashmir)	Ministry of Development of North Eastern Region (DONER); National Informatics Centres	G2C
Digital Gangetic Plain (www.iitk.ac.in/mladgp)	1 State (Uttar Pradesh)	Media Lab Asia; IIT Kanpur	G2C
Drishtee (www.drishtee.com)	5+ States (Haryana, Punjab, Madhya Pradesh, Rajasthan and Bihar)	Drishtee Ltd.	PPP

eChoupal (www.echoupal.com)	6 States (Madhya Pradesh, Karnataka, Andhra Pradesh, Uttar Pradesh, Maharashtra and Rajasthan); 31,000 villages.	International Business Division of ITC Limited	PPP
Gyandoot (www.gyandoot.nic.in)	1 District (Dhar district of Madhya Pradesh state)	Gyandoot Samiti & National Informatics Centres	G2C
Rural e-Seva (www.westgodavari.org)	1 District (West Godavari district of Andhra Pradesh state)	West Godavari District Administration	G2C
TARAhaat (www.tarahaat.com)	4 States (Punjab, Haryana, Madhya Pradesh, Uttar Pradesh)	Development Alternatives	PPP
Village Knowledge Centres (VKC) (www.mission2007 org)	600,000 villages across India by the year 2007	National Alliance for Mission 2007, NGOs, Department of Information Technology, Ministry of Panchayati Raj, Ministry of Agriculture, National Bank for Agriculture and Rural Development, etc.	G2C, PPP

various kind of information, related to community development and utilities. In wake of emerging knowledge society, a range of decisive information, which is still a distant dream to the common citizens, would be accessible if the proposed initiatives are properly implemented. But another aspect needs to be discussed, that is, other than documents on ones vocational and social interests, rural libraries also enhance reading habits of villagers, particularly, the literates and neo-literates. The reading habit helps in personality development, creativity and imagination. The reading habit can also broaden the person's liberal viewpoints. But village knowledge centres or community information centres may or may not provide similar kinds of traits with the citizens. That is why, village knowledge centres can be integrated with the existing rural libraries and where rural libraries do not exist, village knowledge centres can be set up along with rural libraries.

7. INFORMATION LITERACY PROGRAMMES IN INDIA

Information literacy programmes are already in existence in narrower forms in various libraries and information centres in India, in the forms of user education, bibliographic instruction, library instruction, library research, and so on.

Many advocates of information literacy in India have proposed to integrate information literacy programme with the academic curricula of educational systems of India, starting from the school level to the higher education, vocational education, professional education, lifelong education and research degree level. NKC recommendations in the focal areas of libraries, literacy, secondary education, professional education, vocational education, and lifelong education also have enough space for inclusion of information literacy, computer literacy and media literacy components for development of competent knowledge workers as required in the knowledge-based economy.

7.1 Information Literacy Programme at School Level

A study on information literacy programme in India reveals that major initiatives have been taken at the school level. For example, the Jawahar Navodaya Vidyalayas, a network of rural residential schools supported by the Government of India for the rural children covering 6th to 12th classes, are a unique experiment wherein each of the students is to prepare project report using the information resources of the respective libraries. The curriculum is designed to provide opportunities to use information and ICT to facilitate learning process. At present, there are 565 such schools spread over 34 States and Union Territories with a strength of 0.18 million of students [7].

In other cases, most of the schools at junior and senior level have library facilities with ICT components. In many classes, how to use library resources such as atlases, encyclopaedias, dictionaries, periodicals, etc. are usually taught and demonstrated. These resources are now available both in print format as well as electronic format. Erstwhile Indian National Scientific Documentation Centre (INSDOC) (Now, National Institute of Science Communication and Information Resources) developed an audio-visual programme for junior school children about how to find information from such sources. Many Schools have library hour as a part of the curricula, mostly to educate pupil for use of library for the class work and projects. Similarly, many public schools, convent schools and government schools have good library facilities and information infrastructure. In these schools, library classes are allotted for the every class of primary, secondary and senior secondary level, where information literacy competency is provided.

7.2 Information Literacy in Higher Learning Institutions

In the institutions of higher learning in India, user education, library instruction and bibliographic instruction programmes are provided. In universities for research degree programmes, a course on research methodology is included where library research techniques are also taught. Some universities and research institutions subscribe to the electronic resources, on consortium basis or individual basis. The producers or vendors of these electronic information resources regularly conduct user training programmes for use of those resources. The Indian Medlars Centre of National Informatics Centre conducts a user-training programme in every four month on their information products and services, such as IndMed databases, medIND open access journal literature, OpenMED open access archive, UNCat union catalogue databases, etc., which are designed mainly for health professionals and health librarians. Some orientation programmes and refresher courses also impart information literacy competency to the learners. The universities also conduct orientation programmes from time to time for their academics on use of electronic resources.

In the corporate organizations and corporate R&D centres, information literacy competency is an essential trait of the researchers and knowledge workers. The researchers and knowledge workers are being taught the about latest discipline oriented information resources available within the organizations and outside the organizations.

7.3 Information Literacy Programmes for LIS Professionals

The academic staff colleges established in the universities regularly organize orientation/refresher courses for teachers and librarians to imbibe the skills for locating and accessing information in the changing environment.

Many of the government libraries and information centres in India organize orientation programmes for their staff to impart information access skills.

The national documentation centres such as National Institution of Science Communication and Information Resources (NISCAIR) (erstwhile INSDOC), Small Enterprises National Documentation Centre (SENDOC), National Institute of Rural Development (NIRD) and National Social Science Documentation Centre (NASSDOC) play a significant role in orienting library and information science professionals of the country to acquire the skills of access to information.

At the school level, the organizations such as National Council of Education Research and Training (NCERT) and State Council of Education Research Council (SCERT) conduct regular orientation programmes/ refresher courses for the school librarians.

7.4 Role of Library Associations in India

Library associations exist in most of the states and union territories of India apart from those at the national level. State level library associations are very active in public libraries development in their respective states. Some library associations, e.g. Bengal Library Association conduct refresher courses for the in-service public librarians, mostly in the areas of managing and accessing information in ICT environment.

Some library associations at national level are now proactive in spreading the information literacy competency for the librarians and library users. In December 2005, Indian Library Association (ILA) organized 51st All India Conference with the focus on "libraries, information literacy and lifelong learning", where many librarians felt the importance of information literacy in lifelong learning and optimizing the usage of information in the libraries. In this conference, ILA also recommended to form a National Information Literacy Mission and the National Information Literacy Task Force to implement information literacy competency development programmes throughout the country without further delay [5].

In October 2005, an international information literacy workshop was held at the Punjabi University, Patiala, India to promote information literacy in South and South East Asia, with the support of UNESCO and other partners. In September 2003 at Prague, the International Alliance for Information Literacy was formed where India's Networking Alliance for Voluntary Actions (www.navaindia.org), a network of NGOs, became a member.

The Indian Association of Special Libraries and Information Centres (IASLIC), Society for the Advancement of Library and Information Science (SALIS) and Kerala Library Association (KLA), in collaboration with UNESCO, have organized information literacy competency development and sensitization workshops in different parts of India in the consequent years since 2006.

In January 2008, SALIS in collaboration with UNESCO has launched the e-Learning Portal for Awareness Raising on Information Literacy (http://salisonline.org/) [11]. This Portal aims to raise awareness, sensitize and enhance information literacy competency skills of common information users as well as information professionals and educators in the South Asian sub-region. Its objectives are fully in line with UNESCO's mandate to bridge the digital divide and UNESCO's vision of knowledge societies. The Portal covers a number of self-learning modules such as Information Communication Technology (ICT), Information Literacy Models and Standards, Lifelong Learning and Development of Life Skills, Information Literacy Assessment, Information Services for the Disabled People, Freedom of Information, and Right to Information. This portal also provides some sample information literacy programmes for academic libraries, special library, public library and community information centres.

8. CONCLUSION

In the wake of knowledge-driven development of societies in India, a number of initiatives have been planned and implemented to bridge the knowledge and digital divides between information rich and information poor citizens. The urban and rural societies are integrated through another range of initiatives that empower the common citizens with the decision making knowledge resources for their professional, vocational, social and personal life. The knowledge resources, available in the academic, special and public libraries, can be optimally and rationally used with the information literacy competency development programmes of the stakeholders. But in India, training of the trainers, who will deliver information literacy programmes need to be strengthened, as a chunk of library and information professionals are not in a position to handle modern ICT tools and techniques in information handling due lack of personal interests or other reasons. There was a few national level capacity building programmes on the information literacy in the recent past, although the international communities such as UNESCO, IFLA, American Library Association, have already prepared information literacy standards for the various levels of information users. These information literacy standards can be adapted in an emerging nation like India that aims at becoming a knowledge society, where knowledge utilization and knowledge creation capabilities are the driving force in economic and social development. National Knowledge Commission in India has rightly identified different areas of intervention for bringing the whole nation in knowledge and development paradigms. Then information literacy and lifelong learning will bring equal opportunities to the all segments of the society.

9. REFERENCES

1. Abdul Kalam, A.P.J. (2005). ***Address to the Nation on the eve of 56th Republic Day***. Retrieved on on 21 January 2008 from www.presidentofindia.nic.in
2. Central Intelligence Agency (2007). *The World Factbook 2007*. Washington, D.C.: Central Intelligence Agency. Retrieved on 21 January 2008 from https://www.cia.gov/library/publications/ the-world-factbook/
3. Economist Intelligence Unit and IBM Institute for Business Value. (2007). *The 2007 e-readiness rankings: Raising the bar*. London: Economist Intelligence Unit. Retrieved on 21 January 2008 from http://graphics.eiu.com/files/ad_pdfs/2007 Ereadiness_Ranking_WP.pdf
4. Ghosh, Maitreyee. (2005). The public library system in India: challenges and opportunities. *Library Review*, 54(3), 180-191.
5. Indian Library Association. (2005). *Resolutions at the 51th All India Conference*. New Delhi: Indian Library Association. Retrieved on 21 January 2008 from http://eprints.rclis.org/archive/00005896/
6. National Knowledge Commission (2008). *Report to the Nation 2007*. Retrieved on 21 January 2008 from http://knowledgecommission.gov.in/reports/report07.asp
7. Navodaya Vidyalaya Samiti. *Objectives & Salient Features of Navodaya Vidyalayas*. Retrieved on 1 21

January 2008 from http://navodaya.nic.in

8. Press Information Bureau (2007). *Monthly Economic Report, November 2007*. Retrieved on 21 January 2008 from http://pib.nic.in/archieve/others/2007/mernov_07.pdf
9. Sen, Amartya (1999). *Development as Freedom*. New York: Oxford University Press.
10. Sen, Amartya (2001). Reflections on Literacy. In: *Literacy as Freedom: A UNESCO Round-Table*. Paris: UNESCO Publishing.
11. Society for the Advancement of Library and Information Science (SALIS) (2008). *e-Learning Portal for Awareness Raising on Information Literacy*. Retrieved on 21 January 2008 http://salisonline.org/
12. Toffler, Alvin. (1980). *The Third Wave*. New York: Bantam Books.
13. United Nations Development Programme. (2007). *Human Development Report 2007/2008*. New York: United Nations Development Programme. Retrieved on 21 January 2008 from http://hdr.undp.org/en/media/hdr_20072008_en_ complete.pdf
14. Wikipedia, the free encyclopedia (2008). BRIC. Retrieved on 21 January 2008 from http://en.wikipedia.org/wiki/BRIC

3

NATIONAL INFORMATION SYSTEM IN IRAN: SUPERIOR STRIDES IN BUILDING UP AN INFORMATION TECHNOLOGY INFRASTRUCTURE

Abbas Gilvari[1]

After the Islamic Revolution in 1976, Iran began to establish and develop a strong and straightforward infrastructure in Information Technology. While there is not yet planned and implemented a clear Information System strategy at the national level, but during the last decades, many steps have taken. In this article I'm trying to investigate the requirements and inevitable factors of Information Technology and Information System Infrastructure in Iran. Library and Information state of the art, building blocks of Information Technology and steps has taken toward setting up a National Information System is among the discussed subjects.

Keywords: Iran, National Information System, ICT infrastructure, Information Technology Infrastructure, Library and Information Science, Internet use.

1 Deputy of Research & Development, Agricultural Scientific Information and Documentation Center (ASDIC), Agricultural Research and Training Organization, Tehran, Iran

1. INTRODUCTION

Iran, as a pluralistic society, consists of a variety of ethnic groups including Turks, Arabs, Kurds, Balochi, Bakhtyari, Lurs, and other smaller minorities, such as Armenians, Assyrians, Jews, and Brahuis or Brohi (Bureau of Near Eastern Affairs, 2006). The area of 1.6 million sq. km. and population of 70,492,062 (with a growth rate of 1.1 %), made this land as a center for Islamic Shia religion followers (89%). Iran is the second largest economy in the Middle East and the second largest OPEC oil producer. Development and educational growth have been positive in recent years (Gholami, 2004). The literacy rate in this country is more than 96 percent and education is mandatory. The government controls over 80 percent of the economy and has a gross domestic product (GDP) of more than US$561.6 billion (Sadeghnezhad, 2006). Iran's economy is a mixture of central planning, state ownership of oil and other large enterprises, village agriculture, and small-scale private trading and service ventures. In recent years, there has been much progress in rural development, including electrification, public welfare, and road building. In the Middle East and North Africa region, Iran has the second largest population after Egypt, most of its people is young, with increasing hopes and expectations of a better future. The country's health and education indicators are among the best in the region (*World Bank Report*, 2004).

As of November 2006, Iran is subdivided into thirty provinces, 324 sub-provinces, 865 counties, 982 cities and 2378 rural agglomerations (Supreme Council of ICT of Iran, 2006; Provinces of Iran, 2006).

2. NATIONAL INFORMATION SYSTEM

In spite of serious endeavors by librarians and some institutes like National Library of Iran (NLI), IRANDOC,

Jehade_Sazandegi Scientific Information Services (JSIS), RLST and many responsible parties in the last decade, no clear National Information System (NIS) plan has been developed in Iran yet. A symposium entitled "*studying the role of information system on research and development*" was held in Tehran in 1993. 15 papers among the 60 submitted contributions were selected for oral presentation (Mahdavi, 1993). "*Study of the existing problems and bottlenecks of information system*", "*theoretical infrastructure and necessity of establishing a national information system*" and "*policy making and outlining of an information system*" were the common themes in the submitted papers. The first and certified nation-wide information system project in Iran, which was initiated and completed in 1994, was supervised by Horri (1994). This plan as an official document is offered to presidential office. In 1995, JSIS issued the first book on NIS consisting of a collection of both translated and original papers relating to the subject (JSIS, 1995). In 2000, IRANDOC issued the "*proposed plan for designing Scientific and Technical Information System*" (Omidvar, 2001). In this proposal, the NIS is seen as having several subsystems, spread throughout the country. Again in 2001, **High Council of Informatics** (HCI) put high priority on NIS and through an analytical project entitled "*designing national information system*" tried to examine the most important information systems in operation in the country and discovering the existing relations between them (Razeghi Oskoee, 2002).

As pointed out before, while there is no single NIS in Iran, many infrastructures and backbones for implementation of NIS exist. In the following paragraphs an idea of the status of NIS components and their features is given.

3. LIBRARIANSHIP IN IRAN

Despite the long history of libraries, modern librarianship

is rather new in Iran. In 1938, the first course in librarianship (120 hours of teaching), was offered (Soltani, 2002; Ghasemi, 1995). The first Iranian library science department with the aim of training professional librarians (with a master's degree) was set up at the University of Tehran in 1966. After Islamic Revolution, many Library and Information Science Departments (LISD) were established with courses at the undergraduate and master's levels (Hayati, 2005). The doctoral level programme started in 1998, by the pioneering and collaborative efforts of Shiraz and Meshad universities. Up to now, the doctoral level programme in library and information science are offered in Shiraz, Meshad, Tehran and Ahwaz universities. While there is no precise statistics about the number of LISDs, according to some unpublished and ongoing study, there are about 72 library and information science departments (including public, Azad (open) and Payame noor (correspondence to public universities) universities) in Iran (Table 1). 14 (20%) of these departments are located in Tehran (Capital of Iran) and 58 are scattered in other cities. The dominant teaching language is Farsi in all LIS departments. The Associate level programme in Library and information science is now largely closed in most departments with a few exceptions. Fattahi (2006) reported that thee LIS Associate level programme is still active in some LISDs in cities such as Hamden, Beerjand, Bushehr, Zabool, and Kerman. Nearly all LISDs in big and medium cities such as Yazd, Qom, Isfahan, and Tabriz have opened undergraduate level programmes. At universities such as Tehran, Tarbiat Modares, Allame Tabatabaee, Shiraz, Meshad, Hamden and Ahwaz the Master degree programme has been launched[1]. The

1 There are two ongoing researches about the state of affairs of library and Information departments in Iran. Thanks to Dr. Fattahi and Mr. Koolaeian in favor of offering their study results to the writer.

laboratories are equipped with new information technologies and specific subject materials in almost all LISDs.

Table 1: Number of library and information departments in Iran by type

	Type of Department	Number
1	Azad (Open)	16
2	Ministry of Health, Treatment and Medical Education universities	8
3	National Library of Iran (NLI)	1
4	Payame Noor (correspondence to public universities)	20
5	Private Institutes	2
6	Public (governmental) universities	18
7	Scientific-Practical Education Centers (correspondence to public universities)	7
	Total	72

In order to persuade the librarians to adopt new and modern librarianship practices to enhance the value of library services, the Iranian Library Association (ILA) was founded in 1964. The Association was active until 1979, one year after the Islamic Revolution, and published the *ILA Newsletter*. After a gap of 21years, the ILA has been revived and is now known as Iranian Library and Information Association (ILIA) (IRANDOC, 2006; Shabani, 2004). Now ILIA is very active even in the field of Library Training. ILIA have started to publish the *ILIA Newsletter*. There is also another active library association i.e. *Iranian Medical Library Association (IMLA)* which was established in 1993 and is very actively ever since.

A research by Horri (2004) confirms the increase of scientific productivity of Iranian librarians throughout the 3 preceding decades. The study based on 2,490 published papers in the field of library and information science from 1968 to1998 in Iran indicated considerable growth in all categories. The data indicated that the number of published contributions has increased from 113 in 1968-1973 to 862 in 1994-1998. Modem concepts such as "*information storage and retrieval*", and "*information technology*" are seen to be important components in this research. The results indicate that there is a great deal of innovation (Horri, 2004). Many LIS students are now trying to design not only collaborative but also personal web logs. Many LIS students have designed individual home pages.

4. LIBRARIES IN IRAN

Existence of libraries in Iran goes back to the ancient era and establishing such libraries as Saruye Jey in Isfahan, Gondi-Shapur University Library in Ahvaz and the libraries in Ctisphun and Samarqand (Soltani, 2002). During the Islamic period, from the eighth century on, great libraries thrived everywhere in cities such as Shiraz, Saveh, Marv, Nishapur, and Rey and almost all mosques and seminary schools had libraries (Rokneddin Homayun, 1965). In recent years, the number of libraries, of all kinds, has increased and expanded in Iran. In the following paragraphs the current situation of different kinds of libraries in Iran is examined

4.1. National Library and Archives of Iran (NLAI)

The *Library of Dar al-Funun College*, established in 1851, was the first prototype of a national library in Iran. In 1899 another library called the *Nation's Library* was started in Tehran (Wikipedia, The free encyclopedia, 2006). The National Library of Iran (NLI) was officially initiated in 1937. This Library was formerly under the control of the Ministry of Culture and Art (MCA) (Umapathy, 1978) and now, after the merging of NLI and National Documents Organization (NDO) and forming of the National Library and Archives of IR in 2001, is positioned under the direct authority of the Vice-President's Office (National Library and Archives of IR of Iran, 2006). National Library of Iran has several branches scattered across the city of Tehran. The new building of NLI, which is spread out on a land (on the hills of Abbas Abad in north of Tehran) over 90,000m² and specially designed to combine different departments of the library in a single platform, is one of the largest library campuses in the Middle East. It encompasses 5 separate halls, each hall dedicated to a different department and designed so that it is able to adopt with new exchanges in the field of information technology. The present NLI incorporates many different collections from older libraries including many rare and valuable manuscripts. The ultimate capacity of the new building is 7,000,000 documents.

The library has a collection of over 2,000,000 volumes in Farsi and Arabic, 2,500 current periodicals and more than 5,000 old serials. *Namaye Meli* (electronic database of national periodicals articles) and *Ketabshenasi Meli* (electronic national bibliography) are two most important publications of the National Library of Iran. During the last decade the NLI has published and introduced a series of publications including "*Persian Subject Headings*", "*Medical Subject Headings*", "*Persian Cutter numbers*" and development and expansion of DDC and LC schedules in specific fields such as Geography, Islam and Iran History, and also development of Iran Mark. Recently the mechanization and computerization of different sections and activities of the library has begun.

4.2. Public libraries

In 1930, the first Public Library (PL), in the modern sense, was born in Iran. *Baladiye Tehran* (Tehran city) library was established in the municipal office in Tehran. Unfortunately required financial support was not given and the building ended up as a municipal building. In 1965, in *Park_e_ Shahr* in Tehran, a public library was established and after a while and by approval of duma, the Organization of Municipal Public Library (OMPL) was initiated (Homayonfarokh, 1969). In 1996 and after the Islamic Revolution, the Tehran Municipal Art and Cultural Organization responsible for municipal libraries, was established. Now a number of well-stocked and well-equipped municipal public libraries with growing collections have been established in cities such as Tehran, Isfahan and Meshad. About 66 such libraries, with a total collection of about 1,500,000 volumes, exist in Tehran (Iran Public Libraries Foundation, 2002).

Except the municipal libraries, the other public libraries are now under the authority of Iran Public Libraries Foundation (IPLF). The number of public libraries has increased from 290 in pre Islamic Revolution period to 1,640 with a total collection of 12,672,585 volumes and more than 3,949 personnel after the Islamic Revolution. In 2006, the total number of public library members was 1,323,024, and users are 44,137,199 (Tarikhche, 2006; Nourozian, 2006). Altogether, 1,866 computers have been installed in public libraries[1]. At present, about 140 further public libraries are under construction. The total budget of public libraries has increased from US$2,220,000 in the last year to US$22,220,000 in recent year (Malekahmadi, 2006). Recently a generous budget was approved for improving and expanding the facilities in rural Public Libraries. In the last 5 years, two national plans, viz., "*Public libraries development Master plan*" and "*Information technology master plan*" have been developed. The current status of public libraries including classification, training, collection, organizational chart,

1 I would also like to thank Mr. Najafi from IPLF for sending the latest data relating to the public libraries.

personnel and services were studied through the first project. During the second plan, which started recently, all the public libraries will be equipped with new IT tools and as a final point, public libraries will be networked to be able to share their resources.

4.3. Special Libraries

There are many glorious and enriched specific libraries in Iran. These libraries are not categorized as college or public library and are operating under the supervision of specific persons or Institutes. The well-known *Astan Ghods Razavi* (AGR) library in Meshad is one of these libraries. The new building of AGR library with an area of 28,800 square meters was inaugurated in 1994. This library and its branches have a collection of over 5,340,000 volumes in different formats of Books, documents, manuscripts, serials and microfiches and electronic resources (Astan Ghods library, 2006). In June 2006, AGR library and its 37 branches had 303,234 members. Now the main building of AGR library in Meshad has 899,528 Books, 50,486 manuscripts, 34,391 lithography books, 37,244 microfilms and 27,576 audiovisuals (Shakheshaye Amari, 2006). The AGR library is computerized and its activities are automated. Recently, this library announced the initiation of a digital library.

The *Ayatollah Marashi Najafi* (AMN) library in Qom is another large religious library. This library has over 800,000 books, mostly in Persian and Arabic, 2500 periodicals, more than 60,000 manuscripts, and over 16,200 microfilms and microfiches of old manuscripts (Ganjeeneh shahab, 2006). This library is affiliated with the academic theological institutes, which are under the authority of the Ulama Foundation.

Regional Library of Science and Technology (RLST), in Shiraz, is a large library and information center in Iran. RLST was established in 1991 under an agreement between the Islamic Republic of Iran's Ministry of Science, Research and Technology (MCRT) and the Third-World Academy of Sciences. It was intended to act as a regional center for reference, study and bibliographical information and other services in relation to both scientific and technological issues. In the region (Central Asia and Middle-East), the RLST holds a special place. Within a short period RLST has been able to expand its programmes and services among the scientific and technology communities within the region (Regional library, 2006). A set of new databases including *Iran Science Citation Index* has been developed by RLST.

There are also so many other specific and special libraries and information centers such as IRANDOC affiliated with ministries and research or private institutions. It is difficult to give a detailed account of all these here.

4.4. Academic libraries

All the universities and colleges are trying to empower their staff and students with access to libraries. After the Islamic Revolution in Iran, nearly all of the universities are trying to develop their library collections. In Iran, the Academic Libraries (ALs) are under the control of MCRT, while all medical Libraries are under the authority of Ministry of Health, Treatment and Medical Education (MHTME). Davarpanah (1998) in a survey conducted in 1998 examined 55 (of 79) central libraries in the two above-mentioned ministries. He showed that 92.73 % percent of analyzed libraries had computer systems and 90.20% had computerized catalogues. The collections in university libraries add up to 6 million books, half in English or Arabic or other foreign languages. In a survey of 270 university libraries only 1.8% had over 100,000 books. It showed 35.8% of the library staff with academic qualifications of bachelor's degree or higher, of which only 25.3% possessed degrees in library or information sciences. In management positions 1.1% had Ph.D. degrees, but only 0.2% in library science, but progressively more or 5.3% out of 8.4% with master's degrees were trained in library or information science.

4.5 Mosque libraries

Mosque libraries (MLs) belong to mosques and are generally housed beside or inside them. The history of MLs runs parallel to the establishment of mosques themselves in Islam. Books and the other information materials have been the most important source of enrichment of MLs collections throughout Islamic history. The reverence of mosques and thereupon their libraries, operated and managed with the help of volunteers are the most specific features of mosque libraries (Hashemi, 2003).

After the conquest of Moslems upon Iran Empire, Iranians began to establish MLs inside mosque buildings. While there were a lot of MLs before the Islamic Revolution in Iran, it was only after the Revolution that the flourish of MLs began. Now, there are about 57,635 mosques and 7,000 MLs through out the country (Hashemi, 2004; Statistical Center of Iran, 2006). In order to equip the MLs and to provide religious training and education, *Head Office of Culture and Art Centers of Mosques (HOCACM)* was established in 1993. As of now only 1,500 mosque libraries with total collection of 6,253,432 volumes, 5,496 personnel and 525,207 members are under the authority of *HOCACM*[1]. Activities related to collection building, establishing library standards, preparing guidelines and equipping mosque libraries with information technology are among the responsibilities of HOCACM. Recently the *Mosque libraries IT plan* was drafted and this will be implemented very soon.

1 The effort of my dear friend Mr. Hashemi, Head of Mosque Libraries Affair, in making accessible the needed data is acknowledged.

4.6. School libraries

Because of the young population, there are a lot of schools and educational institutions in Iran. While there is no up-to-date and complete statistics about the number of School Libraries (SL), according to an extensive school census in Ministry of Culture and Islamic Guidance (MCIG) in 2002, there exist 4,100 school libraries with a total collection of 7,761,633 titles (11,527,574 copies) throughout the country. 73% of these SLs were established after 1981. 14.8% of these libraries are located in primary schools, 30.4% in guidance schools and 54.7% in secondary schools. There exist about 6,213 library staff in SLs, of whom only 22.3 % had professional library qualifications.

5. STATUS OF EDUCATION IN IRAN

Due to the large proportion of youth and also government attention, education is one of the most important areas in Iran. Numerous training institutes, governmental, semi_ governmental and private, are involved in education and training in all levels. Since the Islamic Revolution of 1979 in Iran, the educational system of the country has undergone qualitative and quantitative changes (Education System in Iran, 2004). Many educational institutions, especially in higher education, paid attention to the electronic learning in recent years. This attention has made some institutes to offer their educational programs - including high school and university entrance exams- , in the distance mode and through the Web.

5.1. School Education

The school system is under the authority of the Ministry of Education and Training (MET). The structure of the educational system under this Ministry is divided into 4 stages: pre-school, primary, guidance and secondary (high school) education cycles. In 2004, a total of 16,030,767 students, 360,855 teachers in 137,669 schools were in different school educational stages (Number of employees, 2005). Pre-school education is a one-year program for five-year-old infants. 439,034 kids were enrolled in this stage in 2005. The five-year primary cycle covers grades 1-5 for children 6 to 11 years old (Compare Students, 2005). This phase is both free and compulsory. A total of 6,648,755 students were enrolled in the academic year 2003-2004 in this stage (Number of Schools, 2005). The guidance (middle) stage covers grades 6 to 8 for children 11 to 13 years old. Like the previous stage, this phase also provides students with general education. Altogether, 4,679,207 students signed up in this stage in 2005 (Number of students, 2005).

Secondary Education cycle is a four-year stage, which covers grade 9 to Grade 12, from age 14 to 17. Secondary education is divided into two main branches, academic/ general and technical/vocational, each of which are divided into other related mainstreams. In recent years, the MET has proposed and implemented a new secondary education system. In this new system and after the guidance stage, students enter a three years secondary stage during which they should complete 96 units in order to be awarded the High School Diploma. Students who are willing to enter the universities and colleges should complete an additional one year of preparation in order to attend university entrance examination known as KONKUR (Education System in Iran, 2004). In 2005, 3,818,814 students were enrolled in secondary schools in Iran (Compare Students, 2005). One important point is that English language, as a second language, is introduced from grade 7. The MET also runs a number of schools outside Iran, mainly in the Persian Gulf region and some European countries.

Recently a Science and Arts Foundation (SAF) has initiated a project (Schoolnet) in order to empower the students with information literacy skills (Schoolnet, 2006). Under this, students all over the country are able to access the Internet.

5.2. Higher Education

Ministry of Science, Research and Technology (MCRT), Formerly Ministry of Culture and Higher Education (MCHE), *Ministry of Health and Medical Education (MHME),* as two governmental Ministries, Payame Noor university (correspondence universities) and Islamic Azad (open) University (IAU), as a private educational institute, are responsible for most post-secondary education in Iran. These universities plus some other related governmental educational institutions offer a wide range of higher educational programmes and courses. Since 1987, masters and doctorate courses have been offered in many different disciplines (Education System in Iran, 2004). At present, there are over 119 universities and Higher Educational Institutes (HEI), 101 IAU institutions and more than 15 Islamic Education Centers (IEC) in Iran representing higher educational programmes (Institute for Higher Education Research and Planning, 2005). The total number of students in sextet subject groups i.e. basic science, human science, medical science, engineering, agriculture and veterinary and art science, in all (governmental and nongovernmental) Higher Educational Institute (HEI), which was 175,675 in 1979, has increased to 2,117,471 in 2005, of which 1,018,980 (51.88%) were in universities and higher education institutes (governmental) and 1,098,491 (48.2%) in Islamic Azad (open) University (IAU) (Statistical Center of Iran, 2006). Details of students in universities and HEI and IAU in the academic year 2004-2005 are presented in Tables 2 and 3.

It is estimated that the number of students will be increased to nearly 3,000,000 in 2006 (Ministry of Science,

Research and Technology, 2006). In addition, there are so many Iranian students who are studying abroad. To facilitate access to faculty and students in universities, ICT facilities and network conveniences have been developed. Nearly all governmental and Azad (open) universities are equipped with Local Area Networks (LANs) and high speed computers and are connected to the National Scientific Network (NSN) through central Servers. About 300 universities and research centers are now covered in the network (Iran's National Scientific Networks, 2006). Recently, in 2006, the Scientific Data Center (SDC) project is proposed. A committee, i.e. the "*Network and Internal Equipment Committee for Universities and Research Centers*" has been established to help the equipment, development and promotion of ICTs in universities, research centers, and Science and Technology Parks (STP) (Komite, 2006). This committee has extended the network access to (more than 26) different universities such as Arak, Eelam, Rafsangan, Zanjan, Alzahra, Gorgan, Yasodj, Kordestan, Qom and many other universities throughout the country, which had no integrated campus network. Disseminating information services to universities throughout the country and facilitating access to needed information necessitate the establishment of this national wide scientific network (Ministry of Science, Research and Technology, 2006).

6. INFORMATION AND COMMUNICATION TECHNOLOGY INFRASTRUCTURE

The first form of Information and Communication Technology (ICT) in Iran was the fax in 1988, and then the computer. Now Iran itself develops ICT Technology. ICT is regarded in Iran as an opportunity for development in different areas. In long-term economic, social and cultural plans such as five-year plans, (the fourth

Table 2: Number of students in universities and higher education institutes (governmental) in Iran by broad field of study in the academic year 2004-2005*

Broad field	All degrees	Associate	Undergraduate	Master's	Prof. / Doctorate	Specialty doctorate
Medicine	91312	25815	28704	2729	28324	5740
Humanities	465690	36540	408167	18038	0	2945
Basic sciences	136923	1090	125463	8552	0	1818
Engineering & Technology	227699	117154	93854	14325	0	2366
Agriculture & Veterinary Sc.	62070	14574	40553	3882	1967	1094
Arts	35286	15672	16720	2700	0	194
Total	**1018980**	**210845**	**713461**	**50226**	**30291**	**14157**

* Table is generated by using statistics gathered from different parts of MCRT website

Table 3: Number of students of Islamic Azad (open) university (IAU) in Iran by broad field of study in the academic year 2004-2005*

Broad field	All degrees	Associate	Undergraduate	Master's	Prof. & Specialty doctorate
Medicine	41528	11936	21958	81	7553
Humanities	498739	130095	349686	17638	1320
Basic sciences	95473	23762	68100	3107	504
Engineering & Technology	352437	175826	172219	4202	190
Agriculture & Veterinary Sc.	80786	24424	50073	2314	3975
Arts	29528	12420	14254	2798	56
Total	**1098491**	378463	676290	30140	13598

* Table is generated by using statistics gathered from different parts of IAU website

Development Plan is under implementation), and also in the Islamic Republic's Twenty-year Vision Document, high attention has been paid to ICT. The theme of the Fourth Development Plan is ***"Stable knowledge-based economic growth"***, and ICT Sector Development Program, as a development tool for furthering the economy and providing job opportunities, support for trade, tourism and so forth, has an important role in achieving the goals. The Ministry of Communications and IT is responsible for the Information and Communications Technology sector in Iran. Its responsibilities include: Telecommunication, Information Technology, Post and Space, Radio communications, data, audio and video transfer, computer link services, creating a suitable basis and support mechanism for information transfer, monitoring, data processing and telemetry methods and Control on the frequency spectrum, protecting Iran's radio frequency rights on a regional and global level, introducing regulations and standards in various postal and telecom sectors communications, etc (Rahmani, 2004).

6.1. Telecommunication

Establishing, developing, maintaining and making use of telecommunication infrastructure, data communication services, national communication network services, and providing fixed rural and urban telephone and cellular phone services, including mobile phone, is the major activity of The Ministry of Communications and IT in the field of telecommunication. On the eve of the Islamic Revolution, there had been 850,000 fixed telephone lines in service in Iran. Installation and operation of the first phase of mobile phone network in Tehran using 176 launcher and receiver in 24 radio stations with a capacity of 9200 lines started in 1994 (Mobile telephone, 2006). In 1995, Iran's communication network capacity exceeded 5 million lines. This number increased to 9.8 million in

2000. During the same period, the fixed telephone analogue network of Iran has been converted to digital in many regions and cities. In the beginning of the year 2000, over half a million mobile phones were in operation, covering more than 230 cities and towns in Iran (Tabesh, 2004). However, as of September 2006, the number of fixed telephones increased to 21,082,715 and mobile phones to 9,928,083 (Sherkate Mokhaberat Iran, 2006). It is projected to increase the number of government and non-government fixed telephones to 36,250,809 and mobile phones to 36,250,678 by the end of Fourth Development Plan (Iran telecom, 2006).

6.2. Information Technology sector

Activities relating to Information Technology (IT) are classified into two types. E-government, E-business and E-health are some super-sector activities in the IT domain. The major organizations, which are active in the field of IT, consist of the Supreme Council of Information Technology (SCIT) and Ministry of Communication and Information Technology (MCIT). SCIT is responsible for major policies and preparation of national guidelines in IT domain, compilation of long-term plans for extension of fundamental and applicable research and also expansion of application of IT in the country. MCIT has activities in major fields of communication, mail, IT and judicial affairs (Rahmani, 2004). Increasing Internet capacity of the country, increasing of data users, connecting more number of villages to data networks, boosting and increasing the number of communication lines, IT office services, electronic cards and high speed ports, and finally developing the courses offered in electronics are among the goals included in the 4th Development Plan.

6.2.1. ICT Laws and Regulations

The history of informatics and its related regulations in

Iran goes back by 30 years. The first law of such nature was the High Council of Informatics (HCI) incorporation law, which was enacted in 1980. This law defined the authority and responsibilities of HCI as the country's highest authority regarding informatics. In 1994, the first regulation on ICT, *the By-law Authorizing Establishment and Supervision of Video and Computer Game Sales and playing Centers*, was officially enacted. In 1998, coinciding with the beginning of the third five-year plan, the ICT was given attention. The first law to provide legal copyright protection for software products was enacted in the year 2000 (Iran telecom annual report 2003, 2004). In 2002, another law named "*Administrative Tasks Automation and Access to the Internet*" was approved. Also the first national plan for expansion of ICT applications named TAKFA was ratified and put into action in this year. The Information and Communication Technology Application program (TAKFA) has been the most important ICT policy initiative in Iran. The Supreme Council on Information and Communication Technology (SCICT), the highest decision making body in ICT policy making in Iran, based on a direct order from the former president, carried out the development of TAKFA which began in late 1999 and ended 2003 (Sadeghnezhad, 2006). This national ICT development plan was to encourage and extend the use of ICT in Iran's private and governmental companies and organizations and establishment of an infrastructure for advancement of ICT throughout the country. Allocation of US$ 20 million for e-Commerce, US$ 20 million for e-Education at the secondary school level, adoption of ICDL (International Driving License) by government as a mandatory skill for all governmental employees and creation of a significant awareness among all government officials regarding the importance of TAKFA was the most achievement of this initiative (Jahangard, 2005). During the implementation,

TAKFA spent US$ 400 million for improvement of ICT infrastructure.

The next substantial step was formulation of Development Plan. The plan called for striving toward accomplishing a *knowledge-based economy* and *worldwide interaction.* In early 2003, the Supreme Council of Cultural Revolution made the preparations for establishing a committee for determining instances of illegal websites in order to have an overview of Internet activities. Later on in April 2003, as a major step toward determining policies for expansion of ICT applications in Iran, "*The Procedure for execution of defined activities for expansion of ICT Application*" was formulated. The *Law of Functions and Jurisdiction of the Ministry of ICT* was passed in late 2003. It was aimed at coordinating the overall ICT efforts and eliminating redundancies (Supreme Council of ICT of Iran, 2006).

The E-commerce Law was the latest ICT-related bill confirmed in early 2004. This law has defined the legal infrastructure of E-commerce and has paved the way for creating the technical infrastructure necessary for Iran to join the nations already capable of doing commerce electronically. In July 2005, the *Techno Crime Regulation Act* submitted to the Islamic Parliament of Iran and approved (Layehe, 2006).

6.2.2. Data Communication Infrastructure

To establish and extend the required network infrastructure further, many programs have been expanded. There were 8,230 KMs of fiber optics laid between the cities in 2003 (Fiber optic network, 2006). Today 34,198 KMs fiber optic has been laid in major cities and between switching centers in Tehran and other big cities (Supreme Council of ICT of Iran, 2006; Sherkate Mokhaberat Iran, 2006). The east-west and Fujaira lines have been developed to link to the international fiber optics network, FLAG, linking Iran to Frankfurt in Germany in the west and to Shanghai in China in the east. The ICT Ministry has drafted and implemented extensive programmes for establishment and expansion of the necessary infrastructure for the National Data Network. National Data Network is currently operational in 85 cities and 210 centers with a capacity of 2000 high-speed ports. By the end of August 2006, the number of ports was expanded to 79,138 (Sherkate Mokhaberat Iran, 2006). Network will be thus able to provide data services to 15,000,000 subscribers by the end of the fourth five-year development plan of the country (Tabesh, 2004).

In order to enhance data communication, the Data Communication Network (DCN) was enhanced by 689 Mbps, and its capacity reached 11,267 Mbps, covering 331 cities by March 2004. At present, in August 2006, the DCN capacity between provinces and inside the provinces is 102,630 Mbps (Shakhesha, 2006). The present numbers of ISPs are 1065, VOIPs are 101, X.25 subscribers are 3,000 and finally ICPs are 39 (Telecommunication Company of Iran, 2006; Sherkate Mokhaberat Iran, 2006). In April 2006, 992,350 registered IP has been reported in Iran (IP Counts by Country, 2006). According to the approved restructuring plan, Telecommunication Company of Iran (TCI) is being divided into a new Specialized Mother Company, and the 31 other companies, which will operate as its subsidiaries (Iran telecom annual report 2003, 2004). They include 3 new companies named as Data communications, Mobile Communications and Backbone Communications Company. The Ministry of ICT is in charge of policy-making for all the sections. In the new structure, the private / non-governmental sector is allowed to operate fixed, mobile, and data communications. Two new private operators, i.e. Iran Cell and Talia, have started to do the job in the mobile section (Supreme Council of ICT of Iran, 2006).

6.2.3. Communication Equipment Industries

The government has invested heavily in the field of communications in the last fifteen years. As a result, the number of telephone subscriptions (fixed) has increased substantially. Currently, licenses for six more independent fixed telephone operators and two mobile telephone operators have been issued. In making this investment, the Ministry of ICT, has procured the required equipment and facilities mostly from within the country (137 manufacturers of communication equipment). Due to this policy, the Telecommunications Company of Iran (TCI) has become the largest market for all Iranian communication equipment manufacturers, leading to the growth in both quantity and quality of communication equipment production in Iran. Currently 120 companies are involved in the design and production of communication equipment and parts including switches, copper and fiber optic cable, radios, antenna, and transport equipment, power supplies, ?connectors, various boards, modems, and multiplexers (Tabesh, 2004).

6.2.4. Internet use

Iran's Internet link started in the early 90s; that is, a little after publicizing it throughout the word (Gholami, 2004; Ministry of ICT, 2006). While the number of Internet users in Iran didn't exceed 250 persons in 1994, it has grown rapidly since the year 2000 (ICT and productivity of the manufacturing industries in Iran). One objective of the Fourth Five- year Development Plan is to raise Internet diffusion rate from the current 5.2% to 30% statewide. There are currently 7,200,000 Internet users, 157 Web hosting companies and nearly 75,000 active websites in Iran (Tahleel, 2006). This number grows geometrically at an estimated annual rate of 70%. Most of these users connect to the Internet through Dial- up services provided by 1065 (virtual and real) ISPs. The rest use Internet-café services (Tabesh, 2004). In a statistical report from Information Technology Company (2006), Iran with 11,200,000 users received rank 20 in Internet use throughout the world.

6.3. Posting Services

Post Company (PC), as a governmental unit, represents postal services in Iran. Good representation of this service is one of the important criteria, among the others, for evaluating the improvement of a country. Activities such as acquisition, execution, supervision over comprehensive programs of postal services, development of post units, private mailbox and other jobs are the main duties of PC. The Islamic Republic of Iran Post Company comprises of 3 parts, which are non-governmental subdivisions, Post-Bank and PAYAM Aviation Services Company. In August 2005, PC received 11,265,000 postal consignments from and delivered 2,710,000 to abroad. Altogether, 778,019,000 postal consignments delivered to abroad last year (Shakhesha, 2006).

6.4. Space Sector

Because of the importance of coordination of space affairs, the discussion about the need for establishment of Space Organization (SO) of the country started in 1998. Finally, the foundation of SO with responsibility and authority of regulations occurred in 2003 (Rahmani, 2004). Increasing the number of earth stations which receive satellite information, amount of selling space services, and providing a part of country's requirements of satellite band-width by national satellites are the most important goals and duties of SO. There are some Satellite Communication Centers (SCC) in Iran. One of the biggest satellite communication centers in the Middle East is located in the town of Boomehen, 35 kilometers north of Tehran. This center provides services to 1250 phone channels and maintains international telephone communication with Europe, Africa, and Asia. Iran also utilizes services of a number of satellite systems such as NOAA-AVHRR and three ground satellite stations, namely Intel Sat in the Pacific Ocean and Inmarsat-A in the Indian Ocean; an independent communication satellite project named Zohreh is also under study (Supreme Council of ICT of Iran, 2006). Creating communication for far reach areas, rural areas, lands, oil platforms and mines; and providing video coverage and facilitating better communication with the countries in the region are among the important goals of Zohreh satellite plan (Zohreh satellite network, 2006).

7. RESEARCH AND CULTURAL STATUS

Within the last decade the volume of scientific activities, research projects, and articles published by Iranians in reputed foreign publications has increased considerably. In 2005, the number of Iranian indexed papers in the citation indexes of ISI was 5,423 in science, 225 in social sciences, 11 in arts and humanities and 5578 in total. Excepting Turkey, Iran's scientific production is ranked highest among all Moslem and neighboring countries in the Middle East (Saboury, 2006). The research criterion in universities and research institutes has also been developed in recent years. The number of finished projects reported by Scientific and Cultural Council of Assessment and Supervision (SCCAS) (2002) which was 5,892 in 2002, has increased to 20,070 in 2004 (Shakhesha, 2005).

There are 2,817 serials being published in Iran in the local language Farsi and some other languages like English and Arabic. Most of these publications are scientific journals (Statistical Center of Iran, 2006). In 2005, 50,813 books were published in Iran, including 11,826 translations, which shows 24.2 % increase than the previous year (Statistical Center of Iran, 2006).

8. CONCLUSION

While there is no NIS in Iran, many steps have been taken forward in recent years. Many facilities and requirements to establish the NIS are made ready during the last couple of decades. Nearly all required infrastructure in order to implementing the NIS is in place. The ICT backbones, including Internet, telephones, organizational networks in universities, banks, economic enterprises, governmental offices and all other needed backbones are prepared. Nearly all the governmental and private sectors are using IT. The number of professionals in Library and Information Science has increased. Network facilities including Local Area Network, Intranets and Extranets are extending rapidly through the cultural, research, and scientific institutions. By implementing TAKFA (The Information and Communication Technology Application) program, a lot of needed capacities and facilities for developing the E-government and automated office in governmental and private sectors are made ready. All universities and academic institutes are connected together and are sharing their bibliographic data through a National network. The extent of computer and Internet use is growing rapidly. Given the importance being attached to IT, it seems likely that the needed infrastructure for implementing a unique standard and establishing a National Information system will be prepared in the next few years in Iran.

9. REFERENCES

1. Astan Ghods library (2006). [Online Available]: http://www.aqlibrary.ir. Accessed: 12/1/2006.
2. Bureau of Near Eastern Affairs (2006). *Background Note: Iran*. [Online available]: http://www.state.gov/r/pa/ei/bgn/5314.htm. Accessed: 11/17/2006.
3. Compare Students in all grades from 1943 (2005).

[Online available]: http://www.sci. org.ir/. Accessed: 9/22/2006.

4. *E-Commerce Policy of the Islamic Republic of Iran (Decree of the Council of Ministers)* (2006). [Online available]: http://www.kafa-iran.com/ICT/ilam001.asp. Accessed: 10/18/2006.
5. *Education System in Iran* (2004). [Online available]: http://www. Salamiran .org /Embassy/ Embassy/ Student Advisory/Iran _ education / Iran_Education_system .html. Accessed: 10/13/2006.
6. Fattahi, Rahmatallah; Zandiravan, Narges (2006). *Rahnamaye gorohhaye amozesh ketabdari va ettela resanidar daneshgahhaye dolati Iran* [Guide to the library and information departments in public (governmental) universities in Iran]. Meshad. (Under publishing).
7. Fiber optic network (2006). [Online available]: http://irantelecom.ir/eng.asp?sm=21& page =11&code=6. Accessed: 10/23/2006.
8. Ganjeeneh shahab, Ashnaee ba ketabkhane bozorge ayatollah Marashi Najafi [Acquaintance with Marashi Najafi glorious library] (2006). [Online available]: http://www.marashilibrary. com/lyb.html. Accessed: 12/10/2006
9. Ghasemi, Farid (1995). Nakhostin kelase amozeshe ketabdari dar Iran [First librarianship course in Iran]. *FasIname ketab*. P: 70-73.
10. Gholami, Roghieh; Moshiri, Saeed; Tome Lee, Sang-Yong (2004). ICT and productivity of the manufacturing industries in Iran. *The electronic journal on information systems in developing countries*, 19, 4. P. 1-19. [Online available]: www.ejisdc.org. Accessed: 9/15/2006.
11. Hashemi, Abolfazl, Gilvari, Abbas (2003). Vazeeyate ketabkhanehaye masajed dar Iran [Status of mosque libraries in Iran]. *Farhang dar maser doshvare tosee*. Tehran: rozname Iran. P. 692-705.
12. Hashemi, Abolfazl, Gilvari, Abbas (2004).

Ketankhanehaye masajede Iran az aghaz ta konon [Iran mosque libraries: from past to the present]. Tehran: Head Office of Culture and Art centers of Mosque.

13. Hayati, Zouhayr (2005). Competency definition for Iranian library and information professionals. *J. of Education for Library and Information Science*, Vol. 46, No. 2. PP. 165-192.

14. Homayoon-Farokh, R.n.d (1969). (The Iranian royal libraries). In Persian Ministry of Culture and Arts, Tehran, Iran.

15. Horri, Abbas (1994). *Nezame meli etelaresani* [National Information System]. Tehran: National Library of Iran.

16. Horri, Abbas (2004). Library and information science research productivity in Iran. *Journal of education for library and information science*, Vol.45(1), P. 15-25.

17. Information Technology Company (2006). Rotbebandi keshvarha bar asase tedad karbaran Internet [Number of Internet users by ranking of countries].

18. Institute for Higher Education Research and Planning (2005). *Amare Amozeshe aali dar yek negah* [Higher education at a glance]. Tehran: Ministry of Science, Research and technology.

19. IP Counts by Country (2006). [Online available]: http://www.itc.ir/ip-count.htm. Accessed: 12/2/2006.

20. IRANDOC (2006). Iranian Library Association (ILA). [Online Available]: http: irandoc.ac.ir. Accessed: 10/29/2006.

21. Iran Public Libraries Foundation, (2002). Tarhe Jame Toseeye ketabkhanehaye omomi Keshvar. Gozaresh marhale avval [developing public libraries pervasive plan: phase one report]. Tehran: Asre_danesh Cultural and Artistic Institute.

22. Iran telecom (2006). *Quantitative objectives of mobile telephone commissioning during the Fourth Development Plan, 2005-2009*. [Online available]: http://irantelecom.ir / eng.asp?page= 23&code=

3&sm=0. Accessed: 11/22/2006.

23. Iran telecom annual report 2003. [Online available]: http://www.irantelecom.ir/default .asp?sm= 64&page= 40&code=7
24. Iran telecom annual report 2004. [Online available]: http://www.irantelecom.ir/default .asp?sm= 64&page= 40&code=7
25. Iran's National Scientific Network (2006). [Online Available]: www.iranscience.net. Accessed: 10/2/ 2006.
26. Jahangard, Nasrollah (2005). TAKFA, Iran's road to knowledge-based development. [Online available]: www.iran-ict.org/Portal/File/ShowFile.aspx?ID =f20f51e1-3e47-4279aceda75be43eff5d http:// unpan1.un.org/intradoc/groups/public/documents/ APCITY/UNPAN006172.pdf. Accessed: 10/22/2006.
27. JSIS (1995). *Nezame meli etelaresani* [National Information System (selected paper)]. Tehran: JSIS.
28. Komite shabake va tajhizate dakheli daneshgahha va marakeze tahghighati [Network and Internal Equipment Committee for Universities and Research Centers] (2006). [Online available]: http://takfa.msrt.ir/ f_committe/committe.htm. Accessed: 9/08/ 2006.
29. Layehe ghanoone jarayem Rayanehi [Techno Crime Regulation Act], (2006). [Online available]: http:// www.itc.ir/aeen/mogharrarat.htm. Accessed: 12/3/ 2006.
30. Mahdavi, Mohammad naghi (1993). *Kholase maghalate seminar barresi naghsh etelaresani dar tahghigh va tosee* [examining the role of information system on research and development]. Tehran: Information Cooperative Committee.
31. Malekahmadi, Mohammad Hossein, (2006). Tarhe IT Ketabkhanehaye omomi keshvar bezodi edjra mishavad [Public libraries IT Plan will start very soon]. [Online available]: http:// www.ictna.ir/news/archives/ 005741.htm. Accessed: 12/13/2006.

32. Ministry of ICT (2006). Internet va Gozaresh az vazeyate aan dar Iran [Internet and its state of affairs in Iran]. [Online available]: http://www.ict.gov.ir/article-fa-1.html. Accessed: 10/26/ 2006.
33. Ministry of Science, Research and Technology (2006). *Hasele yek sal talash dar vezarate olom, tahghighat va fanavari* [Outcome of one year endeavor in Ministry of Science, Research and Technology]. Tehran.
34. Mobile telephone (2006). [Online available] http://irantelecom.ir/eng.asp?page=9&code= 1&sm=15. Accessed: 10/28/2006.
35. Nourozian (2006). Ketabkhanehaye omomi Iran pishanee bakhshe farhang; goft o goo ba dabire kole heiate omanaye ketabkhanehaye omomi keshvar [Public libraries of Iran at the frontal part of culture]. *Koleeat Ketab Mah*, Volume 9(1,2), P. 5-17.
36. Number of employees separated by sex and location From 1997-2003; level of education: primary (2005).
37. Number of Schools in all grades from 1943 (2005). [Online available]: http://www.sci.org.ir/. Accessed: 9/22/2006.
38. Number of Students in all grades from 1943 (20005). [Online available]: [Online available]: http://www.sci.org.ir/. Accessed: 9/22/2006.
39. Omidvar, Madjid (2000). *Tahaye tarhe pishnahadi tarahi nezame etelaresani elmi va fani* [proposed plan for designing Scientific and Technical Information System]. Tehran: IRANDOC.
40. *Provinces of Iran* (2006). [Online available]: http://www.answers.com /topic/ provinces of-Iran. Accessed: 10/15/2006.
41. Rahmani, M. H. (2004). *ICT Sector of the 4th Development Plan*. Translator: A. R. Saghafian. Tehran: TCI Public Relations Office.
42. Razeghi Oskoee, Faranak (2002). Gozareshe porodje tarahie koliate nezame meli etelaat [Designing totality of national information system]. *Khabarname Anformatik*, No. 86, P. 62-64.

43. Regional library of Science and Technology (2006). A Note from the President. [Online available]: http://www.srlst.com/note.htm. Accessed: 12/15/2006.

44. Rokneddin Homayun, Farrokh (1965). *Tarikh-cheh Ketab Khaneh-ha-y Iran va ketabkhaneh ha-y Omumi* (1965). Tehran: Ettehad.

45. Saboury, A. A. (2006). Scientific production in Iran – 2005. *Rahyaft, Science policy quarterly,* No. 37, P. 49-52.

46. Sadeghnezhad, Tohid (2006). Iran ICT use in education. *UNESCO Meta-survey on the use of technologies in education* 64. [Online available]: http://64.233.161.104/search ?q=cache bS67WkhQ0YcJ:www.unescobkk.org/file admin/user_upload/ict/Meta survey/IRAN.PDF+ ICT+in+iran&hl= fa&ct= clnk &cd =16&lr=lang_en. Accessed: 11/5/2006.

47. Schoolnet: Community of the Iranian Schools (2006). [Online available]: http://www1. school net .ir/en/about/ Accessed: 10/27/2006.

48. Scientific and Cultural Council of Assessment and Supervision, (2002). *Avaleen arzyabie khorde daneshgahha va moassesate padjoheshi dolati* [The first Micro-assessment of public universities and research institutions]. Researchers: Jafar Mehrad, Mohammad hossein Dayyani. Tehran: High Council of Cultural Revolution; Scientific and Cultural Council of Assessment and Supervision.

49. Shabani, Ahmad (2004). Naghsh va kaarkard novin anjoman ketabdari va etelaresani Iran dar tosee faaliathaye mashverati va mosharekati ketabdari keshvar [The role and function of ILIA in expanding the library consultancy and cooperative activities]. *Payame Ketabkhane*, Vol. 12, (1,2).

50. *Shakhesha va namagarhaye* ertebatat 1384 [indicator and criterion of Communication in 2005], (2006). [Online available]: http://www.irantelecom.ir/?page=227&code =1

51. *Shakhesha va namagarhaye olom, tahghighat va fanavari* 1384-85[indicator and criterion of science, research and technology in 2005], (2005). [Online available]: http://www .itiran.com/?type=article&id= 6944. Accessed: 10/11/2006.

52. Shakheshaye Amari sazmane ketabkhaneha, moozeha va markaz asnade Astan Ghods Razavi [Statistical criteria in Organization of Libraries, Museums and Document Centers of Astan Ghods Razavi]. [Online available]: http://www.aqlibrary.ir/ statistic/ organization-statistic.aspx. Accessed: 11/24/ 2006.

53. Sherkate Mokhaberat Iran (2006). *Gozareshe pishrafte Haftegie faaliathaye mokhaberati keshvar va ostanha dar sale 85* [weekly report of advances in the country and provinces communication in 2006]. [Online available]: http://www.irantelecom.ir / default.asp?sm=64&page=40&code=7. Accessed: 10/ 11 /2006.

54. Soltani, Poori (2002). Historical aspects of cataloging and classification in Iran. *Cataloging & Classification Quarterly*, Vol. 35(1/ 2), pp. 187- 207.

55. Statistical Center of Iran (2006). [Online available]: http://www.sci.org.ir /portal /faces / public/scien/ scien.Glance/sci_en.educate. Accessed: 11/2/2006.

56. Supreme Council of ICT of Iran (2006). [Online available]: http://www.answers.com /topic / supreme -council-of-ict-of-Iran. Accessed: 11/18/2006.

57. Tabesh, Yahya (2004). Digital review of Iran. *Proceedings of the meeting & workshop on development of a national IT strategy focusing on indigenous content development.* Iran: ministry of Science, Research & Technology; Iranian Information & Documentation Center.

58. Tahleel bazaar hosting Iran [Evaluating the hosting market of Iran]. [Online available]: http://www.ict.gov.ir/ article-fa-1.html. Accessed: 11/24/2006.

59. Tarikhche ketabkhanehaye omomi dar Iran [History

of public libraries in Iran]. [Online available]: http://www.ipl.ir/tarikh.htm. Accessed: 12/13/2006.

60. Telecommunication Company of Iran (2006). Fanavari etelaat [Information technology].
61. The word bank (2004). [Online available]: http://web.worldbank.org/ WBSITE/ EXTERNAL COUNTRIES/ MENAEXT/IRANEXTN/0,menuPK: 312962~pagePK : 141159~piPK:141110 ~the Site PK :312943,00.html. Accessed: 10/23/2006.
62. Umapathy, K. S. (1979). Libraries and librarianship in Iran. *International Library Review,* 10, P. 119-135.
63. Wikipedia, The free encyclopedia (2006). [Online available]: www.wikipedia.org
64. Zohreh satellite network, (2006). [Online available]: http://irantelecom.ir/zohrehtele com network.htm. Accessed: 11/13/2006.

4

MOVING INDIA INTO THE 21st CENTURY KNOWLEDGE ECONOMY: OUTLINES OF A PROPOSAL FOR BUILDING A NATIONAL INFORMATION INFRASTRUCTURE

M N Seetharaman[1]

The convergence of computer and communication technologies has led to the emergence of a global information infrastructure in the form of the World Wide Web. Unleashing an information revolution and pioneering new ways of exchanging information and ideas, Internet is helping to create a global information society and a global knowledge economy. As we move further into the 21st century, information will become a highly critical force, and the speed with which information is created, accessed and put into use will cause even more fundamental changes in the global

1 Consultant, Information Systems & Services, 502, 3rd Cross, 7th Main, HAL II Stage, Bangalore 560 008 (Ph: 080-25285837; Email: mns27@hotmail.com)

economy. India is now on the threshold of moving towards an industrial and beyond the industrial to a knowledge-based economy. The prime mover of India's knowledge economy is the fastest growing information and communication technology sector, which has emerged to make the country a global information technology superpower and a front-runner in the age of information revolution. Economists predict that India will be among frontline economic powers of the world by the year 2050. It is in this context that building a national information infrastructure (NII) assumes critical importance, since a well-established and well-integrated NII can help to sustain and boost India's knowledge economy further. This paper defines national information infrastructure and its goals and objectives, and then proceeds to outline the broad contours of a plan for designing and building the NII in India. Some of the potential applications and benefits of NII for the business, industry, government and the general public are also highlighted.

1. PREAMBLE

I wish to present this paper as a mark of my tributes to Prof. S. Parthasarathy, the living legend and doyen of library and information science in India, on the occasion of his 92nd birthday this year. I have had the good fortune of being his most favourite student among all those who had passed out of the portals of INSDOC since the 1960s. For over 40 years since then, I have been maintaining a close and abiding teacher-student relationship with him and availing of the benefit of his advice and guidance in my professional activities.

I feel I have titled this paper appropriately so as to enable the present day librarians and information scientists to recall and reflect upon the innovative and path-breaking contributions made by Prof. Parthasarathy towards laying the foundation of the key elements of information infrastructure in India upon which it is now possible to build a well-integrated National Information Infrastructure (NII) system on par with those in the developed countries like the United States of America which was the first to conceive this pioneering concept and translate it into a reality, with its "Agenda for Action for National information Infrastructure", legislated during 1993 [1].

Prof. Parthasarathy had the foresight and vision in realizing far ahead of his times the critical role that library and information services will play in supporting the scientific, industrial and economic development of independent India and worked hard along with his contemporaries like Prof. S. R. Ranganathan and Prof. B.S. Kesavan in establishing the Indian National Scientific Documentation Centre (INSDOC), the first of its kind in the country, during the 1950s. INSDOC was the forerunner and the role model for setting up other information centres such as the Defence Science Information & Documentation Centre (DESIDOC), Delhi, the Social Sciences Information and Documentation Centre, New Delhi, the Information Centre for Aeronautics, National Aerospace Laboratories, Bangalore, and so on.

Another significant contribution of Prof. Parthasarathy was the starting of the Associateship Course on Information and Documentation during the 60s, as part of the activities and services of INSDOC, to promote human resource development for meeting the growing manpower needs of special libraries and information centres in the country. Hundreds of successful students of this Course have spread out far and wide both within and outside India, holding positions of importance, and significantly contributing to the growth of library and information science.

Not resting with these achievements, Prof. Parthasarathy went further ahead and played an important role, together with other S&T policy makers and planners, in drawing up a blue print for establishing, for the first time in India, a National Information System for Science and Technology (NISSAT) under the auspices of the Department of Scientific & Industrial Research, Government of India. During the years of its existence, NISSAT was instrumental in establishing a number of sectoral information centres and sponsoring numerous LIS projects and training programmes.

Prof. Parthasarathy also foresaw the inevitable coming of the new era of Internet and the possibility of libraries and information centres offering online information search and retrieval services from remote databases for the benefit of their clientele. Under his leadership and guidance, experiments on conducting online information search and retrieval from databases of the European Space Agency, Frascati, Rome, were successfully conducted during 1976 at the premises of BARC, Mumbai. This successful demonstration paved the way for setting up of "Telesearch", the experimental ESA-UNESCO-NAL online information retrieval facility during 1986 at the Information Centre for Aeronautics, NAL, Bangalore, and similar facilities set up by commercial organizations like Informatics (India), Bangalore.

Despite his advancing years, Prof. Parthasarathy is still active professionally and is a role model for librarians and information scientists to emulate and follow. Imagine a person who even at such a ripe old age travels a lot to attend and preside over conferences and seminars, delivers lectures at library schools, puts in a lot of professional reading and regularly meets and discusses proposals and projects with librarians and information scientists and, what is more significant, establishes library and information study centres. Who else such a person can be other than Prof. Parthasarathy?

All those who know him also know how modest,

unassuming, helpful and kind he is to one and all that come in contact with him, without ever showing off his profound scholarship, knowledge and experience. On this very happy occasion of his 92nd birthday, let all of us who are his students, associates, admirers and well wishers join together and wish him good health and a long life so that he can continue to guide us as before for many more years to come.

2. INFORMATION AND COMMUNICATION INFRASTRUCTURE: A GLOBAL PERSPECTIVE

People everywhere wish to enjoy the tangible benefits of physical infrastructure facilities, in terms of roads, highways, airports, seaports, railways, telecom, power, water supply etc. What is also needed on top of these is an information and communication infrastructure, which is as critical as the physical infrastructure. The global information infrastructure that has been evolving over the last few decades and that is now being used by millions of people all over the world for communicating and sharing of information with each other is in the form of World Wide Web, popularly known as the Internet.

Internet has now become an essential part of our everyday lives, a medium that contains vast quantities of data and information, and a medium that is accessible from almost every point on the planet. Whole populations once separated by distance and time are now finding every aspect of their daily lives - education, healthcare, work, and leisure activities etc. — affected by advances and changes that are taking place on the Internet. For example, students across the world are benefiting from instantaneous access to far-flung libraries, universities, and other treasure houses of data via the Internet. Doctors are reinventing their profession, utilizing tele-medicine to administer off-site diagnoses to patients in need. Citizens from all nations are finding additional outlets for expressing themselves and utilizing the interactive mode of the Internet to voice their opinion and to listen to the views of others. In essence, the Internet has become the vehicle of a new, global digital economy and is pioneering new ways of using the information and communication technologies and promoting new ways of exchanging information and ideas to create a global information society.

Information is now widely regarded as a key strategic resource and an essential ingredient for the security of a nation as well as for its economic and industrial development. Access to and use of information is providing depth and breadth to a nation's key resources to an extent that was not possible or imagined before. As the world moves further into the knowledge economy of the 21st Century, information will become a more vital force than before, and the speed with which it is created, accessed and put to use will cause even more fundamental changes in the global economy. In short, the generation of and access to Information will be the primary rationale for building an all-pervasive national information infrastructure. With this growing recognition, many countries, particularly the developed ones, have sharply focused their policies and programmes on improving their information and communication infrastructure in order to facilitate and support the broadest possible deployment of information resources.

3. INFORMATION AND ECONOMIC GROWTH

For quite some time now, the global economy has been moving away gradually but inexorably from an industrial to a knowledge economy in which know-how is more critical than financial and economic resources. It is reported that over 70 per cent of workers in developed economies are information workers [2]. Efficient production of goods relies more on information and know-how than on any thing else. Most industrial workers need to use their information and knowledge skills more than their bare hands. Knowledge-based products or services can command much higher premium over comparable products, which have little or no embedded-knowledge.

The knowledge economy differs from the traditional economy in that unlike most other resources that deplete when used, information and knowledge can be shared, exchanged and disseminated far and wide. The value of high-tech companies in the software, biotechnology, pharmaceutical, aerospace, automotive, manufacturing and other sectors lies more on the invisible ingredients of knowledge they create than their visible financial and physical assets alone. These companies are moving ahead by setting up their own privately-owned information and communication infrastructure for data communication because their production and distribution systems have become global and so too their markets. Big companies are increasingly dependent on information technology tools more and more to re-engineer themselves and align closely with their suppliers and customers in order to become more competitive in today's fast-changing global marketplace.

Location of an enterprise is no longer that important or advantageous, since technology, processes, products and markets can be created in a virtual environment, offering the benefits of speed, 24x7 operations and a wider global reach. Product cycle times are no longer measured in months and years but in days and weeks, and timeliness and responsiveness are just as important as are quality and cost reduction requirements. The net result of all these developments is that goods and services can be developed, bought, sold and in many cases even delivered over electronic networks through what is popularly known as E-commerce, with many resultant advantages, in terms of quick and timely delivery, cost-savings and improvements in overall efficiency.

4. THE RISING KNOWLEDGE ECONOMY IN INDIA

Historically, India had been largely an agrarian economy, although trade and commerce flourished through the Ages. In his book, *The World Economy: A Millennial Perspective, the* economic historian, Angus Maddison, mentioned that in the 1st Century A.D., India was the world's largest economy, with a 32.9% share of world GDP. Even 900 years later, in 1000 A.D., the GDP of India in relation to the world's was as high as 28.9%. Another estimate of India's pre-colonial economy puts the revenue of Akbar's Mughal empire in 1600 A.D. at £17.5 million, in contrast to the entire treasury of Great Britain two centuries later, estimated at £16 million. However, by 1700, when most of India was ruled by the Mughals, its share of world GDP came down to 24.4%, the largest even at that point of time. The British rule that followed the Mughal's saw a further steep decline of the Indian economy and by 1952 its share in the world economy fell drastically to a low 3.8 % [3].

The wheel of fortune is turning now and India has moved away from the traditional agricultural economy towards a robust and growing industrial economy and is now moving further ahead into a knowledge-based economy. Since the era of economic reforms, which began in 1991, there has been a paradigm shift from the earlier policies of protectionism, self- reliance and central planning to those of liberalization, globalization and market-driven growth. The initiatives in computer and communication technologies aimed at building the key elements of a national information infrastructure are some of the results of these economic reforms.

In recent times, the Indian software development and IT

enabled services have emerged as a niche opportunity for India to become a global information technology superpower and a front-runner in the age of information revolution. India is well placed to offer a range of IT solutions such as Internet based activities, e-commerce and other competitive products and services for many developed or developing countries and many multinational companies. The IT industry is one of the fastest growing sectors of the Indian knowledge economy, with a compounded annual growth of 50% during the last five years and bright prospects for further growth, with an estimated annual revenue earnings of about $80 billion (Rs. 3,50,000 crores) by the year 2008 [4]. The IT sector is creating jobs that did not exist barely five years ago and is likely to create lakhs of additional jobs in the near and long term.

Apart from the fast growing information services sector, which has been fueling the growth of knowledge economy and contributing significantly to the growth of GDP, the Indian manufacturing industry has also been clocking impressive double-digit growth in recent years, thanks to the growing knowledge-based skills of Indian engineers in computer-aided-design, tool design and manufacturing processes and techniques. India is set to become one of the biggest manufacturing hubs of the world, next only to China.

India is also emerging as a force in the knowledge-driven technology sectors and is the preferred destination for most multinationals to set up their R&D and development centres. *The New Scientist* magazine [6] states in its 19th Feb. 2005 *"India Special"* Issue that "over the past five years alone, more than 100 IT and science-based firms have located R&D labs in India. These are not drudge jobs: high-tech companies are coming to India to find innovators whose ideas will take the world by storm. Their recruits are young graduates, straight from India's universities and elite technology institutes, or expatriates, who are streaming back because they see India as the place to be - better than Europe and the US. The knowledge revolution has begun".

5. IMPACT OF KNOWLEDGE ECONOMY AND GDP GROWTH

Thanks to the rising knowledge economy, the Indian GDP, which has been growing at an average rate of about 5.7 % since 1979, 6.8% since 1994, and about 7.5% since 2002, has now grown to 9.2% during 2006-2007. The robust growth in GDP reinforces the view that the Indian economy has finally moved into a higher orbit, and growth rates of 10% and above will become a distinct possibility during the 11th Five Year Plan (2007-2008 to 2011-2012), and beyond. It has been suggested that the fast growing IT services and manufacturing sectors will help to further strengthen the knowledge economy and increase the growth of GDP in the years to come, if only these sectors are able to capture, manipulate, transmit and apply information more effectively.

In its latest assessment of the growth potential of the Indian economy, Goldman Sachs, the global financial services firm, said in a new economic paper released on 24th Jan 2007 [5] that India can sustain an 8 per cent growth rate till 2020. "The implications of projections are that India will overtake the G6 economies, its GDP will surpass Italy, France and the UK by the middle of next decade (around 2015) and will then overtake Germany, Japan and finally the US before 2050, to emerge as the second-largest economy after China".

6. NATIONAL INFORMATION INFRASTRUCTURE AND KNOWLEDGE ECONOMY

While India already has many highly educated and

vocationally qualified people who are making their mark, domestically and globally and are helping to deepen of technological and innovative capabilities among Indian firms, it still needs to increasingly tap into the rapidly growing stock of global knowledge and build an advanced national information infrastructure to further fuel its economic growth and value creation in the context of a global economy that is increasingly information intensive and competitive. It is only through such a national information infrastructure that India can possibly handle and manage the exponential growth of data, information, and knowledge.

The World Bank in its report: *India and the Knowledge Economy* [7] assesses the progress made in India in becoming a knowledge economy and suggests actions to build a dynamic information infrastructure, create an efficient innovation system, strengthen the economic and institutional regime and develop educated and skilled workers. In so doing, the *Report* adds, India will be able to improve its international competitiveness and join the ranks of countries that are making a successful transition to the knowledge economy.

The National Knowledge Commission in its Report [8] submitted to the Prime Minister of India has recommended that there should be a national drive to ensure access to knowledge and learning that can transform the potential for development, lift young Indians to new levels of understanding and competence and make India one of the leading knowledge societies of the world. For this purpose, the Commission recommends that a knowledge network be set up in order to utilize the potentials of research laboratories, professional societies, universities and other institutions of higher learning for the generation and dissemination of knowledge. "The primary objective of this knowledge network is to interconnect all these knowledge institutions through an electronic digital broadband network (minimum access speed of 100mbps or more), with adequate capabilities to encourage the sharing of existing information, knowledge content, coursework, expertise, ideas, innovations, equipment and facilities available with a wider group of institutions, educators and students".

7. PIONEEING INITIATIVES ON ESTABLISHING NATIONAL INFORMATION INFRASTRUCTUE IN OTHER COUNTRIES

The concept of a national data superhighway was first suggested in the initial draft of the High Performance Computing Act (HPCA) of 1991 [9] presented to the United States Senate. The draft outlined a plan to link US supercomputing research centres together on a high-speed network. The notion of building a data superhighway was to stimulate the American economy. The American industry also played an active role in this process, with major U.S. computer companies lobbying for legislation that would extend the Government's high-performance computing and communications programme and the National Research and Education Network beyond the realm of Government, defense research and university laboratories into offices and homes across the US, including libraries, healthcare, education, etc. for the benefit of all American people. These companies proposed building a National Information Infrastructure, a broadband digital network and a public information programme to make Government data more accessible to the public through the NII. Within this context, the Vice President and the Secretary of Commerce of the United States announced the Administration's National Information Infrastructure (NII) initiative in September 1993, envisaging an agenda for cooperation to construct an advanced National

Information Infrastructure through public-private partnership.

The U.S. initiative on the NII project sparked similar initiatives worldwide [10]. The Japanese Telecommunication Council adopted a national strategy in 1994, emphasizing on the development of a fiber optic backbone covering the whole of the country. The aim was to enable adequate access to the Information highway to all Japanese households by the year 2010. This national strategy led to the establishment of "technopolis zones" which would have the infrastructure for high technology industries and would encourage the application of advanced informatics.

In Europe, the European Commission adopted the Bargeman report on the Global information Society in June 1994 and a number of projects were taken up for implementation. In Canada, the Government developed in 1995 through its "*Information Highway*" project a national policy on new information and communication technologies aimed at generalizing the use of *ICT* in every part of life anywhere in the country. The objectives of the policy were to achieve universal access to the "*Information Highway*" in all public places like educational services, community networks, libraries and information banks. Other countries that have taken similar initiatives on building NII include, among many others: France, Portugal, Germany, Korea, Thailand, Singapore and Australia.

In a Working Paper [11] on the policies and programmes for NII in five countries, namely, France, Korea, Japan, Singapore and the United States, the Center for Information Technology and Organizations, University of California, Irvine, USA, presented the view that NII was perceived in these countries as a technological and social vision of the information society of the 21st century, with economic development as the prime consideration.

The key economic consideration was that a country, which is among the prime movers of the information revolution, will be able to take advantage of its new technologies to create vast new markets at home and abroad that can be captured by existing and new firms to create a large number of domestic jobs and also to increase global competitiveness. The first movers can derive competitive advantage because they are able to set technology standards, get to market faster with the latest systems and applications, and exploit the biggest, richest markets around the world.

8. DEFINING NATIONAL INFORMATION INFRASTRCTURE

The term national information infrastructure (NII) or "information superhighway" is a term originally coined by the U.S. government to describe the convergence of telecommunications, information technologies, and the entertainment industry. In a broad sense, NII is defined as an "advanced, seamless web of public and private communication networks, interactive services, interoperable hardware and software, computers, databases, and consumer electronics to put vast amounts of information at users' fingertips" when and where they need it in order to help them to make informed decisions". This seamless web of communication networks was seen as the instrument for unleashing an "information revolution" and an essential step towards the realization of a national information infrastructure, changing forever the way people live, work and interact with each other.

National information infrastructure is not, however, one monolithic, end-to-end network but a totality of high-speed, public and private, interactive and broadband networks, interconnected domestically and internationally. It is the satellite, terrestrial and wireless "conduits" that deliver information and content to homes, businesses and other public and private institutions. One key to making this network of networks a true national and global information infrastructure is a system of open, user-friendly interfaces and global standards, promoting maximum interoperability and connectivity and allowing maximum customer choice of equipment and services.

9. GOALS AND OBJECTIVES OF NII

The *National Information Infrastructure Agenda for Action,* the first comprehensive statement of the US Administration's visions and goals for the NII initiative during 1993, provides an overview of the broad goals and objectives of NII. The purpose of this was to provide a coordinated development of high capacity, interactive communication facilities, which would include means for the Internet, other telecommunications, and a variety of special media services to be made available on a large scale. According to this document, the implementation of the NII is expected to:

- Promote public and private sector investment to increase and expand competition in communication and information markets;
- Extend the "universal service" concept to assure that information resources are easily available to the people at affordable prices;
- Promote technological innovation and new applications in both private and public sectors and continue to fund basic, risky and expensive projects;
- Promote seamless, interactive, user-driven operation of the NII to ensure interoperability and openness of the NII components with efficient, high-capacity multi-media services;
- Ensure security and privacy of information systems,

networks and communication media for all individuals and organizations and ensure network reliability and reduce its vulnerability;

- Improve management of the radio frequency spectrum to ensure that spectrum scarcity does not impede the development of the NII;
- Protect intellectual property rights and balance them with public interest to promote dissemination of information, apply these rights to all forms of information in the electronic environment, and to re-examine and strengthen the copyright laws domestically and internationally;
- Coordinate with other government departments and with other nations on the regulatory policy and on export control policies to remove restrictions and eliminate barriers; and,
- Provide access to government information and improve procurement of information by the government from various sources.

The National Information Infrastructure Protocols [12], a consortium of IT companies and industries in the United States added an additional set of goals for NII, as under:

- To make industrial enterprises globally competitive through a new form of collaborative computing that supports the formation of Virtual Enterprises by industrial establishments, individuals, enterprises, and organizations;
- To provide technologies that allow Virtual Enterprise participants to collaborate regardless of data structures, processes, and computing environments
- To allow companies within Virtual Enterprises to share costs, skills, and access global markets with each participant contributing its core competence

- To enable Virtual Enterprises to provide competitive products, services, and solutions cost-effectively and in a timely manner, regardless of size, organization, geographic or technical boundaries.

10. NATIONAL INFORMATION INFRASTRUCTURE IN INDIA: A PROPOSAL

As a result of several initiatives taken by the Government of India in recent years to create an advanced information and communication infrastructure to accelerate economic growth, most of the key elements required for building a National Information Infrastructure are already in place. Following the Government's new Telecom Policy of 1994 which aimed at improving India's competitiveness in the global telecom market and attracting foreign direct investment, several private telecom companies, both domestic and foreign, have entered this sector and are investing heavily to upgrade the existing infrastructure.

With about 50 million fixed telephone lines and 156 million wireless cellular phones as on date, the telecommunication network in India is now one the largest in Asia and the fastest growing system in the world, with an average annual growth of 20% and an ambitious target of 500 million landline and mobile phones by the year 2010. According to a report in the Times of India (27th Feb 06), the number of personal computers (including note books) sold in the Indian domestic market has crossed 5 million during 2006. With the increasing downward trends in prices, the penetration of PCs in homes and offices is bound to increase further in the years to come.

The Education and Research Network (ERNET) has established several "Points of Presence (PoPs)" at the premier educational and research institutions spread across the country to provide VSAT based network connectivity. A dedicated Packet Switched Public Data Network (I-NET) with international access for computer communication services is also available. ISDN service has already been introduced in the major cities. Other services like Intelligent Network (IN), Frame Relay (FR) and Asynchronous Transfer Mode (ATM) for wide band multimedia applications are also on the anvil. An integrated network service called "SoftNET" has been established in the software technology parks (STPs) to provide a wide variety of value added services for software development and export operations.

In the field of international communications, the existing infrastructure includes satellite earth stations, state-of-the-art digital gateways, optical fiber multimedia submarine cables and multimedia data switches. Fully automatic international subscriber dialing (ISD) service is provided to almost all the countries in the world. Internet subscribers in the country are expected to rise from the present level of about 20 million to 40 million by 2010, and the number of broadband subscribers is also likely to double during this period from the current level of 10 million. Very Small Aperture Terminals (VSAT) and Direct-to-Home (DTH) services are accelerating broadband and Internet services with the added advantage to serve remote and inaccessible areas.

In view of the technical possibility of offering a wide range of services such as multimedia, data, as well as voice over the same platform, the Government of India is planning to deploy *Next Generation Networks* (NGN). Other future services on the anvil are: bandwidth on demand, global virtual private networks, B-ISDN, Mini-M and hand held personal communications. The National Informatics Centre, New Delhi, is providing network backbone and e-Governance support to various Central and State Government Agencies and offering a wide range of information and communication services in the areas of computer-aided-design, geographical information system, biomedical, patent and rural informatics, Internet Data Centre, mathematical modeling and simulation, networking, office procedures automation and web hosting and development.

The Centre for Development of Advanced Computing, Pune has established a Terascale Supercomputing Facility (CTSF) at its Knowledge Park at Bangalore, using an indigenously developed high performance interconnect switch and system software tools to extract maximum performance from the supercomputing cluster of nodes. The applications, which run on this system, are in the areas of Weather Forecasting, Seismic Data Processing, Evolutionary Computing, Structural Mechanics, Computational Fluid Dynamics and Bioinformatics. C-DAC's expertise now extends to advanced Information Technology, IT-enabled solutions in areas like network and Internet software, health care, real time systems, e-Governance, data warehousing, multimedia, digital library artificial intelligence and natural language processing.

The Indian Space Research Organization has established two major space systems: INSAT for communication, television broadcasting and meteorological services, and Indian Remote Sensing Satellites (IRS) system for resources monitoring and management. ISRO has also developed two satellite launch vehicles, PSLV and GSLV, to place INSAT and IRS satellites in the required orbits.

11. STEPS TOWARDS BUILDING A NATIONAL INFORMATION INFRASTRUCTURE IN INDIA

As noted above, a wide range and diversified information and communication technologies are already deployed in India in nearly all sectors of the economy with remarkable impact. Nonetheless, there are still enormous unrealized benefits to be obtained from effective application of information technology, particularly the intertwining of multiple distributed computing applications in many socio-economic sectors, including E-governance, government information delivery, health care, education and training, crisis management, environmental monitoring, design and manufacturing etc. The next logical step to be taken is obviously towards the formal establishment of a National Information Infrastructure as a centralized system by integrating and upgrading, where necessary, the existing information and communication facilities and services.

The National Knowledge Commission, the high-level advisory body to the Prime Minister of India, will be the right and appropriate agency to take up the initiative and prepare a blue print for setting up the NII as a national programme. The Commission may, in turn, constitute several expert committees, as deemed necessary to consider various components and sub-systems of NII and make appropriate recommendations. Major industrial and professional associations, consultants and other knowledge groups may also be commissioned to undertake detailed studies on various aspects of the programme and submit their reports to the Commission. Based on the detailed reports received from these various committees and other expert groups, and on its own internal discussions and deliberations, the Knowledge Commission may then finalize the detailed plan for NII and forward to the Government of India for approval and funding.

Some of the points that need to be factored in preparing the detailed plan are highlighted below:

11.1. The role of the Government of India

The Government of India may assume explicit leadership and allocate financial resources for NII development because NII is for public good and its benefits will accrue not only for the present but also for the future generations as well. Some of the possible roles that the Government is expected to assume may be briefly defined as follows:

As a strategist - in which the Government assumes responsibility for developing a vision for NII and defining its future direction to boost the rising knowledge economy of India;

As a builder - in which the government takes the responsibility to put in place the necessary additional information and communication infrastructure that might be needed to support NII and its programmes and activities. The government has also to develop suitable policies that would attract global information services and telecommunication players to invest, develop and promote India as the 'gateway of information";

As an investor - in which various governmental organizations consider investing in futuristic technology and also help domestic industries and entrepreneurs to grow in the new information environment and knowledge economy;

As an integrator - in which the government ensures that the various programmes and projects are designed to thrive and grow in the environment of the Information Age through close co-operation between government, business, industries and the people;

As a regulator and *facilitator* - in which the government meets the challenges of creating a nation of enterprise through invention and innovations and promoting a level playing field for the business, industry and trade.

11.2. The role of other stakeholders

Although the primary responsibility for building the NII rests with the Government of India, it might be difficult to achieve the goal without the cooperation and support of the other public and private sector stakeholders, including those who will own the information networks. The private sector companies and organizations involved in the creation, publication, transmission, storage, organization, dissemination, recycling or processing of information, or in providing the hardware or software, would be primarily instrumental in constructing the NII. Other stakeholders may include information providers such as digital libraries and information centres, information service providers, content and database developers etc. who wish to offer or share information with others. Other key players who have to be involved in the creation and dissemination of information through NII are universities, specialized academic Institutions, professional societies and associations etc.

11.3. Implementing Agency

The National Informatics Centre (NIC) may be made the nodal agency for building and maintaining the NII, since it is already engaged in many activities and services that are normally associated with NII. Perhaps, it might be desirable to set up a separate National Information Infrastructure Authority under the aegis of NIC.

11.4. Design considerations

According to Computer Professionals for Social Responsibility in the United States, the design factors that need to be considered in planning for NII include the following [14]:

Ease of use - The barriers to use of the NII network need to be minimized.

Enlarging the user communities - NII designers must strive to provide a high level of service to users where they live and work: private homes, libraries, community centers, and businesses. If the service offered to the public is treated as restricted, NII will be unable to empower the individuals and the community to the extent desirable.

Involving the users - It is quite likely that the most significant source of new network services and capabilities of NII would come from the contributions of NII. NII must, therefore, make it easy for individuals and small groups to develop new on-line services that are not made available by any other groups. The need to support individual initiative and entrepreneurship must be kept in view in the design process for NII.

Privacy and security issues - As is the case with reliability, it is difficult to implement privacy and security as an afterthought. Therefore, sufficient safeguards must be included in the NII design to protect the privacy and security of the users;

Development of Standards - The NII will never be a single, static entity but is designed to grow, driven by the general progress of technology and the emergence of information and communication networks throughout the world. Therefore, appropriate standards need to be developed to facilitate the growth of the network and allow for the broadest possible national and international participation in the process.

Reliability - As use of the network expands into more and more sectors of the economy, the need for high reliability, fail-safe design and fault-tolerance will become increasingly important. These critical issues must serve as the central theme of the design at every stage of the process.

Incentives to the private sector - If necessary, attractive incentives by way of tax deductions and relief may have to be offered to the private sector, particularly the small industry segments, for investing on research and development to create new technologies, develop specialized information systems and services and generally strengthen the National Information Infrastructure.

10.5. Other Promotional Measures

The implementation of the NII project will call for several other promotional measures similar to those that were offered by the United States during the initial stages of planning and implementation of the NII project. Some of these promotional measures are briefly highlighted below:

- Investing additional resources, as and when required, on development of high-performance computing and communications technology for application in agriculture, infrastructure, manufacturing, electronic commerce, health, education, digital libraries etc.
- Integrating IT into the business of government;
  - Planning, demonstrating, and providing government-wide electronic mail;
  - Providing intergovernmental tax filing, reporting, and payments processing
  - Promoting e-governance
  - Making government information more accessible to the people
- Implementing nationwide, integrated electronic transfer of information and data
- Establishing an international trade data system;
- Creating a national environmental data index;
- Developing systems and mechanisms to ensure privacy and security;
- Providing incentives for innovation;
- Providing training and technical assistance in IT to Central, State and Local Government employees
- Freeing up and allocation of spectrum to create information skyways and creation of new wireless industries

- Accelerating the growth of broadband services to facilitate high-speed access to information and web-based communication

12. PRACTICAL APPLICATIONS OF NII

The potential applications of NII are too numerous to be listed in detail in a paper such as this. However, a few illustrative examples can be highlighted:

Applications in Industry

It used to be said that nations (and their industries and individual firms) were more or less successful in competition with other nations depending upon the kind of transportation infrastructure they had. Nations with deep-water ports did better than nations unable to exploit the technology of ocean transportation. After World War II, nations with good highways were able to bring goods and services to market cheaper and faster than those without them. And nations with reliable, safe international air transport were able gain from the growth of tourism and global sourcing over those without. By the same logic, NII will play a vital role in sustaining the competitive advantage of the industry and strengthening its leadership in the information technology and software services sector.

Increasingly, economic success will depend on the ability to leverage technology effectively and strategically for competitive advantage. It is for the purpose of increasing the competitiveness of domestic industry in the global market place many nations like Japan, Thailand, and Singapore set up plans to upgrade their existing information infrastructure. Nations that have low cost, reliable communications infrastructures will attract businesses and telecommunications traffic over those that do not. Hong Kong and Singapore have become manufacturing locations and regional headquarters for many multinational corporations because of their telecommunications infrastructures among other factors.

Virtually all industries will use the NII to do their work better, often in quite industry-specific ways that will implicitly increase demand for information infrastructure. Pharmaceutical companies can incorporate communication facilities and services into delivery of drug information to physicians and hospitals, and banks can similarly offer on-line retail banking, bill paying, and investing. Commerce on the Internet has mushroomed over the last several years. This includes the extension of current forms of legitimate business transactions such as financial payment transfers and "e-cash" (electronic cash), and electronic exchanges of global exports and imports.

When fully established and made operational, NII will herald an age of enormous industrial, economic and social opportunities and transform business and industry by enhancing their competitiveness in the era of global competition in several ways, as under:

- Supporting the activities of existing industries; Better computer and communications technologies will enable all industries to operate faster, more flexibly, with greater coordination, and less expensively, thereby enabling them to compete more successfully in the global market.
- Attract new multinationals and encourage existing multinationals to expand: Advanced communications and computer technologies that are created to support NII will allow international businesses to locate manufacturing, engineering and sales outlets closer to markets and still coordinate these distributed and far flung activities with headquarters and regional locations around the world.

- Increase communications traffic over the nation's network thereby enabling cost reductions and / or reinvestment in advanced facilities and services: An advanced infrastructure can attract in-transit communications activity and stimulate greater use of telecommunications through advanced services such as electronic mail, teleconferencing, EDI, packet switching and data communications.
- Develop information industries that can create information products and services for export: Companies that take part in deployment of NII will be the first to create new information products and services primarily for use domestically and eventually for exports to the rest of the world. Information service providers and manufacturers of equipment will have increasing opportunities for exports.
- Handling business transactions with Governments: The delivery and improvement of government services through online technologies will also include the transactions of business with governments such as the submission of taxation returns, small business registrations, all kinds of payments filing of license applications, registrations of patents and trade marks etc.

E-Governance

The Government of India has approved the National e-Governance Action Plan and identified a number of mission-mode projects for implementation. The impact of e-governance and services offered has become already visible. The two top-rated national-level e-governance projects include: railway reservation and tax information network (TIN). Other notable e-governance projects, according to Kochhar & Dhanjal (15), are: **Aarohi** (Uttaranchal), **KDMC** (Maharashtra), **Kaveri-e-com**

(Bangalore), **Tamil Nilam** (Tamil Nadu), **Rural Delivery** (Tamil Nadu), **Sarita** (Maharashtra), **CARD** (Andhra Pradesh), **e-Panchayat** (Andhra Pradhesh), **LR-MIS** (Andhra Pradesh), **Aarnar Sewa** (Assam), **CIC** (Assam), **Land records** (Uttaranchal), **TIMS** (Assam), **Driving license** (Delhi), **Agmarknet and Passport** (Delhi). NII will help to improve and expand these kinds of services in more areas, ultimately leading to a paperless society.

Health Care

The NII holds a great promise for helping to restructure and enhance health care delivery and administration. Implementation of an integrated, wide-area networked information system will be a logical response to the challenges faced by the nation's health care delivery system. NII will play an increasingly important role in helping access to quality health care and in enabling health care providers to streamline their procedures, resulting in considerable reduction in Medicare costs. The benefits of cost reductions in the health care industry will flow to patients, employers, and government and will also help to provide online health care services through applications such as telemedicine.

India is already experiencing a growing surge in medical tourism because of the vast, varied and affordable medical facilities available in the country. The establishment of NII will facilitate the continuous increase in the number of patients from all over the world availing of these medical facilities and contributing towards the national economy.

Home-based enterprises

Business transactions through the NII will allow the home to become the base for a wide variety of entrepreneurial work (and public service) activities. NII will ensure public access to the economic and social benefits of the Information Age not only for those who have computers at home but also to low-income groups and those living in rural areas that have less access to information technology at home. Individuals and entities that heretofore have been predominately surfers of information and publications can now become authors in their own right through NII.

Public services

NII will facilitate connecting every classroom, library, hospital, and clinic in the country so that these public institutions can make use of telecommunications and information technologies to benefit the people, particularly those living in remote areas. It will help to ensure that access is not only available to those who can afford to pay but also to those who cannot afford to pay.

Educational institutions

At present, many public institutions, especially schools, lack interconnection. This deficiency is relevant because economic competition in the 21st Century will demand that a nation's educational institutions are on the cutting edge in providing a 'computer-rich environment' for their students. Computer networks, especially wide-area networks (WANs), give students and teachers the opportunity to communicate and access information stored in databases around the world. NII will remove traditional barriers between student, teacher and professional researcher, and create a learning community of individuals who are collectively interested in a particular subject. The electronic superhighway will increasingly allow experts to share their research and foster an excitement for learning among willing students, and in this process they can also help teachers navigate quickly through the information highway.

Libraries

Public libraries have traditionally served as a repository

of information for citizens. In the Information Age, libraries will play an increasingly important role because a growing economy requires that workers continuously learn new skills. Connecting libraries to the NII is critical to ensuring that the people can obtain information and services and benefit from life-long learning opportunities, regardless of economic circumstances, demography and geography. Information sources accessed through the NII also represent components of emerging universally accessible, digital libraries. The digital library will be a collection of information resources to facilitate producers to make such resources available and the consumers to access them for use and reference.

Authors

The NII can provide benefits to authors by reducing the time taken between creation of their intellectual works and dissemination of their contents. It will open additional markets for authors. A wide variety of scholarly collections can be made available for research and reference by would-be authors. NII by itself will not be successful if there is no content. What will drive the NII is the content moving through it.

Specialized Applications

- Crime Control: NII will facilitate mobile transmission of fingerprints, warrants and other images to and from law enforcement field personnel; tactical use of live mobile video for hostage, arrest, and surveillance operations; vehicle and personnel tracking systems; personnel locator service, utilizing wearable devices containing wireless transmitters, and on-board information and security systems for mass transit vehicles.
- Energy Conservation and Management: The applications of NII in promoting energy

conservation and management can include: remote monitoring, coordination, and operation of distribution and transmission components from centralized locations; managing the consumption of electric power and natural gas; transmissions to monitor and record pipeline flow and pipeline pressure indicators; and teal-time monitoring, alerting, and control in situations involving handling of hazardous materials.

- Pollution control: The problems arising from increasing pollution can be tackled by making use of NII for management and remedial measures in crisis situations like oil-spills; real-time monitoring, alerting, and control in situations involving handling of hazardous materials; and visual inspection of pipes and cables exposed during excavation projects.

13. THE FUTURE OF NII

It is clear that the information superhighway is not simply a national infrastructure, but also a global one; and it is not something in the future, but something that is already here and growing rapidly. Individual countries must expect their NII to be part of the global information infrastructure sooner than later. While attempting to forecast the future of NII, there are several points that are worth noting:

- The NII services that will have the greatest demand in future are those that are already here. The extension and integration of these existing facilities and services will underscore the future of NII.
- Although there will be new facilities and services along the way in future, NII in the short term will focus on extension of existing voice, video and data facilities and services through existing networks.

- The market for NII services will be brighter in the industrial, business and government sectors in the immediate term. It might take a longer time for NII services to be used in many other sectors.

14. SUMMARY AND CONCLUSIONS

Much of the current excitement about national information infrastructure and the convergence of many communications and information technologies have been catalyzed by the Internet. Thus, understanding the Internet may be the key to understanding many of the opportunities in the NII. The Internet is a model for a commercially dominated interoperable infrastructure and is indeed a prototype for much of the emerging information infrastructure, despite its roots in experimentation and its current limitations.

NII of tomorrow will be larger, more powerful, and more complex and more widely used than current computer networks and will evolve from the networks of today, extending the notion of inclusiveness geographically, technologically, and economically. Presently, it is and will always be in a state of flux, as more and more devices, systems, processes etc. emerge in future and be interconnected in some way or other.

15. REFERENCES

1. United States. National Information Infrastructure: ·Agenda for Action. Washington D.C. 1993.
2. David Skyrme and Associates. The Global Knowledge Economy and its implications for markets. Insight No.21. Newbury, England, 1997.
3. Economic History of India. In Wikipedia: the Free Encyclopedia
4. IndiaCore (www.indiacore.com). Information on Indian Infrastructure & Core Sectors: Infotech.

5. Goldman Sachs. Baseline projections for India's growth. Global Economic Paper No. 152. Page 5. Stamford, Conn. USA, Goldman Sachs.
6. *New Scientist*: India Special. The next knowledge superpower - opinion - 19 February 2005.
7. World Bank. India and the Knowledge Economy: Leveraging Strengths and Opportunities: A Report. Washington D.C., World Bank. June 28, 2005.
8. India: National Knowledge Commission. NKC Recommendations on Knowledge Networks. New Delhi, 21 Dec. 2006.
9. Malhotra, Yogesh et al. National Information Infrastructure: Myths, Metaphors and Realities National Information Advisory Council. New Hartford, New York, BRINT Institute. 1995
10. Ho, Thomas I.M. National Information Infrastructure: WWW Resources. Indianapolis, Indiana University. 1995.
11. Kraemer, K.L. and others: National Information Infrastructure: A cross-country comparison. Irvine, Calif. USA, Center for Research on Information Technology and Organizations. Working Paper PAC-110, July 1996.
12. National Industrial Information Infrastructure Protocols Project Office National Information Infrastructure: The White Papers: Information Infrastructure through 2000. Washington D.C., USA, National Academy Press, 1997
13. Gartner Inc. India's ICT Industry: Increasing in global visibility. Stamford, Conn. USA, Gartner, 18 Apr. 2005.
14. Computer Professionals for Social Responsibility: Serving the Community: A Public Interest Vision of the National Information Infrastructure. CPSR Policy Paper on the NII. San Francisco, CPSR. Oct. 1993.
15. Kochhar, S. and Dhanjal, G. (2004), From Governance

to e-Governance: An initial assessment of some of India's best projects, Technical Report, Skoch Consultancy Services, New Delhi. 110008

Additional References

1. Ronald H et al. Information infrastructure: Agenda for Cooperation. Information Infrastructure Task Force. Washington D.C. 1994.
2. U.S. National Research Council. NII 2000 Steering Committee. The Unpredictable Certainty: Information Infrastructure through 2000. Washington D.C., National Academy Press, 1996.
3. U.S. Department of Commerce. National Telecommunications & Information Administration. Connecting the Nation: Classrooms, Libraries and Healthcare Organizations in the Information Age. Washington D.C. 1995
4. Harindranath, G and Liebenau, J: National Information Policies in International Perspective: Vienna, *UNIDO Emerging Technology Services*, V98. 1998
5. The UK National Information Infrastructure: Summary of Report of Parliamentary Office of Science & Technology. London, May 1995.
6. Lovelock, Peter. The Asian NII Experience. In Internet Society: INET97: Proceedings. Kuala Lumpur, Malaysia, 1997.

5

THE AGRIS SEARCH SYSTEM - SOME IDEAS FOR A SEMANTICS- AND KNOWLEDGE NETWORK-ENABLED SIMPLE SEARCH SYSTEM

L J Haravu[1]

It is indeed an honour to this author to be invited to contribute to a festschrift in honour of Prof. S. Parthasarathy, a doyen of the library and information profession in India. There are only a few of the students and associates of the late Dr S R Ranganathan and Prof. Parthasarathy along with Prof. Neelameghan are probably the brightest sparks of the brilliance of Dr Ranganathan. Prof. Parthasarathy whom I have had the pleasure of knowing as our senior in the erstwhile INSDOC and later as a revered professional whose advise was sought on innumerable occasions is a beacon of wisdom. His vision and insight are both profound and yet practical. He has always been self-effacing and reserved except to those who sought his

1 Trustee, Kesavan Institute of Information and Knowledge Management, Hyderabad. E-mail: haravu@newgenlib.com

views like earnest students and I believe this is what has endeared him to many professionals like me. He has also been one of the founding members of the Trust to honour late Mr B S Kesavan, another great professional with whom Prof. Parthasarathy was also closely involved in building the fledgling INSDOC in the 1960s. I salute these professional seers and offer my humble contribution to this festschrift.

1. INTRODUCTION

It is now accepted that there is really no dearth of information for the scholar who seeks it in whatever field of study he may be interested. The proliferation of databases, search engines, subject portals, digital libraries and open access repositories is enough proof of this. The search engine has been the pre-eminent means for information retrieval now for several years since the emergence of the web as the preferred source of information. However, there has also been disillusionment with the results that search engines deliver. The developers of search engines have attempted to build page and site ranking algorithms; database search engines like that of AGRIS (Information System for Agricultural Sciences and Technology) of the Food and Agriculture Organization (FAO) of the United Nations have also attempted to provide its users with search mechanisms and thesauri to help them to increase retrieval effectiveness. Here again the search systems have evolved and changed over time and reflect new thinking in the design of these, based on user studies, analysis of results, and new paradigms and algorithms that are suggested and experimented with.

Recent thinking in this area is concerned with using theories, tools and techniques to build semantics and meaning into search systems. These all belong to the area of research and development that has come to be known as the Semantic Web.

This paper presents ideas about bibliographic database search engines, based on experience of interacting with users of agricultural information over several years.

2. LIMITATIONS OF DATABASE SEARCH ENGINES

The speed and anonymity that generic search engines like Google and Yahoo! offer to searchers even in specialized areas like agriculture has resulted in the inexperienced searcher sacrificing quality for ease of access; relevance for speed and convenience. The challenge that a domain-specific search system such as AGRIS faces is how to differentiate itself from generic ones and yet provide the speed and convenience of the generic ones. It is my view that bibliographic database and other search systems have the following limitations.

- **Searching skills of users vary widely but all of them are treated alike**
- **Multilingual systems such as AGRIS pose other problems as well**, e.g., the need for language analyzers, language-specific stemming algorithms and mapping between thesaurus terms in different languages
- **The human dimension is missing.** Information retrieved by a searcher does not always satisfy needs. For instance results retrieved may have conflicting conclusions. Dated information and those from preliminary experimental findings often do not elucidate; on the other hand they may add to the uncertainty of the information seeker, e.g., in a problem-solving situation. In such situations searchers often seek the intervention of an expert, one whose knowledge is based on long years of experience. Such expertise may not always be available on hand to many seekers, e.g., in a remote research station in sub-Saharan Africa.

3. CHALLENGES IN DESIGNING SEARCH SYSTEMS

- Several factors should be taken into consideration in designing search systems:
- Users need help at various stages of their interactions with the search system and how such help can be provided by the search engine needs to be considered
- Users need guidance to make effective use of thesauri
- The possibility to use web-based ontologies opens new means to improve search effectiveness transparently to the user
- The addition of a human dimension would add greatly to the satisfaction of real needs
- A search engine, if possible, should go beyond just providing a list of 'hits'.
- All intervention by the system should be seen as helping the user

Search systems need also to take into account use environments and the nature of end-users:

- Their preferences
- Searching behaviours
- Purposes sought to be achieved

How these can be factored into the search system is a challenge in the design and implementation of a domain-specific search system such as AGRIS.

4. SOME CHARACTERISTICS OF THE USE ENVIRONMENTS OF AGRIS

In the experience of the author the following characteristics of the environments in which AGRIS is used (and is often) the only accessible database are as follows.

The environment where AGRIS is used is very heterogeneous:

- Many experienced researchers, teachers
- Also many inexperienced users, e.g., students
  - Difficulties in articulating information needs and searches
  - Very generic or too specific searches
- Multilingual, and hence searching and retrieval in not just the five UN languages
- Users work in relatively remote locations
- Access to peers is not always possible. As already pointed out, the possibility to interact with knowledgeable peers after obtaining the search results is an important element contributing to meeting the needs of an end-user

Our experience is, and this is probably true of other database environments as well, that poorly formulated searches result in frustration instead of elucidation. Help on how to modify and re-submit the query to obtain better results is obviously desirable in a search engine.

- Search results do not always resolve uncertainties, they may in fact add to them,
- A majority of users prefer to work with the simple search interface. The use of a simple text box into which users can enter a word or phrase before submitting it to the search engine has become the preferred choice of most users.
  - The Advanced search feature (in the case of AGRIS called the Search Assistant) is used more by professional information specialists rather than subject specialists.
  - Most users ignore the availability of a subject thesaurus (AGROVOC, in the case of AGRIS).

5. SOME IDEAS FOR THE DESIGN OF THE AGRIS SEARCH ENGINE

The ideas presented below are based on observation of and interaction with subject specialist searchers in agriculture and related areas.

- Allow the user complete freedom to articulate his needs in his own words.
- Any intervention (human or machine) at the first formulation stage is counter- productive.
- The user's initial expression of needs must be captured, however inadequately defined it may be.

Following the capture of the users need in the simple search text box, the search engine may be configured as discussed below. Case logic has been used to present the options.

CASE 1

If a single word (term) is entered in the search text box **AND**

If the term is **NOT** an AGROVOC descriptor

THEN

Search the Lucene[1] index for the entered term and

If the results exceed a configured maximum of hits

Then

1. **Display** an alert that the search has retrieved too many hits and only selected results will be displayed and that the search engine will make suggestions to

[1] The AGRIS database uses *Lucene*, an open source search/indexing system.

assist the user to reformulate the search. (Note: all suggestions made by the search engine are marked as optional and the searcher is free to reject the suggestions at any stage of his/her search)

2. **Show** the first page of results sorted by relevance (number of hits to display on a page is a configurable parameter) and **Show** one or more terms that are orthographically near the entered term, automatically selected from the Lucene index.

3. **Display** a suggestion that the searcher may consider using one or more of the displayed terms shown in step 2 or the originally entered term together with one or more of terms displayed in step 2 **OR** allow the searcher to continue to retrieve and display the remaining results **OR**

4. If the searcher accepts the search engine's suggestions, the search is reformulated and results are displayed once again sorted by relevance.

ELSE

Search the Lucene* index for the entered AGROVOC term and

If the results exceed a configured maximum of hits

Then

1. **Display** an alert that the search has retrieved too many hits and only selected results will be displayed and that the search engine will make suggestions to assist the user to reformulate the search. (Note: all suggestions made by the search

engine are marked as optional and the searcher is free to reject the suggestions at any stage of his search)

2. **Show** the first page of results sorted by relevance (number of hits to display on a page is a configurable parameter) and **Show** the terms from the AGROVOC semantic network of the entered term automatically.
3. **Display** a suggestion that the searcher may consider using one or more of the displayed terms shown in step 2 or the originally entered term together with one or more of terms displayed in step 2 **OR** allow the searcher to continue to retrieve and display the remaining results **OR**
4. If the searcher accepts the search engine's suggestions, the search is reformulated and results are displayed once again sorted by relevance.

ENDIF

END CASE 1

CASE 2

If a single word (term) is entered whether the term is an AGROVOC descriptor or not

Then search the Lucene* index for the entered term **AND if** the number of hits is nil then

1. Display an alert that the search did not produce any hits and that suggestions will be made to assist the user to reformulate the search.
2. Display one or more terms orthographically close to the entered term from the Lucene

index (if the term is not an AGROVOC term) **OR** display the semantic network of the term from AGROVOC and suggest that the searcher may consider using one or more of the displayed terms shown or the originally entered term together with one or more terms displayed **OR**

3. If the searcher accepts the search engine's suggestions, the search is reformulated and results are displayed once again sorted by relevance.

END CASE 2

CASE 3

If a string, sentence or phrase is entered in the search text box **then**

1. Parse the string to identify potential single or compound AGROVOC terms that might be searched. Hyperlink each of these to the semantic network in AGROVOC.
2. Use an implied AND between the parsed words/strings. For instance if the entered string is "drought related root rot in sorghum", the parsed output will be "drought$", "root rot" and "sorghum$" (the $ symbol is to indicate right truncation). The search expression will be "drought$" AND "root rot" AND "sorghum$".
3. A search is conducted automatically with the search expression formed.
4. Follow the steps suggested in CASE 1 when the number of hits exceeds a maximum threshold. In this case however, the searcher will be asked to explore the semantic network of one or more of the parsed terms to reformulate the query.
5. If the searcher accepts the search engine's

suggestions, the search is reformulated and results are displayed once again sorted by relevance.

END CASE 3

Other cases based on the availability of an ontology that is structured as an OWL (web ontology language) or SKOS (Simple Knowledge Organizing System) will soon become possible once inference engines and other ontology tools become available.

Our experience shows also that if the purpose of the searcher is known, it is possible to infer the kind of recall and/or precision that the user would be happy with and also the need to ensure that one or more terms (or categories of terms) that should be present in the search query. As far as we know, none of the search engines considers the purpose of the searcher in formulating searches. One possible way of doing this is to ask the searcher to select the purpose of his search from a drop down box. Purposes should be broadly categorized, e.g., 'Survey of the topic', 'problem solving help', 'development of teaching material', 'recent findings', and so on. In addition to the general purpose categories, there could also be agriculture-specific ones, e.g., 'selection of breeding materials', 'items relevant to a specific geographic location/region/soil type'.

Query modification and reformulation

Search systems implicitly assume that a user's need is fulfilled after showing the results. In reality, the user, after looking through his search results, and even after he uses the help and suggestions to formulate his query, may find that the results achieved are not entirely satisfactory. Some of the issues that need to be considered in query modification and reformulation are:

- Can the search system help the user reformulate

his query to obtain better results? Some ideas were presented in the previous section of this paper.

- Can it simulate an interaction with an information specialist or a more experienced peer who then helps in reformulating the query?
- Can the search system use the inherent semantics in a thesaurus or ontology and if so how?
- Can the system provide a means for the end-user to actually enter into a dialogue with a knowledgeable peer to obtain a more meaningful interpretation of the results? This would bring in the human dimension that is presently missing in search systems.
- Can the search system help the user make use of leads implicit in search results? Inferences using an ontology may point (along with other user input) to other terms (from titles, authors, geographic areas) that could be used in a reformulated search. These are methods used by experienced information specialist searchers in delegated searches with success.
- Can the search system allow the selection of one or more result records and ask for *'More like these*? This has already been implemented in some systems, based on the use of terms in the selected records and the relationships of these with other terms in the thesaurus.
- In the reverse case allow selection of one or more result records and ask for *'Not like these'*.
- The possibilities of using ontologies to infer the broad categories into which the entered search terms belong. For instance, in agriculture: **thing** (e.g., plant, crop, species, soils), **action** (e.g., breeding, harvesting, measurement), **condition/property** (e.g.,

diseases), **agent** (e.g., bacteria, viruses), **space** (geographic areas, countries, regions), and **time** (e.g., seasons). This is a facet analytical approach to analysis of a query. Such an analysis could lead to transparent expansion (and or restriction) of a reformulated query. The system presents the categorized (expanded query) and asks which concepts must be present, which may be present and which should not be in results.

The human dimension in search systems

Information, in most cases is entropic. By this I mean that information (as opposed to knowledge) alone does not resolve uncertainty; it is not enough for a user to take action (e.g., redo an experiment or revise procedures, interpret results). The need for a more experienced peer to guide the searcher is felt by students.

Many information use surveys have pointed out that more than information from a database, it is the one-on-one interaction with a senior or more experienced peer that helps. If a search system can build a human interface, many users might benefit. They will be using a knowledge network. The search system would then be going beyond 'hits' alone.

One way of doing this is to build a volunteer group of information specialists and subject experts in different areas of agriculture. If a user is not happy with his search results, or his own knowledge is insufficient for him to resolve uncertainties, he could be given the option to seek synchronous or asynchronous interaction with a member of the volunteer group.

If user exercises the option, the system could search for an appropriate volunteer who might be in a position to guide the user by making available the email, telephone, or online chat of the volunteer and put the end-user in touch with such a volunteer. This would open the doors for knowledge exchange and elucidation and not end with the provision of information alone.

6. FEEDBACK COLLECTION AND ANALYSIS

The collection and analysis of feedback (collected automatically as well as via user input) on user experiences with the search system would be useful to developers of the search system. One possible way is for the system to automatically create a log of search terms (single terms, phrases, strings, etc.) entered by users; the language of the search term used; the instances where users actually used the help/prompts/suggestions that the search system offered and the nature of the help/prompts/suggestions used; the number of hits that a search resulted in; the country or region of the searcher.

Feedback provided directly by the user, aggregated and analyzed over time together with automatically collected feedback provides a knowledge base that is valuable in fine-tuning the search system.

6

ELEMENTS OF A CORPORATE INFORMATION SYSTEM IN THE KNOWLEDGE SOCIETY

Vivek Patkar[1]

Traditionally an information system in the corporate sector is synonymous with the Management Information System. Its standard model provides necessary input to meet the information needs of the top, middle and operational level staff of a corporate. In the forthcoming knowledge society the corporate business would face further heightened competition and it would be imperative to upgrade the functioning of an information system to address the knowledge-centric demands. This paper first outlines the challenges involved in the task by highlighting various facets of the knowledge. It next presents a schematic model of a new information system. Various actions to strengthen the corporate knowledge gathering and creation process are also suggested.

1. INTRODUCTION

It is an acknowledged fact that roads and railroads were

1 Independent Research Scholar. D-1, Anita Cooperative Housing Society, Plot No.612, Sector 6, Charkop, Kandivali (West), Mumbai – 400 067. E-mail: vnpatkar2004@yahoo.co.in

the mainstay of the bygone industrial society since they provided the critical physical and economically efficient support to the production and distribution of goods across the markets. Likewise information systems play a central role in the prevailing information society, which is dominated by the information dependent services and operations. The modern business, has grown into a transnational enterprise and employs an outsourcing strategy for its peripheral activities; it depends heavily on numerous internal and external information systems. In fact, without the support of a Management Information System (MIS) that incorporates sub-systems for operations like inventory control, production scheduling, marketing, payroll and human resource management the smooth functioning of a business is not possible in practice.

Building such an internal corporate information system basically involves putting together the actions of data collection, cleaning, coding, processing and dissemination with the help of suitable technological means for providing relevant and timely information to the organisation. Thanks to the advances in information technology, the versatility and scope of information systems have enhanced tremendously in the last few decades. Online trading operations in stocks and shares, automated banking operations and web-based marketing and selling of goods and services are some new dimensions added to the business operations in recent years. To some extent information systems have been augmented accordingly to serve the corporate staff and customers more extensively while keeping in view their changing needs. The Intranet for providing the staff access to corporate information and setting up a web site for informing the potential customers are examples of this. In the emerging knowledge society, however, the driving force for business functions and transactions would be knowledge. This means it would be essential to upgrade or extend the corporate information system to contain the knowledge element on a much larger scale to meet the demand of all the corporate staff members. This paper first highlights core needs of a business in such a society and outlines various facets of the knowledge. It identifies the parameters for designing a new information system. A number of actions are suggested at the end to help in creating and sustaining the corporate knowledge base.

2. BUSINESS NEEDS IN A KNOWLEDGE SOCIETY

The business environment in the knowledge society would be quite different from what it is. The business will be driven primarily by a knowledge economy. Global competition, demand for personalized goods and services and stringent application of environmental quality standards are some of the important parameters to be honoured by the business in the society, which would be more exacting in its demands. Naturally the major activity of a corporate would be to exploit information and communication technology infrastructure to process the information from diverse sources and available in different formats so as to generate the knowledge that would provide the competitive edge. The corporate workforce in the new milieu would predominantly consist of knowledge workers namely, those involved in assimilating, creating and applying knowledge in their tasks. In such a corporate environment not only the production of new knowledge through innovation and invention but its conversion into productive use will be most valued. Overall the new economy will be mainly propelled by knowledge and know-how rather than by conventional resources of raw material and manual labour and run of the mill kind of information [1].

Some of the important features of business in the knowledge society are :

- Transactions would be based on the intense, multi-faceted and intelligent processing of information,
- Services would be designed to address the specific needs of the customer individually,
- Innovation and creativity would be constantly required on the part of both individual and organisation, and,
- Protection of intellectual property rights of both individual and organisation would be of prime concern.

The above requirements will have far-reaching implications for modifying or extending the existing information systems too. For example, it would be necessary to extract novel and precious knowledge constantly from the voluminous information by employing advanced information technology tools. It would further involve replacement of the policy of uniform product development to serve the masses by individual customization ethos. That would require building more specific and detailed information base. In addition, information systems will have to supply suitable inputs to each and every corporate worker to help sustain their creativity and productivity and renewing themselves periodically. Equally important would be the aspect of exercising extreme care while acquiring and disseminating the information so that no legal violation or infringement of copyright, trademark, patent and other forms of intellectual property is committed. It is clear that traditional MIS will require considerable strengthening to cope with such enhanced needs.

Before turning to the design and operational aspects of new information system let us understand the concept of knowledge that is to be addressed by these systems.

3. SHADES OF KNOWLEDGE

In the new era an information system will have to go beyond information management, and this involves management of knowledge associated with objects that it can identify and handle. Usually this is achieved by processing the data according to the needs of the end user. For instance, in a typical management information system different reports are generated serving the top, middle and field level personnel for policy making, strategy formulation and execution purpose, respectively.

Now something more is needed by these people namely, further mined information to provide them with fresh insight and innovative options to gain the advantage. In other words, new decisive knowledge and actionable knowledge to maintain the lead over the competitors or to excel over previous own performance would be the prime expectation from such information systems support. It would be more than the traditional decision support system that is to be aimed at.

Knowledge is a multidimensional concept and not a physical commodity. It, more often than not, resides in the minds of people. "Knowing" for practical purpose is defined as coordinated and successful action which results in reducing the complexity [2]. *Satisfactory* knowledge for an individual and business organisation is identified as the one having the following characteristics [3]:

- *Distinctiveness*: knowledge must make a difference.
- *Invariance*: knowledge is reliable under a large set of conditions.
- *Usefulness*: knowledge helps individual and organisation to achieve the set goals.
- *Coherence*: knowledge has acceptable links with the exiting knowledge.

- *Formality*: knowledge can be formally expressed and communicated.
- *Conformity*: knowledge acceptance by organisation as a whole.
- *Authority*: knowledge is credible and not questioned for its authenticity.

Conversion of information into knowledge therefore requires different approaches. Knowledge exists in various forms and can be divided in the following broad categories:

- **Explicit knowledge** - exists in accessible forms and can be expressed and captured without much ambiguity. Knowledge stored in the documents in a library is an example.
- **Implicit or Tacit knowledge** - resides in human mind and experience and is often difficult to capture. How to ride a bicycle or how to swim, represents this form of knowledge.
- **Folklore or cultural knowledge** - exists in a variety of forms (e.g. proverbs, poems and symbolic rituals) without any specific source and difficult to decipher. Food with some ingredients (e.g. onion or garlic) is not preferred by some communities due to adherence to a particular belief.

Dealing with the explicit form of knowledge is relatively easy because sources are well defined. Further, subject specific algorithms and methods are available to process the information therein. Classically information systems have been built around this knowledge and are supplemented by primary data collection efforts, say by conducting field surveys as and when found necessary and scanning the gray literature for relevant information. A corporate library or the unit performing the information collection function is normally involved in building such databases to enhance the scope of a corporate information system.

Tracking the implicit or tacit knowledge existing within the organization or outside is a major hurdle in the knowledge base creation process. It is a human construction, and although it is public, it is at the same time to a great extent personal [4]. How to capture such knowledge and handle it profitably deserves more attention now. Efforts are generally concentrated on converting the tacit knowledge into explicit knowledge for preservation and wider dissemination. Periodic interviews and discussions with experts can help in unlocking this knowledge. Encouraging senior professionals to pen-down their experiences are also the attempts in this direction. There are however limits to this process.

Tacit knowledge is further divided into different types according to the degree to which it is communicable:

- Verbalisable but not usually verbalized (e.g. practical intelligence)
- Demonstrable by doing (e.g. professional skill)
- Silenced (e.g. things are not allowed to be said)

One more form of knowledge that relies on the personal construction of meaning is termed as *abduction*. It conveys the manner in which people reason while discovering new meaning or ideas from a given set of observations [5]. Hypertext linking facility provided by the Internet is an example of creation of this type of knowledge where a person can choose only a few select links and derive his own inference by drawing upon his domain knowledge and previous experience. It is possible that application of such knowledge in another case or context can provide useful breakthrough.

Another difficult to capture knowledge is known by the

term *aura*. It means an object, such as originally drawn picture or a chiseled statue is unique and cannot be imitated beyond certain point. Reproduction, or copying, destroys the uniqueness of such things, that is, it destroys their aura is the argument [6]. How to take care of the aura aspect of knowledge in an information system design is a huge challenge.

Tacit knowledge, abduction and aura together form a category of knowledge expressed by the common term '*low knowledge*'. Its focus is on knowledge that depends on individual perception and interpretation. It is believed that further advances in information technology leading to grid and ubiquitous computing environments would help in converting part of *low knowledge* to an explicit form for wider application [7].

4. A FRAMEWORK FOR NEW INFORMATION SYSTEM

In a true system, that is a system in its most generic form, each component is either directly or indirectly linked to the remaining ones and thereby influences the other components of the system. Utmost care is therefore needed while designing each of them keeping in view this interdependence property. A 15-point property framework is proposed (column 2 in Table 1) to define any system [8]. Let us now study the properties of an information system in that framework as given in the third column of Table 1.

Table 1: Properties of an Information System

Sr. No.	System Property	Information System (IS)
1	*Wholeness:* The whole is primary and not the components	IS as a whole serves the purpose and not the raw data, codes and computer alone
2	*Holistic view:* Whole system has	To address the needs of say

	to adapt to the environment	digital working environment all the IS components have to be modified
3	*Unique functionality:* Total functionality cannot be performed by components	Results given by an IS cannot be supplied individually by any one or group of components
4	*Purpose priority:* Purpose served by the system comes first	Results from the IS as a whole are considered first and then that of its components
5	*Support of the components:* Meeting the purpose is the goal and components have to work towards achieving that and not their respective individual goals	All the components of an IS have to perform their assigned tasks to help achieving the ultimate output expected from an IS
6	*Internal interdependency:* Independent existence of components does not serve the system purpose	Every component of an IS depends on some other for either input or output or both to contribute to information processing
7	*Multiplier effects:* Change in one component can have cascading impact within the system	Malfunctioning of one component of an IS can lead to partial or total failure and sometimes wrong results
8	*Performance level:* Optimal performance does not follow from optimal performance of individual components	Output of an IS would not improve by optimizing performance of say delivery mechanism alone
9	*Divorce between cause and effect:* Impact of change may be delayed in time and space	Performance of an IS does not change immediately if say processing software is upgraded
10	*A definite pace of working:* Changing the pace can be counterproductive	An IS works with certain tempo and it cannot be speeded up say by eliminating the step of data cleaning operation
11	*Feedback impact:* Feedback from the environment needs attention	An IS needs to be modified say in data processing to meet the new requirement
12	*Multiple goals:* More than one	An IS can serve the needs of

	objective may be addressed	different levels of management and stakeholders too
13	*Equifinality and flexibility:* Given goal can be achieved by more than one way	An IS can evaluate various options for data collection and processing to meet the ultimate goal of report generation
14	*Natural hierarchy:* A natural hierarchy exists in system functioning	An IS has a definite hierarchy in operations and meeting the information demands by different stakeholders
15	*Increase in entropy:* A tendency to worn out in performance exists over the time and external resources are constantly needed for viable existence	An IS needs periodic review and augmentation of resources like trained personnel and new hardware and software to maintain its performance level

It is thus seen that designing a corporate information system to deal with various types of knowledge described in the third section above should draw upon the system properties so as to ensure the desired degree of support to business operations. In the light of the properties stated in Table 1 and the demands of the emerging business environment, a new corporate information system should have the following features:

- Besides meeting the knowledge needs of the corporate staff, it will have to provide information specific to different stakeholders in different formats.
- Special care will have to be taken to filter the information to avoid any violation of the intellectual property rights.
- Development of novel mechanism to capture and process the implicit knowledge will be needed.
- Changes needed in various information sub-systems should get highlighted whenever a new knowledge-

based alteration takes place in any part of the organisation.

- Suitable mechanism is built in to promptly take the cognizance of consumer feedback and environmental developments.

Based on these considerations a schematic form of a new knowledge based information system for supporting a given corporate operations is shown in Figure 1.

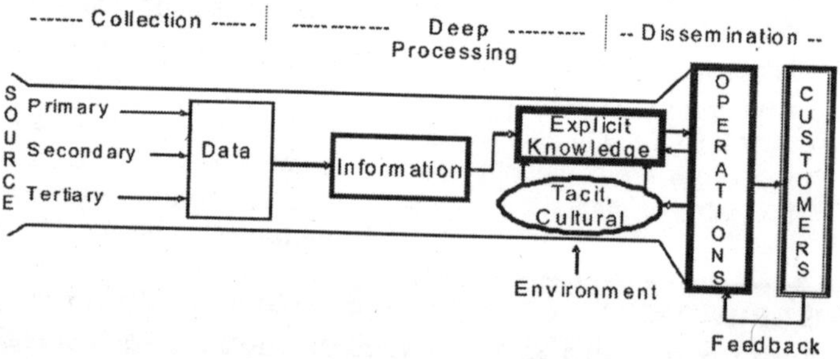

Fig. 1. A Knowledge Based Corporate Information System

It is seen from that knowledge creation component is an exclusively added entity in the design of a corporate information system. Accordingly, the information system will have three main functions: i) data collection, ii) deep processing to convert data into information and knowledge, and, iii) dissemination of knowledge to respective corporate unit. There are feedback loops to help knowledge generation unit to refine and enhance the knowledge base to meet the new demands. The whole information system is a part of the corporate office. Here data both in print and digital forms are collected from the primary (say, by conducting surveys and observations either directly or through outside agency), secondary (say, by collecting from books, trade magazines and standards) and tertiary (say, by referring handbooks and manuals) sources. The corporate library or documentation unit could organize the activity of data collection from the secondary and tertiary sources. The collected data are screened, cleaned and codified for processing. The first level of product thus obtained is information, some of which would be of routine nature and may be passed on to the respective corporate unit for normal operations.

Further, as shown in Figure 1, the information is proposed to be additionally subjected to various knowledge extraction processes using subject specific algorithms, methods and available computing power. At this stage extensive application of techniques (simulation, geographic information system, virtual reality and expert systems) to derive knowledge from the information is expected. Data Mining is one more advanced tool that is considered useful for this purpose [9]. These efforts are to be augmented by converting the tacit and folk or cultural knowledge obtained from the environment and from within the organisation by applying various strategies. The final product thus created is explicit knowledge. It is to be packaged suitably and supplied to various operational and management units for consumption. Feedback received from the customers both in the explicit and indicative form is to be processed further by the knowledge-handling unit.

It is obvious that the proposed knowledge-handling unit is to be staffed by professionals who have domain knowledge and are trained to process the knowledge. It can also become a part of the knowledge management unit, if already existing. The task of protecting the intellectual property rights of the organization should receive due attention in the process and that task can also be entrusted to this unit. This unit therefore should have close links with the research and development unit of the organisation. Moreover the proposed information system should achieve seamless integration with the document management system and enterprise resource planning system, if implemented.

Library professionals with suitable training can act as knowledge mediators or information architects or knowledge preservers to contribute substantially to this knowledge-centered activity in the corporate setting [10].

To illustrate the role of a knowledge-handling or generation unit of a corporate information system, let us consider the sales operations for a given product. Here the standard geographical information system software supplemented by data mining techniques can be used to perform integrated analysis of the voluminous sales figures where spatial, temporal and sales personnel variations are examined with respect to customer profiles and economic changes. The resulting output available both in text and advanced graphic forms would help in understanding the relation between various parameters and provide new insights, which are normally not apparent. It is likely that this fresh knowledge can lead to developing completely new marketing strategy. Results obtained from its implementation and also the experiences of the marketing staff are to be suitably processed for refining the knowledge. It would serve articulating marketing strategies and provide relevant inputs to product design and fabrication operations too.

5. ACTIONS

It is clear that sizeable amount of useful knowledge remains with the personnel and unless it is made either explicit or transformed into working knowledge the desired level of output from the information system cannot be ensured. Towards that end some basic actions, not necessarily in the stated order, that would help the business in knowledge capturing and knowledge conversion process are suggested here.

1. To convert tacit knowledge into tacit knowledge with wider base is one useful starting strategy. For

this purpose organizational structure needs modification. Instead of long hierarchical structure, small teams consisting of professionals need be formed to address a task or sub-task so that personal knowledge and experience gets shared among the team members [11]. Consulting firms are found gainfully employing this method.

2. To widen the stock of the folk or cultural knowledge the staff should be moved around places periodically through a suitably designed human resources development policy.
3. To obtain the benefit of knowledge of senior professionals or staff members internal seminars and symposiums where they are encouraged to share their experiences and inform about the approaches taken to address tricky issues in their career should be arranged. A systematic attempt to record, document and build such in-house knowledge repository need be promoted.
4. To archive the corporate or official e-mails with relevant subject headings or descriptor as it has become a major mode for communication and knowledge transactions. Knowledge derived from that say, by the method of content analysis, is expected to help in litigation matters, knowledge management and dealing with customer queries for instance [12].
5. To suitably augment the online product information system that would provide the virtual guidance to the customer whose inner urge is to get the first hand feel of the product like touch, smell and real look before taking a decision.
6. To design an identifier tag for a product giving built-in information so as to assure the customer the

authenticity that need not have to be anchored in the aura concept as far as possible [13].

7. To continuously upgrade the methods for knowledge creation and adopt advances in the information technology tools to generate new knowledge.
8. To strengthen the corporate library infrastructure to codify, classify, validate and organize the knowledge both internal and external including that regularly downloaded from the Internet for efficient retrieval and repackaging. Special emphasis need be given on the web mining and content management operations besides promoting the information literacy within the organisation.
9. To network with professional bodies and academia to understand the emerging trends in knowledge development and deployment.
10. To implement a practice of conducting and recording the "Exit" interview of a departing professional who has served for a reasonable period so as to obtain his/her valuable views on various aspects of business operations. That would ensure against the loss of knowledge due to the mobility.
11. To plan the involvement of customers say through the Internet in product design and innovation where their tacit knowledge and latent expectations can be tapped for the long-term benefits [14].

6. CONCLUDING REMARKS

Graduation of an information system into knowledge system is not so simple. The process involved is complex because knowledge comes in different shades and significant amount exits in the non-explicit form. Development of suitable knowledge conversion and processing strategies is required for this purpose. Higher level of transparency or visibility in the operations of the business organisations would be the demand of the future society. Compulsory disclosure of information with regard to corporate social responsibility obligation fulfillment is one example and such demands are bound to increase. It is thus envisaged that dissemination of critically processed information to meet such demands would also become the prime task of the information professionals. It may be noted that the new information system as proposed is generic in nature and can be adopted by any organisation with marginal changes.

It is clear that human involvement is the active force that can create new knowledge and it needs to be nurtured and facilitated by the information and communication technology [15]. The strategy should be to develop ways and means to unlock the knowledge from the human mind as far as possible and to assimilate it formally in the information system to serve the organisation in the long run. A corporate library/documentation centre either alone or in collaboration with the unit dealing with information management can play a significant role in this process [16]. Advanced tools from the information technology, library science and information management fields can help in knowledge refinement and value addition to the information system to serve the business in the new scene.

7. REFERENCES

1. Neelameghan, A. "Information Economy and Knowledge Society: An Introduction." *Information Studies.* 5(2) April-June: 107-124.
2. Zeleny, M. "Knowledge of Enterprise: Knowledge Management or Knowledge Technology?" *International Journal of Technology and Decision Making.* 1(2) 2002: 181-207.

3. Heylighen, F. "Objective, Subjective and Intersubjective Selector of Knowledge." *Evolution and Cognition*. 3(1) 1997: 63-67.
4. Polanyi, M. *The Tacit Dimension*. London: Routledge & Kegan Paul; 1967.
5. Leake, D.B. "Abduction, Experience and Goals: A Model of Abductive Everyday Explanation." *Journal of Experimental and Theoretical Artificial Intelligence*. 7 1995: 407-428.
6. Benjamin, W. *Illuminations*. Edited and with an Introduction by H. Arendt, translated by H. Zohn. London: Jonathan Cape; 1970.
7. Patokorpi, E. "Low Knowledge in Cyberspace: Abduction, Tacit Knowledge, Aura, and the Mobility of Knowledge." *Human Systems Management*. 25(3) 2006 July-September: 211-220.
8. Haines, S. G., *The Systems Thinking Approach to Strategic Planning and Management*. New York: St. Lucie Press; 2000.
9. Patkar, V.N. "Data Mining Applications in Library and Academic Institutions." *Information Studies*. 11(3) 2005 July-September: 145-156.
10. Deegan, M.; Tanner, S., *Digital Futures: Strategies for the Information Age*. London: Library Association Publishing; 2002.
11. Nonaka, I. and Takeuchi, H. *The Knowledge-Creating Company*. New York: Oxford University Press; 1995.
12. Perachio, G. "Why Businesses must Consider Email Archiving." *Library + Information Update*. 5(10) 2006 October: 245-25.
13. Patokorpi, E. and Kimppa, K. "Dynamics of the Key Elements of Consumer Trust Building Online." *Information, Communication and Ethics in Society*. 1(1) 2006: 17-24.
14. Yakhlef, A. "Immobility of Tacit Knowledge and the Displacement of the Locus of Innovation." *European Journal of Innovation Management*. 8(2) 2005: 227-239.

15. Laise, D; Migliarese, P.; Verteramo, S. "Knowledge Organization Design: A Diagnostic Tool." *Human Systems Management.* 24(2) 2005 April-June: 121-131.

16. Patkar, V. "The Primacy of the Library in the Emerging Knowledge Society." In *Knowledge, Library and Information Networking*, ed. by H.K. Kaul and I.V. Malhan. New Delhi, DELNET – Developing Library Network; 2006; p.32-49.

7

IMPORTANCE OF ARCHIVES AND ARCHIVAL COLLECTION DEVELOPMENT

A. Ratnakar[1]

The absence of archives in many organisations, especially in India has resulted in a very difficult situation for researchers and writers of corporate history. In this paper the various steps involved in establishing an archive and the material to be collected are presented.

1. INTRODUCTION

History tells us about our past, our ancestors' lives, and culture of the society of that period. On a larger canvas it reveals the state of a nation, its diversity, its problems, its struggles, its follies and success. It reveals the mistakes that might have happened and helps the later generations to learn from those mistakes and take a different path. Historians dwell deep into the past (that is as far back as they can go) using the material evidence available to them. For them evidence in the form of documents (on clay

1 O 13, 'Niveditakunj', Sector X, R K Puram, New Delhi 110022, India. E-mail: aspari_r@hotmail.com

tablets, parchments, engravings on metal/rock, paper documents, and in recent years, microforms) are the most important sources as research material. They draw their thesis, opinions and conclusions usually based on the material available to them. Hence, records pertaining to the past are as important as the nascent information being generated in different disciplines of knowledge. The place where such records of the past are housed is called "archives" a term derived from the Greek word "Arkons" where official records were housed. Normally unpublished documents constitute a large proportion of the records in an archive. The earlier practice of archives set up by the governments housing only official records has now changed. There are archives of different nature catering to particular groups. Government archives, institutional archives, business archives and personal archives are some such examples.

In the era of Internet, mobile phones, laptops and palmtops, the collection of documents pertaining to historical records is not given the same importance as current and recent records. Access to such records is certainly not easy especially in a country like India. This is especially so in such fields as history and social science disciplines. While some records pertaining to religious scriptures exist in centres of worship, documents pertaining to institutions, individuals, official rulers, and early business houses are limited. Wherever some activity is seen in this regard, it is bear minimal. The tradition of maintaining documents for posterity did not get rooted perhaps due to the tradition of oral transmission of knowledge from "Guru" to his disciple. Much of the knowledge generated and transmitted got diluted over a period of time and today we are facing the consequences and repercussions of it. When one is researching into the past, be it about an individual, institution or the nation, lack of documented information is experienced time and again. Researchers have to depend on material available in archives outside the country. In an editorial in Current Science [] Balaram writes: "A clear sign that an historical record is not a matter of grave importance. The careful maintenance of a written record and the building up of archives and repositories of documents is, undoubtedly, a Western practice. Oral history is more popular in India, with every story embellished in the retelling. Organizations, which retain every file in dusty and disorganized disarray, usually discard them by the truckload in periodic cleaning operations. There is no resident archivist, who sifts through the piles of paper looking for the bits that may help a future chronicler to piece together an authentic and interesting story. I felt the absence of a written record, files of correspondence and photographs, most acutely when confronted with the self-imposed ...."

Exceptions to this are the records available as inscriptions on stone and other materials like parchment, palm leaves and metals. However these belong to a much earlier period and records during the 17th to 19th century are scarce. To some extent the National Archives of India fulfils the requirement mainly with regards to official records. So also the archives belonging to a few Business houses like the Tatas, and Godrej and banks like Reserve Bank of India and State Bank of India. Researchers still have to depend on material available in archives outside the country.

2. CREATION OF AN ARCHIVE AND COLLECTION DEVELOPMENT

Once the importance of archives is realized and a decision taken to start one, following actions will have to be taken to make it successful:

- Formulate a Policy

- Draw a Plan of action
- Build necessary Infrastructure
- Collect the material
- Organise the material collected
- Make the material available to users
- Maintain the collection
- Continue Collecting material

3. FORMULATION OF POLICY

A policy is to be framed regarding what material is to be collected and how it is to be made accessible. It is important to take cognizance of the possible copyright restrictions that might have been imposed either by the donor or any agency under which the archive is set up. Perhaps some documents of sensitive nature may not be made public though available in the archives.

Plan of Action : A plan, both in terms of immediate and long-term actions, has to be drawn keeping in mind the available resources and the urgency. An over enthusiastic plan, however good it may be, will be not effective. It would be better to phase out the programme and carry out each step paying attention to quality and sustainability.

4. BUILDING INFRASTRUCTURE

Apart from having an allocated budget for the activities of the archives, another important requirement is having qualified staff (archivists) from the beginning so that the work is carried out in a professional manner. Providing sufficient space to house the documents following the norms set for preserving archival material is of paramount importance. Proper lighting, dust free rooms with temperature and humidity control are some other issues to be taken care of. Comfortable reading space for the users will greatly enhance the usage of the archives as environment plays an important part in the usage. In the fast changing modes of access to information, one has to keep in mind the possible requirement to use the latest technology available for both preserving and making available the documents to the users.

5. COLLECTION OF MATERIAL

Based on the type of archives and its policy, decision will have to be taken regarding the type and the extent of material to be collected. This varies from one archive to another depending on the type of the archives and its framework. Generally documents related to the following areas are to be collected.

6. INFORMATION TO ARCHIVE

Background to Starting : The background information regarding the starting of an organization is most sought after when a historian is researching about any organization. Documents pertaining to the reasons for starting an institution / organisation, information about its founders, their interaction with each other while establishing the organization, agencies connected with the starting of the institution (could be a single body or multiple agencies – government(s), individuals and philanthropists) are all of primary importance.

Founders : Any material related to the founders of an organization will have to be collected from various sources – from the family records, official documents, personal correspondence, contributions to their own field and related fields.

Information on Location : Records related to the choice of the location of an organisation, its original location, any controversies regarding the location, photographs of the site before starting the institution, drawings of the building plans, construction activities, will all be relevant.

Achievements of individuals / institution : Progress and achievements of an organization at every stage indicate milestones of progress of an organization.

Financial Information : Records pertaining to the finances of an organization will throw light on the stability of an organization at any particular point of time. The funds received from various sources - the founders, individuals, official agencies / government bodies will indicate the interest of various people in starting and developing an organization.

7. TYPES OF RECORDS USEFUL TO ARCHIVE

Reports : Annual reports of institutions, Council /Board /reports, reports of the various committees set up at different periods of time for special purposes, audit reports, reports from other organizations form important part of archival collection.

Biographies : Biographical material about the founders of the organization which appear as periodical articles, books and obituary notices will throw light on various factors pertaining to the founding of an organization.

Correspondence : Correspondence between the founders and others connected in establishing the organisation forms an important source of history of the organisation. There could be different views among the founders in respect of the constitution, functioning, policy to be laid, etc and these could be found in the letters exchanged between concerned people.

Information from Newspapers and Journals : Important events about Institutions are covered by newspapers and also written in journals. These sources will give at least some information which is not available in the records of an organisation or if the organisation does not make it available for whatever reason. However one should be very careful in drawing conclusion from such secondary sources.

Oral Histories and Recordings : Oral history recordings form a very important part of the collections in any archives. Recordings of the interviews with the persons who were involved with the founding of the organisation or those who were in the organisation in the early periods will give much information, which will be tacit knowledge of the persons. Recorded talks given on radio, convocation addresses, lectures delivered during any programme will also be useful information to archive.

Photographs, Films : It is important to collect photographs of the founders, site of the institution before and after construction, construction of buildings (Early and later), notable visitors to the organisation, Council / Board Members and Heads of the Institution / Departments and outstanding members of the organization. In the present times, with the technological advances, video films of various programmes of an organization are also an important source of information.

Financial records : Records pertaining to the initial funding for starting the organization, the contribution from different sources, regular finances received for annual expenditure, budget details should be persevered carefully as these will indicate the growth of an organization.

Collection development is not a one-time task but an ongoing activity in an archive. One keeps finding new material pertaining to early period and also material of current interest. Older institutions which do not have an archive have a much more difficult task in building their archives than the newer ones. The new institutions should take advantage of this fact and should start collecting any material of relevance as discussed above without allowing the available sources to get lost for various reasons.

REFERENCE

1. Balaram, P.(2007). Current Science, Vol. 92, p 5

8

MOBILE PHONES, WIMAX, WEB 2.0 AND YOUTUBE IN SOCIAL NETWORKING

A. Neelameghan[1]

Information devices, products and services focus largely on delivery of relevant information to the literate, relatively homogenous groups, for instance academics, researchers, and scholars. Providing relevant information to the public at large, in some cases composed of multi-cultural, multi-lingual, semi-literate individuals, with varied information requirements and limited capability to use information search instruments, it is a different ball game. Add to these user groups, especially in developing countries, the large proportion of illiterate or semi-literate and marginalized communities, information delivery issues become even more complicated. In recent decades, developments in information and communication technologies (ICT) are found to create digital divides on the one hand and offer means of improving information delivery to these communities, on the other.

Briefly discusses the role of ICT in networking among

1 Former, Professor, DRTC/ISI, Bangalore-560059. **Contact**: 216, 16th Cross, 4th Main, Banglore 560055; E-mail: anm2002@vsnl.net

people at local, national and global levels, supporting the formation of communities of common interests and practices, sharing and exchange of information in mutual collaboration for common good. In this context, discusses the spread of mobile / cell phone, SMS, and wireless technologies (e.g. WiMax) even into rural areas, with particular reference to India and emerging technologies, such as, Web 2.0 and YouTube which encourage collaborative and participative cultures via the Internet.

1. INTRODUCTION

Information devices, products and services are designed and updated to facilitate exchange of information, and interconnect people strengthening cooperation and collaboration among them so that they may realize their individual hopes and dreams and collectively the broader developmental goals of the society. These devices, products and services focus largely on delivery of relevant information to the literate relatively homogenous scholar groups and individuals – for instance, academics and researchers. Many of them can use library catalogues, indexes, and conduct searches in databases and on the Internet/WWW. However, serving the public at large, in some cases multi-cultural and multi-lingual, with varied information requirements, with limited capability to use information search instruments, it is a different ball game. And when you add to these potential user groups, especially in developing countries, the large proportion of illiterate or semi-literate and marginalized communities, information delivery issues become even more complicated. Developments in information and communication technologies (ICT) create digital divides on the one hand and offer means of improving information delivery to such communities.

Information exchange has been practised ever since *Homo Sapiens* formed families, groups and communities.

In the very beginning, markings - pictorial and other - on cave walls and stones informed group members about the environment - animals in the vicinity e.g. of likely danger and/or to be hunted for food, existence of ponds and water falls, useful vegetation etc. The knowledge so gained enabled the early men to survive and build on the knowledge and pass it on to subsequent generations.

Drum beats, tolling of bells, town criers, the muezzin and the like announce or call to people to assemble, hear messages and/or initiate action. These assemblies facilitated identifying individuals and groups with common interests, faith, and practices and also to build on this commonality and widen the group composition. In later times, clubbing, partying, and other social gatherings, further facilitated face to face interactions and networking.

Exchange of letters and use of other communication media – telephone, fax, telegram – widened the networking – across national boundaries and even globally.

Interactions among peoples of different cultures was supported with the expansion of travel facilities, business and trade, colonization, conferences, international relations, etc.

In scholarly communications, citing the work of others is a common practice and it has spawned networks of scholars, academics and researchers. Applications of information and communication technologies (ICT) and global connectivity via networks and network of networks e.g. Inrternet has enabled and supported dissemination and exchange of information globally. There is mutuality and synergism between globalization and almost seamless access and exchange among people with commonality of interests and practices. Collaboration and cooperation – real and virtual – within and across communities has given rise to e-communities / web-based communities. An e-community is a community that uses ICTs for sharing / exchanging information, expressing viewpoints, comments, etc. on matters in which the members of the community have commonality of interest or stake. Positive features of such exchanges include: acceleration of empowerment, creation of more level playing field, facilitation of the expression of and greater visibility to the needs and aspirations of the participating people, and better awareness of and potential for use of the tacit knowledge of the communities for the welfare and good of the society at local, national and international levels.

There is increasing awareness that equity and justice require that the vast numbers of marginalized and rural communities, falling outside this communication space, need to be connected and empowered and the valuable tacit community knowledge they possess be utilized. There is also increasing awareness that the less privileged and hitherto unreached neglected rural communities should be adequately compensated and not merely exploited while using and benefiting from their tacit knowledge.

2. SPREAD OF WIRELESS TECHNOLOGY AND CELL PHONE USE

Front-runners among the ICT applications for rural connectivity are wireless and mobile communication technologies. Features of these devices of particular interest to multi-cultural, multilingual, semiliterate and illiterate communities include:

- Exchanging messages in the local language;
- Dissemination of text, images, multi-media learning materials, etc. also in local languages;
- Enhancement of collaboration and cooperation and facilitation of joining voices / forces, that is

connectivity for collaboration even at global distances;

- Recording, collection and use of the knowledge and experience of the marginalized communities; and
- Relatively lower cost of the equipment and service.

The spread of telecom facilities – wireless technology and cell phones – into the rural areas is enabling rural traders, consumers, and others to obtain market information for products, to contact district officials not only to get information but also obtain certificates and other documents. Information kiosks and tele-centres are also playing useful roles by providing information and connecting people in rural areas among themselves and with NGOs, government offices, etc. Mobile phones are seen to bridge the digital divide in developed as well as developing countries. In a recent report on GSMA, a recommendation was the extension of mobile phones to different segments of the peoples of Africa. This is considered the fastest way to bridge digital divide in the countries of that continent (Biniyat, (2006).

2.1. Mobile Communication

2.1.1. Spread in Rural India

According to a study commissioned by Nokia, conducted by the Center for Knowledge Societies (CKS), and the report authored by Dr Aditya Dev Sood, "mobile communication is revolutionizing economic and social life in rural parts of the country, generating a wave of local entrepreneurs, and creating greater access to social services.

Mobile phone market is rapidly growing; as many as 6 million new mobile subscriptions are added each month and the forecast is that by the end of 2007, 20 per cent of the Indian population will own a phone and the mobile network may cover three quarters of the population by the end of 2008. The average number of subscribers to wireless phones per month increased from about 5.3 million in 2007 to about 6.9 million currently (Pai, 2008). "Cellular phones are perhaps now ready top penetrate that large chunk of the mass-market: the bottom of the pyramid – from where it is believed the next 250 million subscribes will emerge." Pai also looks at the still perssisting low teledensity (23.2%); and the shortfall in revenue from value added services vis a vis the expectations. Nevertheles,"There are several rural innovations that have come a long way in demonstrating that some of the value added services are life-changing (and even life-saving, in some cases). The key is to scale and proliferate these applications as widely as possible."

The CKS report further notes that new users of mobile phones, a good proportion of them are from rural areas, "with scarce infrastructure and facilities, high level of illiteracy, low PC and internet penetration;" but they found their incomes rise," as a result of increased productivity made possible through mobile communications." Mobile phones are not to be considered merely as a communications device, but "as a new and essential form of infrastructure that will transform a host of other service sectors in rural economies around the world." Dr Sood adds.that the new mobility could help bridge the socio-economic digital divide between rural and urban areas.

The *W3C Workshop on the Mobile Web in Developing Countries*, held in Bangalore, India, on 5-6 December 2006, emphasized that the ***real goal*** of providing ICT in developing countries is not to connect people all people to the Web "but to provide services (health, banking, government, education, business, trade sectors) and the most appropriate way to provide such e-services on mobile phones is with SMS-based applications. The reasons for this include:

- Easy to use (everybody knows how to send an SMS)
- Low and predictable cost (no cost for receiving a message, low and known cost for sending a message;
- Availability on all phones
- A standardized platform to ease service development
- Cheap service development and hosting
- Much scope and wide audience
- Easy reachability and "discoverability" of existing services (search engines, portals, etc)"

There are, of course, limitations to such applications. For example, "limited capabilities (text-only, limited size, basic services like single query-answer only, etc.); interoperability problems between operators; problems relating to availability of Web browser and configuration; user interface; and cost." Therefore, for adopting the Web as the platform for developing future services requires finding solutions to these problems.

2.2.2. A Karnataka Project (reported by Frederick Noronha, 2007)

ICT applications - primarily computers and electronic communications - imply centralization, language, complicated methods of participation, and design issues.

A project in south Karnataka plans to record 'stories' digitally, and share them across the digital divide. Using mobile phones with simplified icons, which villagers would find easier to deal with, seeks to zero in on what kind of information local users find useful.

Ramnath Bhat, working in communications-based NGO Voices, is part of the Story Bank project, in association with University of Surrey, U.K. It is part of a larger project called 'Bridging the Global Digital Divide'. It is currently based in the rural area of Buddikote, in Kolar Gold Fields area in southern Karnataka..

The project is to use the Nokia N80 mobile phone, together with easier-to-use software for villagers, including backward classes, to create multimedia content. The project aims at making it simple to create and access digital content.

The phone interface is modified and uses icons to make easy the process of creating content. There are separate icons for recording ambient sound, for voice and for clicking pictures or taking video. With these, even an unlettered villager will be able to record small video clips with audio tracks. These digital stories will be then sent to a nearby central server, connected to a touch-screen.

3. WIMAX FOR WIRELESS BROADBAND ACCESS

Amit Sharma, President, Motorola India, says: In rural India where 70 percent of the population is spread out, telecom penetration is only about 2 per cent and data connectivity is practically non-existent. Internet connectivity, though growing, is still low. India has just about seven million Internet subscribers of whom only 1.3 million have access to broadband connections, way below the target of 20 million set for 2010.

"Fortunately, an alternative is available. India can avoid the unwieldy and challenging process of hardwiring its 3.2 million square kilometers — the seventh largest area in the world — by using next-generation broadband wireless technologies such as WiMAX. WiMax will allow India to make the leap from voice (2.5G) to voice/data/video/TV (4G), both cost-effectively and quickly.

"WiMAX is a global, standards-based technology that can provide wireless broadband access to both urban and rural areas." It could be the way forward for developing countries to provide data services to the masses, given their limitations of infrastructure and time.

Another useful feature is "WiMax can also complement mobile devices.... India has over 130 million mobile phones against less than 20 million PCs. .... PC usage is restricted to the educated elite and businesses. However, every electrician, carpenter and delivery boy is today comfortable with, indeed dependant on, a mobile phone to conduct his/her business. In the future, more consumers will access the net on their phones than on PCs; even more so, when WiMax makes high-speed data, video and TV possible on handheld devices.

"The early gains of partial wireless connectivity in rural India can be seen in the stunning success of ITC's e-choupal project, which has empowered thousands of farmers in remote hamlets by enabling them to optimise price-discovery through access to updated information. WiMax could accelerate the pace of such connectivity thousand-fold, unleashing the potential and the power of the rural economy...... With a constructive public-private partnership, WiMax could become a truly powerful engine of socio-economic transformation."

4. USE OF SMS - WARANA UNWIRED

Sean Blagsvedt and Rajesh Veeraraghavan report : "We have run an experiment replacing a PC based system for helping a rural sugarcane cooperative with a mobile phone based system. The new mobile system replicates almost all of the PC based functionality. It is cheaper, adds additional functionality and is more popular.

"Warana is a village located in rural Maharashtra. The sugarcane cooperative is serving about 70,000 farmers across 75 villages. The government of India in 1998, started a pilot experiment to bridge the digital divide by setting up the Warana Wired Village project.... This cooporative effort has established 54 kiosks to connect 40,000 farmers across the different villages. Financial input: Government of India 50%, government of Maharashtra 40% and the Warana Cooperative 10%; the total amount spent on the pilot project was about $500,000.

"The original goals of the project were to give internet access to farmers, to allow farmers to check market prices so that they can sell the produce to the market that was offering them the best price.

"The Cooperative then started using these kiosks for remote bookkeeping. The farmers used the kiosks to check their sugarcane output, track their fertilizer outputs, issuing harvesting permits and to get their pay stubs. There is a kiosk operator who serves as the intermediary to give access to these farmers.

"The kiosks are still running 8 years after their original installation... So the question was: Can we preserve the functionality of the existing PC-based system while making the entire system cheaper and more effective? .... We replaced the client PCs with SMS enabled phones. On the server, we attached a smart phone through USB to their PC server. So, we have an SMS gateway that receives incoming SMS messages and converts into database calls and the response was also converted to an SMS message and the result sent back to the phone that sent it. The authentication was through the SIM card (essentially the phone number).

"**Results:** We found that all the existing application scenarios could be converted using the SMS-enabled phones. The system is now available 24 hours, and farmers use the data on a few occasions even at odd times like 3.30 in the morning. The solution is truly mobile and the farmers are using it in places like tea shops, front of the farmer's fields and in the kiosks. In most cases they use the kiosk operator (who is now the phone operator) as the intermediary to send the SMS messages. There is a potential saving of over a million rupees ($22,000) which is a big deal in these contexts if the cooperative completely switched from the PCs to the mobile phones. This is primarily due to the savings from the maintenance costs of the PCs.

"We are working with the Warana cooperative to see whether they want to scale this to all of the 54 villages they are operating. We hope this will lead to many more SMS applications throughout the world."

5. WEB 2.0

The term Web 2.0 was coined by O'Reilly Media in . It does not refer to an update to the Internet/WWW "technical specifications, but to changes in the ways systems developers have used the web platform." It became more widely known and adopted through a series of Web 2.0 conferences, the first one in 2004. Web 2.0 is generallly perceived as a "second-generation of Web-based communities and hosted services such as social networking sites, wikis and folksonomies that facilitate collaboration and sharing between users."

According to Tim O'Reilly, "Web 2.0 is the business revolution in the computer industry caused by the move to the internet as platform, and an attempt to understand the rules for success on that new platform." Tim Berners-Lee (WWW creator) and others have questioned use of the term Web 2.0.

A Web 2.0 web-site may exhibit some basic common characteristics such as the following:

- "Network as platform" — delivering (and allowing users to use) applications entirely through a browser.
- Users owning the data on the site and exercising control over the data.

- An architecture of participation that encourages users to add value to the application as they use it. This stands in sharp contrast to hierarchical access-control in applications, in which systems categorize users into roles with varying levels of functionality.
- A rich, interactive, user-friendly interface based on Ajax or similar frameworks.
- Some social-networking aspects.
- Enhanced graphical interfaces such as gradients and rounded corners.

The concept of Web-as-participation-platform captures many of these characteristics. Bart Decrem, founder and former CEO of Flock, calls Web 2.0 the "participatory Web" and regards Web-as-information-source as Web 1.0.

The Wikipedia article describes the technical aspects – architecture, servers, software, protocols etc. - and notes some of the criticisms, of Web 2.0.

A useful feature is the facilitation of collaborative language learning. For instance, "in second language learning, Web 2.0 technologies have been described as new and emerging technologies. Technologies such as on-demand video, file sharing, blogs, wikis, and podcasting have become very popular with language educators and students. Users of these technologies have emphasised their collaborative and community-building aspects, and suggested they are a natural ally for a constructivist learning methodology. A number of events sposored by the IATEFL Learning Technologies SIG in the UK, Japan and India have focused on the use of Web 2.0 technologies to enhance language learning environments.

6. YOUTUBE

Henry Jenkins in his *Nine* Propositions *Towards a Cultural Theory of YouTube* writes: " YouTube has emerged as the meeting point between a range of different grassroots communities involved in the production and circulation of media content. Much that is written about YouTube implies that the availability of Web 2.0 technologies has enabled the growth of participatory cultures. I would argue the opposite: that it was the emergence of participatory cultures of all kinds over the past several decades that has paved the way for the early embrace, quick adoption, and diverse use of platforms like YouTube. But as these various fan communities, brand communities, and subcultures come together through this common portal, they are learning techniques and practices from each other, accelerating innovation within and across these different communities of practice. ... [T]he most powerful content on YouTube comes from and is taken up by specific communities of practice and is thus in that sense a form of cultural collaboration.

Yochai Benkler describes the YouTube as a hybrid medium "space where commercial, amateur, nonprofit, governmental, educational, and activist content co-exists and interacts in ever more complex ways" (The Wealth of Networks) .... it potentially represents a site of conflict and renegotiation between different forms of power.

Jenkins adds: "YouTube represents a site where amateur curators assess the value of commercial content and re-present it for various niche communities of consumers. YouTube participants respond to the endless flow and multiple channels of mass media by making selections, choosing meaningful moments which then get added to a shared archive." The contents gain greater visibility and circulation through YouTube than they get via the broadcast and cable channels from which they originated or when promoted via blogs, Live Journal, MySpace, etc.

Further "YouTube operates, alongside Flickr, as an important site for citizen journalists, taking advantage of a world where most people have cameras embedded in their cellphones which they carry with them everywhere they go. We see examples of stories or images in the past year which would not have gotten media attention if someone hadn't thought to record them as they unfolded using readily accessible recording equiptment: and disseminated as a product of this powerful mixture of mobile technology and digital distribution. ...YouTube may embody a particular opportunity for translating participatory culture into civic engagement.

6.1. Participatory Culture and Shifts in Cultural Economy

YouTube induces shifts in the cultural economy: ".... the grassroots culture appropriates and remixes content from the mass media industry; the mass media industry monitors trends and pulls innovations back into the system, amplifying them and spreading them to other populations. Yet as they do so, they often alter the social and economic relations which fueled this cultural production in the first place. We will see increasing debates about the relations between the gift economy of participatory culture and the commodity relations that characterize user-generated content. .... These sites may be seen as a way of economic exploitation as they outsource media production from highly paid and specialized creative workers to their amateur unpaid counterparts.

6.2. Cultural Competency

"In the age of YouTube, social networking emerges as one of the important social skills and cultural competencies that young people need to acquire if they are going to become meaningful participants in the culture around them. We need to be concerned with the participation gap as much as we are concerned with the digital divide. The digital divide has to do with access to technology; the participation gap has to do with access to cultural experiences and the skills that people acquire through their participation within ongoing online communities and social networks. ... A participatory culture is not necessarily a diverse culture. As John McMuria has shown us, minorities are grossly under-represented — at least among the most heavily viewed videos on YouTube, which still tend to come most often from white middle class males. If we want to see a more "democratic" culture, we need to explore what mechanisms might encouraged greater diversity among participants, whose work gets seen, and what gets valued within the new participatory culture.

7. CONCLUDING REMARKS

Mobile communications – cell phone and other wireless technologies - is rapidly changing the economic and social life in rural areas, generating a spate of local entrepreneurs, and enabling greater access to social services. We have given a couple case studies

Web 2.0 is generallly perceived as a second-generation of Web-based communities and collaboration and sharing between users. It is being adopted more widely with collaborative contributions from and through a wide range of people who have some information to share.

The YouTube, which is using Web 2.0, is emerging "as the meeting point between a range of different grassroots communities involved in the production and circulation of media content." Application of YouTube calls for understanding of other than one's own culture. Young people need to acquire such cultural competencies in order to become meaningful participants in the culture around them. As quoted above "We need to be concerned with the participation gap as much as we are concerned with the digital divide. The digital divide has to do with access to technology; the participation gap has to do with access to cultural experiences and the skills that people acquire through their participation within ongoing online communities and social networks."

8. REFERENCES AND ADDITIONAL READINGS

1. Benkler, Yochai (2006). The Wealth of Networks: How Social Production Transforms Markets and Freedom; Yale University Press. (http://www.benkler.org/Benkler_Wealth_Of_Networks.pdf)
2. Bhatnagar, S., and Schware, R. eds. (2000). Information and communication technology in development: cases from India. New Delhi: Sage Publications
3. Biniyat, Luka (2006). Mobile fastest way to bridge digital divides in Africa, says GSMA. (Vanguard). Posted to the *Web*, Monday, April 03.
4. *Blagsvedt, Sean and Veeraraghavan, Rajesh http://research.microsoft.com/~rajeshv/ warana.htm*
5. Chester, Greg. and Neelameghan, A. (2006). Information professional: knowledge and skill development for serving marginalized and rural communities. *Webology*, 3(3); article 29. Accessible at: http://www.webology.ir/2006/v3n3/a29.html
6. Cobo, J.M. (1987). *Study of the problem of discrimination against indigenous populations.* United Nations Special Rapporteur.
7. Harkin, James (2006). Social networking. *The Guardian,* April 15. http://www.guardian.co.uk/commentisfree/story10...1754398.00.html
8. Hirwade, Mangala and Rajyalakshmi, D. (2006) E-content awards: and initiative for bridging the digital divide in India and worldwide. D-Lib Magazine, 12(11): 10p. http://www.dlib.org/dlib/ November/hirwade/11/hirwade.html
9. Jenkins, Henry (2007). *Nine propositions towards a cultural theory of YouTube.* (http://www.

henryjenkins.org/ 2007/05/9_propositions_towards_a_cultu.html)

10. Kumar, B.R (2006). AIR's broadcasts did make a difference: a phenomenal success was achieved in production through sustained broadcasts during the 'Green Revolution period'. *The Hindu Magazine*, 2006-12-31; p. 14.
11. Kumar, S. (2001). Indigenous communities' knowledge of local ecological services. *Economic and Political Weekly*, 28 July.
12. Mckie, Rob (2005). Ancient legends give early warning of modern disasters: the new science of geomythology is being harnessed by researchers who believe folklore can save lives. *The Observer* Guardian Newspapers Limited; 4 December
13. Matsuura, Koichiro (Director General, UNESCO). Message on the occasion of the International Day of the World's Indigenous People, 9 August 2006.
14. Neelameghan, A. (2006). E-Communities, Community Knowledge, and Knowledge Management. *KnowGenesis International Journal for Technical Communication,* 1(2): 21-27
15. Neelameghan, A. and Chester, Greg (2006). Environmental knowledge and marginalized communities: the last mile connectivity. *Webology*, 3(1), March.
16. Noronha, Frederick (2007). *Villagers and Dalits seek to create 'stories' of their own.* Posted on 2007-02-09
17. Pai, Sridhar T. (2008). A VAS landscpape: where do we go from here? It, 2008 February; p. 58-62
18. Rose, J. (2000). Multipurpose community Telecentres in support of people-centered development. Information Studies, 6(1), 5-28.
19. Seshia, Shaila, Garoupa, Catherine, Lenzer, Benjamin, and Gulati, Namrati, eds [2005]. *Traditional wisdom in natural resource management: the only*

way to conserve. Dehra Dun, Uttaranchal: Rural Litigation & Entitlement Kendra.

20. Soni, Vikram (2005). Tribal people and preserving prime forests. *The Hindu,* 29 November.
21. Swaminathan, M.S. (2005). Mission 2007: every village a knowledge centre. *The Hindu*, 25 November. Web 2.0. *Web 2_0-Wiki.htm*
22. Wolf, Richard K. (2006). The black cow's footprint – time space and music in the lives of the Kotas of South India. Delhi.

9

THE PEOPLE'S NETWORK: WHAT IS IN IT FOR US?

K.Sankaraiah[1]

Information age brings with it challenges as well as opportunities. Information technology, which is widely believed to usher in information age, if allowed a free rein, may exacerbate the digital divide. The People's Network (PN) in the UK is seen as an answer to some of the problems that accompany information society. This paper begins with an explanation of the PN, its origin and background. It deals with PN's broad aims and objectives, together with how they are being realized. PN's progress has been under review with a few informal attempts and a couple of major formal ones, having the official stamp. The paper also draws attention to some faint dissenting voices on the network in UK. It further attempts to see how India can draw lessons from the UK experience. The public library that emerges out of the PN is looked at in some detail. It also briefly looks into the sustainability aspect of PN.

1 Regional Librarian, British Council Libraries, South India (Retd.) Chennai. **Contact :** 'Padmalaya', 58, Fathima Nagar, 3, Kurinji Street, Valasaravakkam, Chennai-600 087, Tel. : 044-24861240, E-mail : sankariahk@dataone.in

1. WHAT IS THE PEOPLE'S NETWORK?

The People's Network (PN) is the IT-based network of public libraries in the four major constituent parts of the United Kingdom - England, Wales, Scotland and Northern Ireland. It has connected public libraries to the Internet and to a host of online services. Peter Brophy, Chair in Information Management at the Manchester Metropolitan University describes it "as a turning point in the history of the public libraries in the UK" and says "it marks a leap forward in their evolution in the UK." It is widely seen as an answer to some of the challenges of the information society. Information age and information society, many believe, S. Arunachalam, among them, may further widen the digital divide if left unchecked. So PN aims to enhance the role of the public library as a key agent in enabling all citizens, irrespective of their background, to prosper in the information society and to benefit from the new opportunities offered by the information and communication technologies (ICT) It has opened up to all people, a whole new world of information and opportunities, mostly free of cost, doing away in the process, with distinctions and barriers of all kinds. In short, PN presents a new vision of society in the information age where library service is repositioned and reequipped for the new millennium.

2. ORIGIN

The PN project was launched in 2000 after a great deal of study and in about two years' time, it became operational. The delivery of the PN project in time and to the budget was in itself a technological feat and management miracle. During the two decades preceding PN, the public library system in the UK was at a relatively low point in standing and performance. Budgetary cuts had resulted in closing down of a few libraries, low intake of library materials and reduction in opening hours. But with a new government taking over in May 1997 public libraries turned the corner. The government grasped the opportunities the ICT promised for increasing the prosperity and improving the quality of life for all sections of society and the key role the public library could play in transforming the community. A plethora of reports of vision of a new networked public library followed. In 1997 the Library and Information Commission (LIC) England, which is presently named MLA, published a seminal report called *New library: the People's Network*. LIC christened and designed the network and was its chief architect. The publication of the report was described as "a defining moment" in the history of public library movement in the UK.

3. BACKGROUND

Historically, PN was preceded by a series of initiatives for co-operation among public libraries during the period, 1960-1980, for purposes such as inter library cooperation, cooperative cataloging, and cooperative technical, trade, commercial and business information services. A couple of prominent examples were Birmingham Libraries Cooperative Mechanization Project (BLCMP), London and South Eastern Library Region (LASER) LASER was a key player in the setting up of the **Electronic Access to Resources in Libraries (EARL)** consortium for public library networking in 1995. (Both LASER and EARL ceased to function in 2001) Besides, during the early 1990's there were other initiatives to increase the use of ICT in libraries. The main reason for this was the desire to improve the learning opportunities available for UK citizens either through formal education courses offered by colleges and universities or by lifelong learning available through public libraries. These pre-PN initiatives had resulted in a number of cooperative activities not only between individual libraries but also between libraries and non-library agencies. To explore the ways in which ICT could assist libraries, a number of projects were taken up under an umbrella programme called **e-Lib**. It covered areas including digitization, preservation of images, electronic journals, resource discovery as well as education and training of librarians and the study of the impact of electronic library development on library and information staff. The e-Lib programme aimed for "a sea-change, a cultural shift to see libraries taking these new technologies in an enthusiastic way". All this goes to prove that PN was neither sudden, nor sprang up in a vacuum.

4. AIMS AND STRATEGIES

The PN has lofty aims. Broadly, they fall under the following areas:

a. Enhancing education and lifelong learning opportunities
b. Enriching citizens' information and involvement in society through fostering a politically and culturally informed society
c. Supporting business and the economy and training and employment of citizens
d. Nurturing social cohesion through community history and community identity
e. Building the National Digital Library

Of course, PN tries to achieve these aims and objectives through the individual public libraries spread across the UK.

5. EDUCATION AND LIFE LONG LEARNING

PN laid a great deal of emphasis on education as the main catalyst to face the challenges and grab the opportunities thrown up by the information society. As it has been well established, ICTs change radically the way people work, live and interact with one another. PN takes note of the fact that technology not only affects information handling, but its substantial impact is felt in all walks of life - trade and commerce, health and education, art and culture, defence and security, research and development, employment and management. In education, for example, the focus is now shifting from formal to non-formal methods – self-learning, lifelong learning and the like. Education is no longer seen as a series of injections, administered at set times in life, but as a continuing process from cradle to grave. A single job for lifetime is fast becoming anachronistic in the climate of constant change or "discontinuous change", to borrow Charles Handy's famous phrase. Self-reliance in the use of information is the best guarantee against insecurity in and out of job or career. According to an estimate, about a fifth of all the work-force in Britain change their career every year. PN aims to help not only the adult and working population, but also the aged and the disabled who want to pursue a vocation suited to them or just a hobby, personal interest or reading for pleasure. Besides, public library has always been an adjunct to formal education. Until April 2006, public libraries were very much part of an online network of schools called the **National Grid for Learning (NGfL)** and by virtue of this association, public libraries supplemented learning for young children. In many large public libraries, homework clubs are very popular. With PN coming in, students, parents and library staff assisting them in their homework, have access to almost unlimited number and range of information resources available in multimedia. The early introduction to independent learning in the library for children is expected to promote a more rounded education in them while also imparting the skills needed for learning independently in later years. Through PN the image of the public library as an educator has gone up in the eyes of the people in the UK.

6. CITIZENS' INFORMATION AND INVOLVEMENT IN SOCIETY

Prior to PN, many people, particularly young people had distanced themselves from public libraries, which they considered as outdated and irrelevant to the needs of the day. But the networked public library system changed this perception. It is now seen as a gateway for citizen communications - an opening to the networked society, promoting healthy democracy and social harmony. PN is the conduit for delivering official information, for interactive communications with government, both local and central, voluntary organisations, and private sector agencies and interest groups. Communications in all directions - vertical, horizontal and sideways - are possible within the community and without, thanks to PN. Citizens get in touch with local bodies and government departments. Further, PN makes life easy for people, by helping them to pay taxes, renew driving licenses and passports online. **DirectGov** is a holdall homepage that tells citizens about easier ways to find key services, e.g. to find the nearest school, library or training centre. It can also work in the reverse direction as a channel to obtain feedback for the government on the range of its services and policies. In short, PN works as an interface between the authorities and the citizens and of course the public libraries are its public face.

7. BUSINESS AND ECONOMY AND TRAINING AND EMPLOYMENT

PN is designed to be a powerful instrument for improving the overall well being of the public. Successful business firms do exploit information as an organizational resource. However, a large percentage of businesses in Britain are small and medium size enterprises. Besides, there are millions of self-employed people, who cannot afford their own independent information services. Traditionally, public libraries have had huge print based resources. These are now being supplemented by remote databases on trade and commerce through the Internet. Through its public library outlets, PN helps people to skill and re-skill themselves as and when necessary - from basic ICT skills to advanced level competencies and expertise. UK's unique institution, **University for Industry (UfI)** offers over 900,000 training courses to the citizens through a service called **learndirect**. These range from very simple to highly advanced and cover the whole gamut of fields. These courses are offered from over 600 learning centres. Nearly two thirds of these centres are located in public libraries. PN does not overlook literacy, numeracy and even foreign languages for people who need or want to learn them. In fact, PN aims to promote a culture of learning and re-learning among people. This is the surest way to create wealth and prosperity. Of course information about employment opportunities is made available widely through libraries. There is ample evidence to show that people in great numbers are able to get jobs through PN.

8. SOCIAL COHESION, COMMUNITY HISTORY AND COMMUNITY IDENTITY

An area in which public libraries support both the acquisition and a sense of community is that of community history. Public libraries keep collections of local history, genealogy and family history through a long tradition of storing archives, records, maps, photographs and films. They have long been custodians of people's identity and community's self-image. People of all ages are eager to know their roots. Libraries have always helped people to trace their ancestry. Today, digital technologies have come in handy to libraries in converting this largely paper-based information to new formats. By connecting all the libraries electronically, PN is making these resources widely accessible across the country. In addition to keeping records and documents and disseminating them, public libraries have been serving as community centres where "extension activities" like exhibitions, cultural shows and meetings are organized. Moreover, files of much sought after information pertaining to the locality are kept and are constantly updated e.g. important people like authors, experts in several fields, information on help e.g. how to register birth and death, electoral rolls, 'what's on' type of information.

9. THE NATIONAL DIGITAL LIBRARY

Big Lottery Fund, formerly **New Opportunities Fund, (NOF),** has provided finance to create a huge collection of information in digital form. Significant collections like photographs, rare books and maps from public libraries as well as collections from museums and galleries have been digitized to create online collections accessible not only to library users and researches but to all citizens, supporting cultural awareness and identity. As a result, libraries are in a position to put up virtual multimedia exhibitions with images, narrative, background information for visitors who can feel proud of their cultural heritage.

10. PN'S THREE MAIN ELEMENTS

The three 'C's behind PN are connectivity, competence and content and they represent: (a) **ICT** infrastructure; (b) library staff training; and (c) digital content creation respectively. PN is a 170 million pounds project, the largest funding ever in the history of public libraries in UK. To this huge amount was added another a $4 million (2.6 million pounds) gift from the Bill and Melinda Gates Foundation. This fund was specifically meant for purchasing ICT hardware (terminals and printers) for libraries, situated in areas of social deprivation. An idea of the scale of the PN can be gained by the following facts regarding the three main elements.

a. ICT Infrastructure

In England alone, there are 3500 public libraries offering over 20,000 computer terminals. Over 30,000 computer terminals with broadband Internet access provide millions of hours worth of Internet use every year throughout UK. With the Gate's Foundation's grant, another 1903 Internet terminals in 413 libraries across UK were added. Ancillary facilities such as photocopying and scanning form part of this offer. Connectivity by broadband or ISDN and or wireless as appropriate is provided in all public libraries, including mobile libraries.

b. Staff training

More than 40,000 public library staff members have been trained to use computers and also to train and guide members of the public in online searching to meet their information needs. All libraries have established ICT learning centres, ranging in number from 2 to 6 publicly accessible Internet terminals in small branch or community libraries to between 10 and 50 + Internet terminals in large and medium sized libraries situated in towns and cities. The basic training covered (l) grounding in ICT fundamentals including trouble shooting (2) health, safety and legal issues (3) information retrieval techniques (4) using IT for reader development (5) managing ICT resources in libraries and (6) using IT for professional development of staff. All these basics were covered under a programme called **European Computer Driving License**

(ECDL) In addition to the basic programme, training for selected staff members was imparted for advanced roles such as; Net navigator, in-depth search skills; Information gatekeeper, web design skills; Information consultant; information manager. The training was spread over three years and had a dramatic impact on the quality of library service.

c. Digital Content Creation

The third key element of the PN is the creation and dissemination of digital content. The guidance provided on content development in the LIC's second major report, ***Building the New Library Network*** identified three main strands, (a) Cultural enrichment, b) citizens information and involvement and (c) re-skilling the nation. The digital content of learning resources is delivered free at the point of use to every reader and involves the development of "a community bank" of learning resources and materials in electronic format of well over a million pages, tens of thousands of audio and video clips, innumerable pages of text and many hundreds of new learning packages on a diverse range of topics. The sources for these materials range from libraries, museums, galleries to educational institutions and cover; information on local services; directories of education and training provision; unique heritage collections in library and other cultural institutions, museums and galleries; learning materials; community websites; ancestry, genealogy, family history; public record office holdings.

11. MODERNIZATION OF TRADITIONAL SERVICES

One of the latest developments in PN is that in October 2005 three important online services were launched. These are traditional public library services but now are being offered in a revamped way. These are:

a. Enquire

This is an online enquiry service in real time, like instant messaging or a chat session with a librarian. The PN uses OCLC's **Question Point** software for this service. There is a tie-up with American and Canadian libraries to offer this service 24 X 7. This service stresses the role of public libraries within the democratic process and encourages the citizens to use libraries and online library service to find out about local issues, among other things.

b. Discover

This is a personalized service through the Net to access resources including collections from museums, libraries and archives, national e-government services, etc. It includes often hard-to-find objects in databases.

c. Read

A one-stop-shop for books and reading which includes online directory of library-connected reading groups and *reader 2 reader* opportunities for chat, discussion, voting for best reads and reviews of readers' favourite books. It helps readers to pick up books of their choice, recommended by other readers.

12. EVALUATION

Having pumped in a large amount of money into PN, it was only to be expected that the managers would want to find out how the "*digibaby*" was doing. A great deal of evidence had been collected for evaluating the effectiveness of the PN at the local, regional and national levels during the three year period, 2003-2005, following the roll-out of computer terminals. Peter Brophy carried out two studies. However, the major evaluation called **Books and Bytes:** new service paradigms for the 21st century library carried out by the well known research and consultancy centre, the Tavistock Institute, London over a two year period (April 2002 march 2004) was a comprehensive survey, covering two of the three major areas of PN, viz., IT infrastructure and ICT training for library staff (ICTL) Important findings of these surveys are:

- Following the installation of PCs and other hardware peripherals in public libraries, there was a sudden surge in the use of the equipment.
- In the year 2003, 10% of the use of the Internet in the whole country originated in the PN. 27% of the PN users had never used the Internet before.
- In the first few months of PN, 25000 readers had started a new course of study or training or gained a qualification online, 8000 users have found new jobs; 52,500 people have used the service for activities supporting their community.

These numbers are large, considering the size of the population of UK. The demand was so heavy that some libraries had to resort to rationing use by introducing advance booking systems, and time limits for sessions to control demand at peak hours. Not only was there increased use, but the increased use was noticeably by people from groups previously under-represented and un-represented among the public library users. In other words, the PN succeeded in broadening the public library user base, attracting new users including teenagers, unemployed people, asylum seekers, refugees, old and disabled people, people who could be categorized as socially and digitally excluded. As a result of the PN, public libraries, using Mobile libraries with the custom-made wireless connectivity, were able to reach out to people in the far-flung rural and remote areas. PN is a success story, according to majority of the participants of the survey. Libraries have helped many thousands of adults and young people to become confident and competent in using technology. Library staff now provide services that address digital citizenship, discover and use relevant resources, by creating portals to information resources in areas such as health, helping students to find and use websites and resources suitable for school curriculum. They create interactive learning environments and activities supporting reader development. This service has a knock-on effect on the traditional services, which have registered a greater demand. Users appreciate efforts of staff members who help them acquire new skills, knowledge and qualifications to improve career prospects or just pursue a hobby. As a result of PN, people's perception, especially that of the younger people, of the public library has changed. "PN has helped to redefine the library from an outmoded institution of the 20th century to a new, high tech, reinvigorated library of the future. " The media has by and large, endorsed these findings.

13. CYNICISM, SKEPTICISM AND OPTIMISM

All this is not to say that all is entirely hunky-dory. There are a few problems, although minor. Many of them are structural, strategic or human. Firstly, adoption and progress of IT in the 210 library authorities in the UK are uneven. Even prior to PN, while some of the libraries had adopted IT and offered IT-based services to users, some were not enthusiastic and so were wary and slow in the adoption of technology. Secondly, many users, especially older ones, were apprehensive that introduction of PC meant end of print-based libraries. Thirdly, some of the librarians at the top of the hierarchy were not wholeheartedly convinced of the need for IT. Historically, there was little staff turnover at senior levels over a period of time. The brighter students coming out of the library schools were attracted towards the private sector with the result there were significant pockets of conservatism in the profession. A project of PN's magnitude required a revolution in staff attitudes, which was missing. To achieve the goals of PN, a proactive promotion of services to the larger groups was called for. Some staff members were unable to rise up to the occasion. Fourthly, the early emphasis was mainly on the core PN programmes like the IT infrastructure, basic staff training and content creation. But challenges of leadership, understanding, vision and change remained untouched. These strategic aspects were left to be addressed by another report, *Framework for the Future,* which came out in 2003. On the whole, the reviews were critical of the "non-reflexive and non-learning culture of the library profession". The less enthusiastic minority had little sense of commitment to a vision of the future library. Finally, in spite of the resistance to change from a small percentage of staff, PN threw up a paradigmatic shift in the perception of ICT, not merely as a means for information collection and retrieval but also "as an empowering tool that can be used for social and community purposes". The evaluation contained a word of caution that as home access to the Net rises, the high levels of demand experienced in the initial stage might not be sustainable.

14. NEW LIBRARY

It will be interesting to look at the *new library* that emerges out of PN Public library has been at the heart of the community almost from its inception over 150 years ago. *Framework for the future* describes it as "public anchor for neighbourhoods and communities". Long hailed as people's universities or street corner colleges, public libraries are now recognised as the communications backbone of the information society. Public libraries enjoy an unrivalled reputation as safe, welcoming and neutral spaces open to all. In conjunction with a number of previous and parallel activities in public libraries, PN has crystallized and brought to the fore a vision of an all-pervading modern institution. PN has effectively turned the public library "inside out". In the process, it has begun to shape new professional identities. With a recharged, committed and enthusiastic librarian at the helm, the new public library is fully equipped to play multiple roles, unseen and not thought of before.

(a) The newly emerged library under PN setup is, first and foremost, a treasure trove of information. Technology enables it to answer queries online on an almost unlimited range and variety of subjects, a place to access virtually everything that the new technology can deliver. It creates and promotes knowledge as well as it acquires it.

(b) The new library does not invalidate print and other traditional media. It only tops these up with new formats. So, the new public library continues to serve the public as a hybrid library. It promotes reading in newer ways, adopts new techniques for reader development and promotes information literacy. There is an underlying strong faith in the public library as a physical place.

(c) It is a much busier information centre under PN umbrella and will continue to exist in the foreseeable future, with the librarians not just discharging their duties passively, but as inspired professionals with active responsibilities. An air of dynamism pervades throughout the new library with new facilities including video conferencing for users.

(d) It is a place for education for all, including those who have never stepped inside before. Babies with their mothers and other members of the family reading books, young children doing their homework, adults learning new vocations and seeking to better their prospects, retired people (euphemistically called silver surfers) pursuing their hobbies and even differently abled people trying to get in touch with relatives living far away.

(e) Libraries have always had a training function and this has been more firmly established under PN. People of all ages and backgrounds are trained by librarians to use computers for a variety of purposes.

(f) It promotes social cohesion and thereby tries to bridge the digital divide by providing a level playing field for the information haves and information have-not's. It enables citizens to participate more actively in democratic governance, otherwise termed digital democracy.

(g) The new library is a more formalized gateway to the world. Even the remotest rural library is equipped to enable users to get into the information super highway.

(h) It provides advice on careers and helps people to find jobs online.

(i) It empowers citizens with information about rights and entitlements, enables them to keep in touch with their political representatives. It makes life easy for people in a variety of ways by providing what are called citizen services.

(j) In case of housebound people, it reaches out to them with library materials and even lends laptops where necessary; and much of this is free.

This is just a snapshot of what the reactivated public library can do and is indeed doing under PN. There are many more possibilities in store, thanks to the ICT revolution. Chris Batt, Chief Executive of MLA: the Council for Museums, Libraries and Archives, which manages PN describes the public library as the heart and brain of the information society.

15. LESSONS FOR INDIA

Are there any lessons we in India can learn from the PN? The answer is yes, there are. Britain was one of the earliest countries to have grasped the potential of the ICTs. Fortunately for us too, realization of this truth has dawned on the sections of society that matter. Now there are champions who speak for the ICTs. The championing has, however, to be more widespread than it is today. There is an incipient interest that libraries can play a role in bringing about change, although the opinion leaders in the country may not associate this feeling with PN of Britain We are witnessing increased interest in ICTs particularly in literate circles and largely concentrated in urban areas. Of late our country has been doing much to take a quantum leap to become an IT super power. State governments are vying with one another in adopting IT. Many have installed or toying with the idea of installing 'kiosks' to introduce citizens' services as part of e-governance e.g. **e-seva** centres in many towns and cities in Andhra Pradesh. NGOs are not lagging behind in this effort as is evident in initiatives like the Pondicherry Information Villages project of the MS Swaminathan Research Foundation. Yet another major initiative to connect the less developed parts of India to the Internet is the **n-logue**. To quote its website," 'n-logue' was incubated by the telecommunications and computer network (TeNet) group of the Indian Institute of Technology Madras and disseminating innovative, affordable communication technologies to the rural poor of developing countries". It helps entrepreneurs in rural India to start **access centres** using low cost wireless technologies. These kiosks are present in states like Madhya Pradesh, Himachal Pradesh, Rajasthan, Andhra

Pradesh, Karnataka and Tamil Nadu. Its well-wishers would, however, like to see a more rapid spreading of the movement. Successive governments at the Centre have been taking a series of steps, for about a decade now, to explore the possibilities of introducing ICTs into the country. The IT Action Plan, prepared by the National Task Force during the NDA rule talked about **IT for All** by 2008, universal access to the Internet and conversion of every PCO into a 'tele information centre.' A National Knowledge Commission (NKC) was constituted in June 2005 with the mandate to devise and introduce reforms expected to transform India into a strong and vibrant knowledge economy in the coming years. It has a time frame of 3 years up to October 2008. Shades of policy aims of PN can be seen in the terms of reference of the NKC. Dissemination of knowledge, focus on universal elementary education, creating a culture of learning, especially for the skilled workforce, boosting literacy levels and using ICT to improve education and spread of knowledge are some of them. As part of NKC, a Working Group on Libraries and Library Services has been created for the first time. The latest in the series of attempts is a recent policy initiative by government of India to start 100,000 **Common Service Centres (CSCs)**, broadband-enabled computer kiosks that will offer a range of 'government to citizen' and 'business to customer' services, besides providing access to the Internet. They are expected to begin to serve India's 600,000 villages by March 2008. In an article in *The Hindu*, Chandrasekar regrets the absence of reliable statistics of Internet access and generally of IT penetration in India for planning the expansion in a systematic way.

Except the NKC, none of the initiatives envision a role for pubic libraries. But an encouraging sign is that the powers that be have become aware of the potential of the ICTs and in particular the Internet to tackle the problem of digital divide and eradication of poverty. There is however, no evidence to connect this inspiration to British experience. But obstacles to overcome the problems in the provision of ICTs and libraries are huge and at times look insurmountable. Successive governments have placed on the statute book many a noble legislation, e.g. Right to Information or employment guarantee scheme. Unfortunately the required awareness of these laws and strategy to help the common people is missing. Can the illiterate or semiliterate rural people know how and where to access this information deplores Raha. It is the public libraries, neutral places, as they are, with friendly and committed staff can make a difference.

Moreover, talking about PN in the Indian context, one cannot help making a comparison between the two countries. Britain and India are like chalk and cheese. Britain is smaller in size and population than some of our individual States. Britain's literacy is 99% where as India's hovers around 60%. India is a veritable Babel of Tongues, whereas English is spoken and understood through the length and breadth of the UK. Visiting public library is the fifth most popular past time in UK. According to the Indian constitution, education is on the Concurrent List, meaning that both the Central and State governments have responsibility for it. Only 13 out of 28 States and 7 Union Territories have passed public library legislation and among these laws, there is a great divergence in the library systems each state opts for. Above all, India is a poor country, despite the claims to the contrary. This multiplicity of problems seems to suggest that PN model does not suit India. But, the message should be welcome. Indeed, PN has a universal appeal.

16. LOOKING AHEAD

It is no exaggeration to say that the People's Network is

nothing short of a revolution for public libraries in the UK. It couldn't have come at a more opportune time in their history. As was mentioned before, during the two decades preceding PN, their stock was at low ebb. PN has dramatically changed all that. It highlights the educational role of the public libraries. Its single most important aim is to give equal opportunity for all to better their lot and through it, to tackle some of the social imbalances including the digital divide. Questions of its sustainability are often raised. With the profile of the public library having gone up, thanks to the introduction of ICTs, they have become attractive to do business with for their potential partners like the local authorities, media and the private sector. The new alliances should give the PN the much-needed support in the long run. Ultimately, however, it is the love and patronage of the user, the central figure in the scheme of things, which will sustain the public library. The satisfied customer is its potential supporter, advocate and champion. Already over 60% of the population of the UK use public libraries; with the introduction of PN, the volume of use and the number of users are growing. Librarians, charged with new enthusiasm have to continue to take a proactive role in promoting public libraries creatively. They have to not only bring users to the library, but also have to take the new libraries to the users. This is the central message of the People's Network.

17. REFERENCES

1. Arunachalam. S. Information for research in developing countries - information technology: a friend or foe? *International information and library review*, Vol. 35, 2003, p.133-147
2. Batt, Chris. Public libraries in a wired world. *APLIS*, Vol. 13(4), December 2000, p.158-165
3. Big Lottery Fund. *Books and bytes: new service*

paradigms for the 21st century library: an evaluation of the People's Network and ICT training for public library staff programme, carried out by the Tavistoek Institute. 2004.

4. Brophy, Peter. *The people's network: a turning point in public libraries: First findings.* Resource:Dec 2002
5. Brophy, Peter. The people's network: moving forward. *MLA,* April 2004.
6. Chandrasekhar, C.P. India is online, but most Indians are not. *The Hindu,* 25 Sept. 2006. p.13

Department for Culture, Media and Sport (DCMS)

7. *"New Library: the People's Network": the government's response.* April 1998. HMSO, CMD, 3887
8. *Libraries for all: social inclusion for public libraries: policy guidance for local authorities in England.* DCMS, October, 1999.
9. *Framework for the Future: libraries, learning and information in the next decade,* 2003-2013. DCMS, Feb 2003
10. Dolan, John. Inside out: the shape of new library. In *Building community information networks strategies and experiences ed. by Sheila Pantry.* p.84 - 91 Library Association Publishing, 1999.
11. Halper, Sally. Evaluating the impact of the People's Network. *Update* Vol. 3(12), Dec 2004, p. 34-35
12. Holman, Tom. Framework : the next stage. *Update,*Vol. 5(6), June 2006, p.32-35
13. Kendall, M and Cravan, J. Time will tell how to measure the impact of the People's Network. *Update* Vol. 4 (12), Dec.2005, p.30-32

Library and Information Commission (LIC)

14. *New Library : The People's Network* 1997
15. *Building the New Library Network.* 1998.
16. People's Network : You've come along way, digibaby.

A review of the Evaluation of the People's Network and ICT training for public Library Staff Training Programme. Interim report of the New Opportunities fund, 2003. *Update,* 3(5), May 2004, p.5

17. People's Network: new paradigm needed to release full potential : review of Books and Bytes. *Update,* Vol. 4(1-2), Jan-Feb 2005, p.2
18. Raha, Subir. The obligation to inform. *Deccan Chronicle (Chennai edition)*, 17 Nov. 2006, p.7
19. Sankaraiah. K Empowering information users through information literary: role of public libraries; paper presented at *National Seminar on the Role of the Public libraries in rural development,* organised jointly by the Madras Library Association, Pennington Public Library and Raja Rammohan Roy Library Foundation, 16-18, August 2002.
20. Tedd, Lucy A. Library co-operation and ICT in the UK : an overview. *Information services and use* Vol.23, 2003. p.199-210.

10

INTELLECTUAL PROPERTY RIGHTS AND LIBRARY AND INFORMATION PROFESSIONALS

S. Amba[1]

1. INTRODUCTION

Intellectual Property Rights (IPR) related issues have been increasingly becoming important, particularly since the coming into force of TRIPS and its implementation in India. Advances in digital communication and technologies have been major factors that necessitate a proper understanding of all the issues involved. These have led to a situation in which the need for awareness of IPR-related issues among library and information professionals (LIP) assumes great importance. This paper attempts to examine some of the principal facets of IPR, their impact and implications for library and information work and service. As is to be expected the emphasis is on the areas of patent information and copyright. However, an attempt has been made to touch on other facets also.

1 Deputy Director (Retd.), Central Leather Research Institute, Adyar, Chennai 600 020. **Contact** : No. 225, III Street, Ramnagar North, Velachery, Chennai–600042

The term 'property' generally brings to mind two types of property – immovable property such as land or buildings and movable property such as jewelry, shares, stocks, automobiles, etc. '*Intellectual property*' can be considered a third category of property. Intellectual property is increasingly being recognized as of prime importance in the economy of nations. The basic features that apply to other types of property, viz., that the owner of the property is free to use it as he/she wishes, provided the use is not against the law, and *to exclude others from so using that owned property* apply just as well to intellectual property also.

What exactly is 'intellectual property'? The term is reserved for types of property that result from creations of the human mind, the intellect. Rights of ownership are granted by the State. However, unlike the conventional rights, the rights of the owner are limited to a specific period of time with a view to maintain a balance between two "contradictory" perspectives. These are:

i) The individual's right to enjoy the fruits of his/her intellectual endeavours; and

ii) The need for the society to apply the outputs of the intellect for betterment of the society as a whole.

The 'time feature' distinguishes intellectual property and differentiates it from other types.

2. INTERNATIONAL SCENARIO

Before examining the different types of intellectual properties, it would be in order to briefly describe the major international organizations, international agreements and conventions concerned with IPR.

2.1 World Intellectual Property Organisation (WIPO)

The international body, which is exclusively concerned

with various aspects of intellectual property, is the WIPO which was established in 1967 to promote the protection of IP throughout the world through cooperation among states and in collaboration with other international organizations. In 1974, the WIPO became a specialized agency of the UN and is headquartered in Geneva. WIPO is responsible for promoting the development and harmonization of IP-related legislation, standards and procedures among its member states and handles the administration of 24 international treaties. In 1996 it signed the cooperation agreement with the World Trade Organisation (WTO). The five strategic goals of the WIPO as given in their website www.wipo.int are –

- To promote an IP culture;
- To integrate IP into national development policies and programmes;
- To develop international IP laws and standards;
- To deliver quality services in global IP protection systems; and
- To increase the efficiency of WIPO's management and support processes

2.2. Trade Related Aspects of Intellectual Property Rights (TRIPS)

It is a treaty administered by the WTO and sets minimum standards for many forms of intellectual property. TRIPS was negotiated in 1994 at the end of the Uruguay Round of the General Agreement on Tariffs and Trade (GATT) treaty. The TRIPS agreement introduced intellectual property law into the international trading system for the first time and remains the most comprehensive international agreement on intellectual property to date. The TRIPS Agreement is applicable to all WTO members. The basic principle is that of national treatment. i.e. treating one's own nationals and foreigners equally. The obligations under TRIPS apply equally to all member states; however, developing countries were allowed extra time to implement the applicable changes to their national laws. The transition period expired in 2005 and India has amended its intellectual property laws to conform to TRIPS regulations. TRIPs also specifies enforcement procedures, remedies, and dispute resolution procedures. Though it does not expect all members to have identical rules on intellectual property, it expects all members to comply with the minimum standards set by it and laws of the member countries should not contravene the provisions of the agreement. (Details can be accessed at http://www.wto.org/english/tratop_e/trips_e/tripfq_e.htm)

2.3. Patent Treaties

2.3.1. Patent Cooperation Treaty

Generally, patent rights are 'country dependent' or territorial in that the right is given only within the country. To have rights in other countries it is necessary to apply for and get the patent granted. The **Patent Cooperation Treaty** (**PCT**) is an international patent law treaty, concluded in 1970. It provides a unified procedure for filing patent applications to protect inventions in each of its 135 contracting states. A patent application filed under the PCT is called an **international application** or **PCT application**. A single filing of an international application is made with a Receiving Office (RO) designating the countries where patent protection is sought. The millionth international application (or PCT application) was filed at the end of 2004. (http://www.wipo.int/pct/en/treaty/about.htm). The advantage is that by filing one application, the applicant will obtain an international filing date for his application and that filing date will have the effect of a regular national filing in each country. India is a member of the PCT since December 1998.

2.4. Copyright Treaties

2.4.1. Berne Convention

The earliest Copyright Convention is the Berne Convention for the Protection of Literary and Artistic Works of 1886 of which India is a member. The convention is based on the principle of national treatment meaning that under national law one cannot discriminate against works from countries that are party to the Convention. It also adheres to the principle of automatic protection in that it would not be necessary to register the work.

2.5. The Universal Copyright Convention (or UCC)

Adopted at Geneva in 1952, UCC is one of the two principal international conventions protecting copyright, the other being the Berne Convention. The UCC was developed by UNESCO as an alternative to the Berne Convention for those states which disagreed with aspects of the Berne Convention

2.6. The Rome Convention

This convention for the protection of performers, producers of phonograms and broadcasting organisations was accepted in 1961. It secures protection in performances of performers, phonograms of producers of phonograms and broadcasts of broadcasting organizations. Though India is not a member of the Rome Convention of 1961, the Copyright Act 1957 is fully compliant with the provisions of the Rome Convention.

2.7. TRIPS (Copyright)

The main effect of TRIPS, with respect to copyright, is that it imports most of the provisions of *the Berne* Convention. The only provisions of the Berne Convention which have not been incorporated into TRIPS concern moral rights. The *IFLA Committee on Copyright and other*

Legal Matters (CLM) has issued a document entitled "*Tips for TRIPS: A Guide for Libraries and Librarians to the Agreement on Trade-Related Aspects of Intellectual Property Rights (TRIPS)*"

2.8. WIPO Copyright Treaty (WCT) (1996)

The WCT is a special agreement under the Berne Convention. Any Contracting Party (even if it is not bound by the Berne Convention) must comply with the substantive provisions of the 1971 (Paris) Act of the Berne Convention. The WCT mentions two subject matters to be protected by copyright,

(i) computer programs, whatever may be the mode or form of their expression, and

(ii) compilations of data or other material ("databases"), in any form, which by reason of the selection or arrangement of their contents constitute intellectual creations.

2.9. WIPO Performance and Phonograms Treaty (WPPT)

This deals with intellectual property rights of two kinds of beneficiaries: performers (actors, singers, musicians, etc.), producers of phonograms (the persons or legal entities who or which take the initiative and have the responsibility for the fixation of the sounds).

The WCT and WPPT are together known as the "WIPO Internet Treaties. These treaties are part of the WIPO Digital Agenda, which sets out a series of guidelines and goals for WIPO in seeking to develop practical solutions to the challenges raised by the impact of new technologies on intellectual property rights. India is not a member of these treaties.

3. CATEGORIES OF INTELLECTUAL PROPERTY

- Marks, logos, names etc. – Trademarks

- Designs – e.g. a new shape for a bottle – Industrial Designs
- Geographical names indicating a product – Geographical Indications
- Protection of new plant varieties
- Layout of design of integrated circuits.
- Inventions e. g. a new product or process of manufacture – Patents
- Literary, artistic and scientific work e.g. Books etc. Performances, broadcasts etc – Copyright and Copyrights Related Rights

3.1. Trademarks

A trademark is basically a sign that is used to distinguish the goods or services offered by one undertaking from those offered by another. Two main characteristics of a trademark are that it should be

(a) Distinctive; and

(b) Not deceptive.

International protection for trademark is through the Madrid system governed by two treaties – the Madrid Agreement and the Madrid Protocol. Trademarks can be registered at the office of the Registrar of Trademarks and Designs. At times even if it is not registered prolonged use will give the necessary protection. India enacted its new Trademarks Act 1999 (the TM Act) and the Trademarks Rules 2002, with effect from 15th September 2003, to ensure adequate protection to domestic and international brand owners, in compliance with the TRIPS Agreement. The term of a trademark has been increased to 10 years, renewable upon expiration. A digital database on CD-ROMs of 1,50,000 Trade Mark Certificates and 1,250 Trade Marks Journals has been created in the Office of the Controller General of Patents, Designs & Trade

Marks. (www.patentoffice.nic.in). Information professionals especially in the private sector have to be aware of such rules and databases.

3.2. Industrial Designs

This relates to the ornamental or aesthetic aspect of a useful product. It is concerned with shape, texture, colour, pattern etc. of an object that could be consumer oriented or industrial. It protects the appearance of a product. The International Agreement for this is the Hague Agreement. In India, the Indian Design Act, 1911 has been replaced by the Design Act, 2000. The term for a Design is 10 years from the date of registration. This period can be extended by 5 years if application is made before the expiry of 10 years.

3.3. Geographical Indication (GI)

It is a notice stating that a given product originates in a given geographical area. Often this may imply a certain quality. It is used to identify goods having special characteristics originating from a definite Geographical Territory. The International Agreement for this is the Lisbon Agreement.

To differentiate between trademark and GI, we could take the following hypothetical example – Rice from the Nellore area referred to as Nellore Rice could be taken to be a GI but such rice can be marketed under the Trade Mark "Diamond". In December 1999, the Parliament passed the Geographical Indications of Goods (Registration and Protection) Act, 1999. It prevents unauthorized use of a Registered Geographical Indication by others. The Registration is valid for 10 years. The Controller General of Patents, Designs and Trade Marks, is the Registrar of Geographical Indications and administers the Act. The Geographical Indications Registry is located at Chennai.

GI have been given for many items in India such as Mysore Silk, which has got a GI registration. The example given below illustrates how a LIP can be involved in this. The CLRI was approached with regard to GI for Kolhapuri footwear, which is a traditional handcrafted footwear, produced for centuries in the bordering areas of Maharastra and Karnataka - Athni, Nippani and Kolhapur. The library was asked to get as much documentation as possible regarding this. In the *New Sunday Express* of 25th February datelined Bangalore there was a news item that GI was being sought for 'monsooned coffee'.

3.4. UPOV: (International Union for the Protection of New Varieties of Plants) (1991 Convention).

Protection of plant varieties is another aspect of IP rights and as such seeks to acknowledge the achievements of breeders of new plant varieties by giving them an exclusive right for a limited period. India is interested in a *Sui Generis* system and is concerned with Breeder's rights and Farmer's rights. The Latin term *"sui generis"*, means "of its own kind of class". The first registrations are underway in India under the 2001 Protection of Plant Varieties and Farmers' Rights Act. The Act is India's sui generis system for the protection of plant varieties as required under the Agreement on Trade Related Aspects of Intellectual Property Rights (TRIPS). As the name implies, the Act provides a range of safeguards for farmers and gives them rights on a par with plant breeders as a result of campaigns by NGOs such as the Gene Campaign.

In *the Hindu* dated Dec. 7th 2006 there was a report that twelve varieties of crops, including Rice, Wheat and Maize will be registered by February 2007, in the first phase of the registration under this Act. A list of 35 crops have been prepared out of which 12 would be registered first by the Protection of Plant Varieties and Farmers Rights Authority. No other aspect of intellectual property has generated such discussions as this as it strikes at the very heart of India. The ethics and economics of this category of IP have been discussed at various national and international fora. Information professionals in agriculture related organizations whether academic or commercial would definitely have to well versed in this matter. There is a plethora of articles relating to this both in print as well as in electronic format and compilation and organization for retrieval would definitely be required.

3.5. Domain Names Protection

As a result of the Internet's popularity, Indian courts have dealt with a large number of domain name disputes in the last few years. The Supreme Court of India held that domain names are subject to the legal norms applicable to other intellectual properties such as trademarks.

3.6. Patents and Patenting

Patents are one of the oldest forms of intellectual property. It is the protection given to an invention – a "product" or the "process" of manufacturing a product. Granting a patent is based on two fundamental ideas:

a) Human effort should be rewarded; i.e. one is entitled to fruits of one's labour;

b) The product invented / process developed should not be the sole possession of the inventor in perpetuity. It should be for the 'public good' i.e. knowledge should be in the 'public domain'.

Some of the things that cannot be patented are:

- Things that exist in nature – such as the discovery of a new comet.

- Machines that defy the laws of nature – machines that defy the law of gravity
- Scientific theories or mathematical models
- Methods or schemes for doing business
- Methods of medical treatment and diagnostic methods
- The mere discovery of a new property or new use for a known substance
- Invention contrary to law or morality or injurious to public health

Three criteria have to be fulfilled for an invention to be patented. These are:

- Novelty – the invention must be new or novel
- Non – obviousness i.e. an inventive step should be involved
- It must have utility

A patent specification discloses the details of the invention for which the patent protection is sought. The legal rights in a patent are based on the disclosures made in the specification. Specifications can either be -

Provisional: A provisional specification does not disclose the complete description of the invention as time might be required to develop it further. The provisional specification is filed to claim the priority date of an invention. Or

Complete: The document, containing the detailed description of the invention along with the drawings and claims is called as the complete specification. Also the description regarding prior art is included in the complete specification.

The Patent Act of 1970 is in force with amendments in 1999, 2003 and 2005 to bring it in line with TRIPS requirements. Patents are filed with the Controller General of Patents, Trademarks and Designs. The head office is in Kolkata with regional offices in Delhi, Mumbai and Chennai. Filing of an application is the first step in the patenting process. Once a patent is filed it is examined against the three criteria mentioned earlier. If the criteria are satisfied it is published and is open for opposition. If there is no opposition then the patent is sealed or granted. An important point to be noted is the concept of priority date. That is, if two people have invented / developed an identical product, the person who files his application first gets the priority and exclusive right to commercially exploit the invention. The date of application determines the priority date. Currently, the term for **patents in India** is 20 years from the date of filing of the application for the patent. It is the responsibility of the patentee to maintain an issued patent by paying the annuities until the patent expires. After the 20 years term the invention claimed in the patent falls into the public domain.

The Patent law does not allow algorithms or business methods to be patented. Further, software per se cannot be patented – it has to be embedded software and the device as a whole has to be patented.

3.6.1. The role of the Information Professional vis-à-vis patents

It has been mentioned that *novelty* is one of the criteria for granting patents. Novelty means that the information contained in the patent should not have been published earlier. The information professional can help at two stages – one before filing of the patent to ascertain if information is already available in published form or create an awareness in the applicant for the need for novelty and advise them in filing a patent before the matter is submitted as a dissertation or as a paper; the other is checking for novelty in patents relating to the field of interest of the parent organization so as to aid in the opposition process.

It has been stated that information contained in a patent is not available elsewhere. It has been estimated that 80% of the information contained in a patent document is never published elsewhere and at times it is the only source of information. If one considers that nearly a million patents are granted annually it is easy to imagine the vast store of technical information that has to be tapped by the information professional. A patent document contains not just technical information but also other useful information.

Let us just see what they are: As the patent document is both a technical as well as a legal document, four categories of information can be found in a patent – bibliographic; technical; legal and database and retrieval oriented. Every patent document must contain a description of the "prior art" in that area. That is, it describes the developments in the field in which the patent is taken and as such contains useful research and technical information. There are two types of "prior art" references those given by the applicant and those given by the patent examiner. This is more so in the US Patents. In the US, the "duty of candor" principle postulates that all prior art documents that are in any way considered relevant to the patentability of the invention must be disclosed. Failing to do so may result in litigation and penalties. Hence, patent documents are a fertile field for identifying documents of interest.

The patent contains technical information in that it gives the details of the invention (both textual and illustrations) and also describes the claims made by it. The legal aspect is covered by details of the country of publication; patent number; application date; grant date; title; details of the applicant/inventor; etc. The international classification number; the national classification number and INID codes are useful in the context of retrieval.

3.6.2. What are the International Patent Classification and INID Codes?

The Strasbourg Agreement (of 1971) concerning the International Patent Classification provides for a common classification for patents for invention including published patent applications, utility models and utility certificates. The International Patent Classification (IPC) is a hierarchical system in which the whole area of technology is divided into a range of sections, classes, subclasses and groups. The Classification is periodically revised in order to improve the system and to take account of technical development. The current, 8th edition containing approximately 70,000 groups entered into force on January 1, 2006. The Indian patent classification is more than 55 years old and all fields of technology are classified under 208 classes which have been grouped into 66 groups. The IPC is a useful tool in the retrieval of patents from different databases.

Since patents can be in different languages there may be differences in terminology to describe the data elements. To overcome this, a common code for identifying the different data elements, the INID code was developed. These codes were standardized by the International Co-operation in Information REtrieval among PATent offices (ICIREPAT) which ceased to exist in 1979, when its functions were transferred to the WIPO PCPI (Permanent Committee on Patent Information). INID stands for Internationally agreed Numbers for the Identification of (bibliographic) data. These are numerals and are indicated immediately before the corresponding bibliographic data elements. A few examples:

[11] Patent Number

[22] Date of filing the patent application

[51] International Patent Classification

[54] Title of invention

Information professionals can utilize the INID codes when retrieval of patents in different languages is to be done or when creating an in-house database of patents. This would be useful in the context of exchange of data or in the merging of databases.

3.6.3. Equivalent Patents/Patent Family

A patent for the same invention can be taken in more than one country. These are called as equivalent patents. A patent family is all of the **patents** and patent applications resulting from a specific patent application. When the Web did not exist, the *Chemical Abstracts* was the most useful tool in identifying equivalent patents.

3.6.4. Sources of Information

Only a few of the web sources are listed here. These are the www.uspto.gov for US patents; www.espacenet.com which is the gateway for Europe's network of patent databases. The website of the European patent office http://ep.espacenet.com/ is extremely useful and gives worldwide access. Further, it is also possible to search INPADOC's database of patent families through this website. Information on several million patents is thus accessible. The WIPO intellectual property Digital Library web site provides access to intellectual property data collections that include PCT (Patents), Trademarks, Industrial Designs etc.

In India, the Patent Information System at Nagpur can be approached for information. The details of the Patent Office India can be found in www.ipindia.nic.in. Till the Patents (Amendment) Act of 2005 all information on Indian patents was published in the Gazette of India Part III Section 2. However, this has been discontinued and details of all patents applied for, granted, opposed etc are published in the Official Journal of the Patent Office. http://www.patentoffice.nic.in/ipr/patent/journal_archieve. The documentary sources of information on Indian Patents prior to 1972 have been detailed in a paper by Amba published in World Patent Information in 2001.

The Patent Facilitating Cell of the TIFAC (DST) brings out the *IPR Bulletin*. Two databases are brought out by TIFAC which are also available online against subscription. These are Ekaswa- A Database of patent applications filed in India as published in the issues of the Gazette of India (Part III Section 2) from January 1995 onwards and Ekaswa- B Database of patent applications notified for opposition in the Gazette of India (Part III Section 2) published from January 1995 onwards. They can also be contacted for supply of patent documents (www.tifac.org.in). The Intellectual Property & KnowHow Informatics (Patents) Division, National Informatics Centre, Department of Information Technology is also a very good source of information and for supply of patent documents. The website is http://pk2id.delhi.nic.in/. The NISCAIR has brought a bibliography of Indian Patents from 1972 on CD ROM called the INPAT database. The CSIR brings out the *Journal of Intellectual Property Rights*, which in addition to articles also covers what is happening in the patent arena.

We have all been hearing a great deal about biopiracy and multinationals making use of traditional knowledge in taking patents especially in drugs, pharmaceuticals and agriculture. **Biopiracy** refers to the appropriation, generally by means of patents, of indigenous biomedical knowledge by foreign entities (including corporations, universities and governments) without compensatory payment.

IPR regimes permit only formal systems of knowledge. India has strong and worthy informal systems such as shrutis and smritis. This knowledge has to be codified if such moves are to be prevented. India is one of the 180 – odd nations that is a party to the international treaty - Convention on Biological Diversity, which came into force on 29th December 1993. India has passed the Biological Diversity Act 2002 which came into force as of 15th April 2004. Under this, every local body shall constitute a Biodiversity Management Committee and maintain a People's Biodiversity Register which shall contain comprehensive information on availability and knowledge of local biological resources, their medicinal or any other use or any other traditional knowledge associated with it. The library professionals especially those in public libraries in rural areas need to get involved in such endeavours.

Another effort is the Traditional Knowledge Digital Library (TKDL) Project at NISCAIR. The examiners of patents involving neem, turmeric etc contended that they could not search relevant traditional knowledge as prior art. The reason for this non-accessibility were that a) such information was not compiled and arranged in an orderly fashion b) the prior art was confined to texts which were in the English language. The TKDL project has been established to overcome this. The TKDL database makes available the information from various sources. TKDL gives modern names to plants/diseases/processes mentioned in literature relating to Indian systems of medicine. A classification system, Traditional Knowledge Resource Classification has been developed for Indian systems and is structured on the lines of the IPC so as to facilitate retrieval of information. (www.niscair.res.in). The importance can be seen when one considers the following.

India (CSIR) fought a successful but costly legal battle in

1999 to revoke a US patent for the use of turmeric to heal wounds — a property well known in India for generations. Recently, India won a 10-year-long battle at the European Patent Office against a patent granted on an anti-fungal product, derived from neem, by successfully arguing that the medicinal neem tree is part of traditional Indian knowledge. In 1998 the US Patent Office granted patent to a local company for new strains of rice similar to basmati, which has been grown for centuries in the Himalayan foothills of northwest India and Pakistan and has become popular internationally. After a prolonged legal battle, the patent was revoked four years ago.

The information professional thus has an important role to play in documenting knowledge and dissemination of such knowledge, etc.

3.6.5. Scientometric/Infometric studies

The economic well being of a nation is increasingly being assessed by its patenting activity both within and outside the country. Patents are now one of the indicators of a nation's progress and its industrial development and capability. Increasingly, the assets of a company are being judged also by its patent portfolio. The number of patents held by residents as compared to those held by non residents is a clear indicator of the level of development of technology in the country. In a World Development Report of the World Bank, the number of patent applications filed is considered to be one of the "selected World Development Indicators". Study of and analysis of patenting activity in countries is increasingly being carried out by information professionals as is evidenced in journals such as Scientometrics, etc. A study of the patenting profile of Indian leather and allied patents first from 1912 to 1972 (60 years) and again from 1972 till 1997 was carried out by Amba and analyses were done by patentee, subject, country, etc. These have been published in the journal Library Science with a Slant to Documentation 1981 and World Patent Information 1999. A study on global leather patents in relation to trade has been published in World Patent Information in 2006. Such studies have been carried out in other fields also by other information professionals.

Another area would be the citation pattern of patents. A study on the extent of patent citations was done in 1978 and published in 1979. This showed that there were not many citations to patents probably because of inaccessibility and the pattern did not change much. Perhaps, studies of recent literature may show a difference because of access to websites to patent documents. Equivalent patents had been mentioned earlier. These were studied to ascertain whether equivalent patents of which an Indian patent is one cite the same references and extent of examiner references. It was found that it was not necessarily so. The foreign patent would have references which were not given in the Indian patent. This study was published as a poster paper in ISSI Conference, Sydney. Patent documents give references to both patent as well as non-patent literature. Studies have been carried out on the extent and pattern of referencing the two types of literature. Studies have also been done on the referencing patterns of applicants and examiners. Access to patent literature could be another area of study. These are just a few areas which would be of interest to information professionals.

3.7 Copyright

What follows is concerned mostly with printed material and not with music or videos. Copyright and neighbouring (related) rights as it is generally known is a right given by the law to the creators of literary, dramatic, musical and artistic works. It aims to prevent unauthorized use. It also covers rights relating to broadcasting, performances, etc. There is no copyright in ideas. Copyright subsists only in the material form in which the ideas are expressed. The rights under copyright are exclusive rights i.e. the creator of the work alone has the right to exploit it. The copyright can be assigned or transferred. As in the case of other IP there is a time clause for copyright also. In India, it is 60 years after the death of the author. Another concept to be borne in mind is the concept of common law countries and civil law countries. In the former, it is not necessary to 'fix' or register a work e.g. India, whereas in civil law countries such as the USA it has to be registered.

Two types of rights are spoken of in the context of copyright. These are economic rights and moral rights. Economic rights are the right to copy the work which includes storing it electronically, the right to issue copies of the work, to rent or lend it and to make adaptations or translations. If anyone other than the copyright owner performs these activities without permission or license unless it falls under a statutory exception than that would amount to infringement of the copyright. Moral rights give the creator of a work the right to be identified as the creator and the right to prohibit destruction or degradation of the work. Four rights are recognized under moral rights. These are i) paternity rights – Right to be identified as the author of the work ii) integrity rights – Right of authors to object to derogatory treatment of their work iii) The right for everyone not to have a work falsely attributed to them iv) Commissioner's right of privacy in respect of a photo or film made for private or domestic purpose. Moral rights are stressed more in Europe whereas in USA emphasis is more on economic rights. In India, (and some other countries) the term 'Copyright' is restricted to economic rights, but moral rights are also separately protected, under section 57 of our Copyright Act, as author's special rights. The Act also provides the authors certain moral rights like the right to claim authorship and to restrain or claim damages in respect of any distortion, mutilation etc., of their works.

Another concept talked of in the context of copyright is Public domain. Public domain comprises the body of knowledge to which no person or other legal entity can establish or maintain proprietary interests. This body of knowledge and creativity is considered to be part of a common cultural and intellectual heritage, which, can be exploited or used by anyone.

3.7.1. Protection in India

Copyright of nationals of countries who are members of the Berne Convention, Universal Copyright Convention and the TRIPS Agreement are protected in India through the International Copyright Order. That is, copyrights of works of the countries mentioned in the International Copyright Order are protected in India, as if such works are Indian works. India is a member of the following international conventions

Berne Convention for the Protection of Literary and Artistic works.

Universal Copyright Convention.

Convention for the Protection of Producers of Phonograms against Unauthorised Duplication of their Phonograms.

Multilateral Convention for the Avoidance of Double Taxation of Copyright Royalties.

Trade Related Aspects of Intellectual Property Rights

The Copyright Act, 1957 came into effect from January 1958. This Act has been amended five times since then, i.e., in 1983, 1984, 1992, 1994 and 1999 and as mentioned earlier it conforms to international conventions. Rights have been mentioned till now. There are, however, statutory limitations to these rights. This is because a balance has to be struck between the society's need for knowledge and the need to reward creativity. When does infringement of copyright not take place? When can a work be copied? These are spelt out in Article 52 of the Copyright Act. These are termed as "fair use" of copyright. Some of them of relevance to us are:

- Single copy for private, personal and non-commercial purposes for research and study, criticism or review whether of that work or any other work
- The making of copies or adaptation of a computer program by the lawful possessor of such computer programme to make back-up copies purely as a temporary protection against loss, destruction or damage in order to utilize the computer programme for the purpose for which it was supplied.
- Use of work for the purpose of reporting current events in a newspaper etc. or broadcast
- The use of the work for the purpose of a judicial proceeding
- The reproduction or publication of a work prepared by the Secretariat of a legislature.
- The reading or recitation in public of any reasonable extract from a published work
- The reproduction by a teacher or a pupil in the course of instruction or as part of the questions to be answered in an examination, in answers to such questions
- The making of not more than three copies of a book (including a pamphlet, sheet of music, map, chart or plan) by or under the direction of the person in charge of a public library for the use of the library

if such book is not available for sale in India.

Sections 107 of the US copyright Act deals with "fair use". To determine fair use it is necessary to consider the following –

i. The purpose and character of use
ii. The nature of the copyrighted work
iii. Amount and substantiality of the portion of the copyrighted work
iv. Effect of use upon the potential market for value of the copyrighted work.

An international yardstick has been provided in Article 9(2) of the Berne Convention against which exceptions to rights can be measured. This is referred to as the three-step test. Exceptions must be confined to special cases; should not conflict with normal exploitation of the work and should not prejudice legitimate interests of the author.

There is no copyright in the US for papers emanating from federal government funded research. However, in India all government work is under copyright.

The concerns of the Third World extend to copyright also. Increasingly, copyright issues have gone beyond the printed world into the digital world – video piracy is something that is talked about practically everyday in the daily newspapers. Piracy is a cognizable offence in India punishable with imprisonment of 6 months upto 3 years and/or a fine of Rs. 50,000/- upto Rs. 2,00,000/-. An action against piracy can be initiated by informing the Police about its happening. The law casts duty on the Police to take cognizance of any report/ instance of piracy and empowers the Police to initiate ex-officio action. Any police officer, not below the rank of a sub-inspector may, if he is satisfied that there is an infringement seize without warning all copies of the work. A campaign against piracy has been initiated by the Federation of Publishers' and Book Sellers Association of India. It was reported in February 2004 in The Hindu that losses due to piracy ran into Rs. 450 Crores. The Department of Education has put up a copy of the study on piracy in India carried out during 1996-1997. It makes very interesting reading (http://www.education.nic.in/copyright/maincpract6.asp). As part of its annual report to the U.S. Trade Representative, the International Intellectual Property Alliance estimated that illegal copying of books abroad cost the book industry about $606 million in 2005, roughly the same level as 2004.

As per the Copyright Act 1957, a Copyright Enforcement Advisory Council ahs been set up in the states to review periodically the progress of the enforcement of Copyright Act. Special cells for enforcement of copyright have also been set up. Under the Amendment of 1994 Copyright Societies for different categories of works have been set up. The Indian Reprographic Rights Organisation (IRRO) has been set up for books/literary/artistic/photocopy rights. (www.ifrro.org)

3.7.2. The role of the Information Professional vis-à-vis copyright

This is discussed in the context of the five activities given below:

- Provision of copies
- Budgeting factors
- Creation of websites
- Digitization activities
- Transfer of copyright

Even the now accepted traditional activity of providing photocopies has to be considered in the light of current developments. The question is: If a library has members from the industry and supplies photocopies to them of articles for their R&D work is there a violation of copyright as it is not being used for academic purposes? If a commercial firm is sponsoring a doctoral student, would supply of photocopies be termed commercial? **The purpose for which the photocopy is made decides whether it is commercial or not.** This has to be clarified first and policies drawn up by the library. The Copyright Act does not spell it out clearly. Answers to such questions have been elaborated clearly in the following website: http://www.bl.uk/services/information/copyrightfaq.html#1-1. LIP have to get together and develop guidelines as has been done by the LACA: the Libraries and Archives Copyright Alliance, UK which brings together the major professional organisations representing librarianship, archives and information science professions. (www.cilip.org.uk/laca)

Consortia have expanded access in a big way and therefore procurement of individual articles instead of the whole journal is also gaining ground. We will have to budget for paying copyright fees for articles which are downloaded and this may run into thousands if a couple of articles are being considered as fees may vary from as much as \$22.00 to \$ 60.00. It appears that India is thinking of setting up a central clearance centre for copyright on the lines of the Copyright Clearance Center of the USA. This was one of the recommendations given in the report on copyright piracy prepared by the Department of Secondary and Higher education, Government of India. **(http://www.education.nic.in/cr_piracy_study/cpr10.asp). The Copyright Clearance Centre** (CCC) is a not-for-profit U.S. company that provides collective copyright licensing services for corporate and academic users of copyrighted materials. CCC has agreements with rights holders, publishers and authors, and acts as agent for them. This enables CCC to represent thousands of publishers and hundreds of thousands of authors and other creators.(www.copyright.com).

Librarians as part of their information services create ports / gateways for their users. There has been much discussion on whether such an action infringes copyright. Deep linking and use of frames cause most problems. Many websites have given clear guidelines regarding linking to their sites. These have to be studied by the information professionals and permission obtained before linking. It would be in their own interests and that of the organisations which they represent if the information professionals look into this and obtain permission if necessary as otherwise what would be an exercise to help the library users may turn out to be a contentious copyright issue. Further, guidelines have also to be drawn up regarding linking by others to the library website.

Coming to digitization projects in libraries, it is essential that the information professionals get prior permission from the author before embarking on this exercise. Care has to be taken to ensure that the material that is being digitized is either out of copyright or that permission has been obtained. Obtaining permission at times becomes very time consuming and involves a great deal of labour but it still has to be done. Even identifying whether the material is out of copyright is not easy as the date of death of the author will have to be ascertained. Photographs in newspapers pose a special problem as permission might have been obtained originally for reproduction of it only once. Hence, digitization would require permission from the newspaper as well as the photographer. Further, questions as to whether a library can make copies for research purposes of fragile documents and make them available in the library or campus intranet will have to be resolved.

Orphan works pose another problem. At times, the work is not out of copyright but it is not possible to trace the author or the publisher. In such cases, the library has to take great care to document the steps taken to trace them.

The Copyright Act does not discuss this problem.

In Institutions where scholarly publications are the norm and signing of copyright transfer forms the accepted procedure, information professionals can make the scholars aware of the Author's Addendum to Copyright transfer forms which deals with Authors' Retention of Rights as given by SPARC, Science Commons etc. Further, wherever possible, the LIP would have to make the scholars aware of programs such SHERPA/ROMEO which describe the policies of various publishers regarding copyright and posting papers in institutional repositories whether it should pre-prints or post – prints and so on .

Librarians are thus caught in a dilemma. The basic philosophical underpinning of the profession is to acquire and disseminate information. Freedom of access to information is the basis of our work. However, copyright laws work against this. Hence, librarians have to first become familiar with laws relating to copyright so as to fulfill professional obligations without running into rough weather.

The impact of IPR and the need for their awareness has been discussed in the above paper. It is hoped that IPR issues would become an integral part of the Library and Information Science curriculum.

4. NOTES AND REFERENCES

1. Amba S. Documentary sources of information on Indian Patents. *World Patent Information* 23, 1;2001; 25-27
2. Butler, Rebecca. Copyright law and the Internet. *Library Trends* 52, 2; 2003, Fall;307-317
3. Chakrabarti, S, Amba, S and Ramasami, T. Study of a landscape of global leather patents and analysis of technology linkages to trade. *World Patent Information*

28, 3; 2006; 226-234

4. James, TC. Digital technology and libraries. A copyright law approach. *Annals of Library Science and Information Studies.* 52,1; 2005; 1-7
5. James, TC. Copyright laws of India and the academic community. Journal of Intellectual Property Rights. 9,2004; 226-241
6. James, TC. Indian Copyright Law and Digital Technologies. *Journal of Intellectual Property Rights* 7, 2002, 423-435
7. Poynder R. Patent information on the Internet. *Online and CD ROM Review*, 22,1; 1998, 9-17
8. Sangeetha, MA; Chakrabarti, S and Amba, S. Indian leather patents: an analysis. *World Patent Information* 21,2; 1999; 69-73
9. Shkolnikov, Tanya. To link or not to link: how to avoid copyright traps on the Internet. *J. Acad. Librarianship* 28, 3;2002, May; 133-140
10. Trippe, Anthony J. Patinformatics. *World Patent Information.* 25, 2003; 211-221
11. See The *New Sunday Express* of 25th February 2007 [for information on Geographical Indications]
12. See *Scientometrics.* [A Springer journal for articles on patent citations, patent analysis etc.]
13. See *The Hindu* dated Dec. 7th 2006 [for information on registration of plant varieties]

Related Web sites

- www.wipo.int [For information on WIPO and all international treaties on IP]
- http://www.bl.uk/services/information/copyrightfaq.html#faq
- http://www.wto.org/english/tratop_e/trips_e/tripfq_e.htm
- http://www.patentoffice.nic.in/ipr/patent/journal_archieve
- www.ipindianic.in

- http://pk2id.delhi.nic.in/
- www.tifac.org.in
- http://ep.espacenet.com/
- www.uspto.gov
- www.espacenet.com
- http://copyright.gov.in/
- www.ifrro.org
- http://www.education.nic.in/cr_piracy_study/cpr10.asp
- www.copyright.com
- www.indianembassy.org/policy/ipr/ipr_2000.htm
- www.ala.org/ala/washoff/Woissues/copyrightb/copyright.htm;
- www.cilip.org.uk/laca
- www.patentoffice.nic.in

11

RIGHT TO INFORMATION ACT IN INDIA

K.N. Prasad[1]

0. PREAMBLE

Right to information is deemed a fundamental right of a citizen in many countries. During the past decade a large number of countries have adopted 'Freedom of Information' laws to facilitate their citizens and corporate entities, the right to demand information from their respective government. There are now about 75 countries that have adopted "Freedom of Information" laws, and an equal number of countries have also guaranteed the right to information in their constitution. In a ruling of the Inter-American Court of Human Rights, freedom of information is considered a basic human right implicit in the right to freedom of expression. This, it is hoped, will have immense effect on those countries that have not yet adopted such directives. Freedom of Information is considered an important tool to promote democracy and fight corruption. (1)

1 Executive Officer, Sarada Ranganathan Endowment for Library Science, 702, 42nd Cross, 3rd Block, Rajajinagar, Bangalore 560 010. Ph: (080) 23305109; E-mail: srels@dataone.in

1. INTRODUCTION

"The key to wisdom is this – constant and frequent questioning ... for by doubting we are led to question and by questioning we arrive at the truth" said Peter Abelard, the medieval dialectician, theologian and philosopher.

Information being power, people tend to withhold or manipulate information for their advantage. People need information to enforce accountability of their rulers. This was recognized by the Supreme Court in its landmark decision in S.P. Gupta's case in 1980 much before the enactment of the Right to Information Act in 2005 in India. The rationale behind the Right to Information Act is that no democratically elected government can survive without accountability and the basic premise of accountability is that the people should have information about the functioning of the government. It is only then that they can fulfill their responsibility and make democracy really effective. (9)

"The real Swaraj will come not by the acquisition of authority by a few but by the acquisition of capacity by all to resist authority when abused" said Mahatma Gandhi. "The right to information lies at the very foundation of civil liberties and underscores the fact that an elected government and its actions are open to questioning and accountable to the people who put them in power. Accountability in a democracy means, among other things, that every citizen must have a right to answers. It presupposes a transparency in the public functioning of those who hold the reins of power whether it is at the village level or at any higher level"(7)

The right to information has been recognized as a fundamental human right of the people who are committed to parliamentary democracy, that is, the government of the people, by the people and for the people. Since the people of India have chosen to have parliamentary democracy, they are entitled to the right to information. If the people of the country want to know in what stage a government project is, or what policies they have adopted, they have a right to know. The right is particularly significant when probity and good governance are talked about.

2. WHAT IS "RIGHT TO INFORMATION (RTI)"

The right to information is a right to have access to information held by the government relating to the rights of individuals. This information could be in the form of records, files, registers, maps, data, drawings, and electronic data. The government has a positive duty to give certain types of information without waiting to be asked for it. This would include information concerning projects that may directly affect people, e.g. on environment, health, agriculture, weather conditions or just about any of the services provided or functions performed by various public bodies.

The Supreme Court of India has declared having access to government–held information as a Fundamental Right. It is an integral part of the Right to Freedom of Speech and Expression guaranteed by the Constitution. The right to information lays the foundation upon which to build good governance, transparency, accountability and participation. Most importantly, the Fundamental Right could be the key to eliminate corruption.

The key concepts of the Right to Information include:

- Transparency and accountability in the working of every public authority;
- The right of any citizen of India to request access to information and the corresponding duty of the government to meet the request, except the exempted information;

- The government to pro-actively make available key information to all; and
- It is the responsibility of all sections of people – citizenry, NGOs, media.

Every public authority shall maintain all its records duly catalogued and indexed in a manner and form which facilitates meeting the right to information under the Act and ensures that all records appropriate to be computerized are, within a reasonable time and subject to availability of resources, computerized and connected through a network all over the country on different systems so that access to such records is facilitated.

RTI covers central, state and local governments and all bodies owned, controlled or substantially financed; and non-government organizations substantially financed directly or indirectly by funds provided by the appropriate government. It also covers executive, judiciary and legislature. It includes information relating to private body, which can be accessed under any other law for the time being in force.

RTI includes the right to: (i) inspect works, documents, records; (ii) take notes, extracts or certified copies of documents or records; (iii) take certified samples of material; (iv) obtain information in the form of printouts, diskettes, floppies, tapes, videocassettes or in any other electronic mode or through print outs.

RTI Act, 2005, proposes: (i) application to be submitted in writing or electronically, with prescribed fee to Public Information Officer (PIO); (ii) envisages PIO in each department / agency to receive requests and provide information; (iii) information to be provided within 30 days, 48 hours where life or liberty is involved, 35 days where request is given to Assistant Public Information Officer, 40 days where third party is involved and 45 days for human rights violation information from listed security / intelligence agencies; (iv) time taken for calculation and intimation of fees excluded from the time frame; (v) No action on application for 30 days is deemed a refusal; and (vi) No fee for delayed response.

The following are exempt from disclosure: (i) information, disclosure of which would prejudicially affect the sovereignty and integrity of India, the security, strategic, scientific or economic interests of the State, relation with foreign country or lead incitement of an offence; (ii) information which has been expressly forbidden to be published by any court of law or tribunal or the disclosure of which may constitute contempt of court; (iii) information, the disclosure of which would cause a breach of privilege of Parliament or the State Legislature; (iv) information including commercial confidence, trade secrets or intellectual property, the disclosure of which would harm the competitive position of a third party, unless the competent authority is satisfied that larger public interest warrants the disclosure of such information; (v) information available to a person in his fiduciary relationship, unless the competent authority is satisfied that the larger public interest warrants the disclosure of such information; (vi) information received in confidence from foreign government; (vii) information which would impede the process of investigation or apprehension or prosecution of offenders; (viii) cabinet papers including records of deliberations of the Council of Ministers, Secretaries and other officers ; (ix) information which relates to personal information the disclosure of which has no relationship to any public activity or interest, or which would cause unwarranted invasion of the privacy of the individual; (x) notwithstanding any of the exemptions listed above, a public authority may allow access to information, if public interest in disclosure outweighs the harm to the protected interests; (xi) infringes copyright, except of the state;

(xii)where practicable, part of record can be released; (xiii) intelligence and security agencies exempt – except cases of corruption and human rights violation; (xiv) third party information to be released after giving notice to the third party; (xv)most exempt information to be released after 20 years (with some exemption); (xvi) provided that the information, which cannot be denied to the Parliament or a State Legislative shall not be denied to any person; and (xvii) not withstanding anything in the Official Secrets Act, 1923 nor any of the exemptions, a public interest in disclosure outweighs the harm to the protected interests.

Right to Information Act, 2005 is to provide for setting out the practical regime of right to information for citizens to secure access to information under the control of public. authorities, in order to promote transparency and accountability in the working of every public authority, the constitution of a Central Information Commission (CIC) and State Information Commissions and for matters connected therewith or incidental thereto(2).

The Central Information Commission has ruled out disclosure of any information relating to medical tests under the RTI Act, which terming the relationship between a doctor and the patient as "fiduciary". The disclosure of diagnostic information to a private citizen can only be supplied by the party concerned directly and not by the confidante (17).

3. RTI IN KARNATAKA

The Karnataka Government enacted the Right to Information Act (KRIA) in 2000. The corresponding rules were notified in July 2002. The Government departments are obligated to make certain information available to the public without being requested to do so. In practice, many departments do not comply with this law. These departments are also expected to publicize the procedure for obtaining information from them. When access to information is denied, credible explanation and reasons must be given.

A complete list of Competent Authorities who can provide information can be obtained from www.kar.nic.in/vsb. The KRIA allows any citizen to obtain certified copies of any records, in print or in any electronic format. Applications must be made in writing in 'Form A' specified under the Karnataka Right to Information, Rules Clause 4(1). If one doesn't receive any communication from the Competent Authorities within 15 working days from the date of submission, he can appeal to the Appellate Authority, the immediate superior to the competent authority. If neither responds, he can complain to the Under-Secretary of the Department of Personnel and Administrative Reforms, which is the department responsible for administering the KRIA. If one is aggrieved by the order of the Appellate Authority, he can complain to the Karnataka Appellate Authority (KAT), which should dispose appeal within 30 days from the date of receipt of appeal. There have been instances of citizens appealing before the High Court when none of the authorities responded to their requests. (6)

The Karnataka Information has one of the highest case disposal rates in the country. With three commissions on board, it handles about 200 cases every month. Bangalore is one of the few cities to have an RTI bank and an RTI clinic. The RTI bank stores all information pertaining to the city procured from various government agencies. Citizens can access the information here free of cost. (Address: RTI Bank, Mahiti Adhyayana Kendra, No.54, 17th Cross, M.C. Layout, Vijayanagar, Bangalore 560 040.) The RTI clinic is a free facility that one can contact to clear doubts on the Act. The RTI Clinic functions on the first and third Saturdays of every month.

Almost three decades ago, Karnataka was the first to make an attempt to bring in legislation to provide the public the right to information. However, it was aborted. Unlike the Central Bill, which merely gives freedom of information, the Karnataka Bill gives every citizen of the State a Right to Information. Armed with this Act, the society in general and consumer groups in particular can play a major role in disseminating information, bring the guilty to book and empower the citizens. It can also make public institutions function on democratic lines.

KRIA prohibits supply of information, which is too general in nature and is not required to be collected by public authority. Secondly, if any information is published as required by any law or rules and regulations the same will not be provided. (12)

There have been success stories of individuals changing the system. Awareness is building up. Civil society activists and citizens have formed a group called 'KRIA Katte'. This is a network of civil society organizations, activists and interested citizens. An e-group has also been formed to share, discuss and act on the basis of RTI.

A RTI-related order finds fault with the official practice of storing sale deeds together with private documents like GPAs and wills. (3)

The RTI scene in Karnataka was quite active right from 2000. However, the introduction of the Central RTI Act eliminated several problems with the introduction of an autonomous Information Commission, which was not present in the earlier Act. (4)

A six metro survey on implementation of Section A of the RTI Act by an NGO – Centre for Civil Society shows that New Delhi is most proactive in releasing information to public, way ahead of Chennai and Bangalore. While Delhi released 65% of the information required, Chennai comes second at a distant 33% followed by Bangalore disclosing 29% information. Kolkata was found to be the least transparent local government, disclosing an average of 7% of the information required. (16)

It may be interesting to note that spurred by the social importance and success stories of the RTI Act, the Education Department has written to the Directorate of Secondary Education, Directorate of Pre-University Education, and registrars of all Universities in Karnataka to take necessary steps to include RTI in the syllabus. This will enable students to become informed citizens. (15)

Recently the Central Information Commission has asked the government for more autonomy. Even in Karnataka, the Karnataka Information Commission (KIC) apart from asking for financial autonomy is also planning to forfeit the state logo and have one of its own to be used in matters of correspondence. This will prevent people from assuming that KIC is an arm of the government (5).

4. CASE STUDIES

a. The Central Information Commission has ruled that marks sheets and model answers to set questions should be disclosed under the RTI Act after the entire process is complete. This is likely to set a precedent for banks and educational institutions (14).

b. Using the potent tool of RTI Act, a citizen in Bangalore revealed that the Corporation of Bangalore had granted permission to a builder for construction of a 14-storey building which contravenes the existing rules regarding height of such buildings (19).

c. In a historic case involving an officer of the Central Forensic Science Laboratories, the CIC has ruled that any activity of a public servant in an official capacity is of direct concern to public activity and, therefore, for public interest, should be revealed to the public (11).

d. Bangalore University is set to pay a heavy price for letting lakhs of files gather dust for over 25 years. The Karnataka Information Commission has taken note of Bangalore University's failure to digitize its documents, as mandated under the RTI Act, and asked the University to explain why it has not done so. The Karnataka Information Commission has also threatened the University with a hefty penalty if it does not digitize the data soon. What triggered the direction is university's failure to provide information and allow inspection of files under RTI. (18)

e. The Second Administrative Reforms Commission (ARC) which has social files and notings per se are not confidential and are accessible to the public unless exempted under Section 8 of the RTI Act. ARC recommends – "Every government servant shall in performance of his duties in good faith, communicate to a member of public or any organization full and accurate information which can be disclosed under RTI Act." Dealing with the confidentiality of the information, the ARC has asked each ministry / department to identify information which deserves to be given a security classification. The commission has recommended an amendment to the RTI Act to reclassify 11 items exempted under Sec 8(1) and 9 as top secret, secret, confidential and restricted.

5. AMENDMENTS

No one wishes to have amendments to the Act, which will destroy its real structure and make it ineffective. Once the amendments are made the Act will lose its importance. The amendments are not just about file notings. They seek to completely exclude people from the decision-making process. One cannot participate in governance. Even after a decision is taken, one would only have access to limited information. Substantive file notings will be provided only in the case of social and developmental projects. Many may believe that file notings will not affect information sought by a common man is not true. Almost all information is connected to file notings.

The government also wants to keep all information related to personnel out of the purview of the RTI Act.

One accepts that information concerning security of the country, ongoing investigations, and private information needs to be excluded. But such areas are already excluded from disclosure in the existing Act. (13)

6. EVALUATION

Activists built up a national campaign against the Bill seeking to weaken the RTI Act by putting notings on official government files out of its purview. Section 2(f) of the Act specifies that information means: "any material in any form including records, documents, and memos, etc. The DoPT's website has repeated this definition and has added," but does not include file notings".

As former President Dr. A.P. J. Abdul Kalam said, "This will harm decision-making as officials would be more cautious or even refrain from rendering objective, frank and written advice on files."

The other major apprehension is that the information obtained using the RTI Act could be misused. "Government decisions often involve crores of rupees," noted a senior bureaucrat. "While the process of decision-making is on, file notings related to that should not be publicly revealed or else, vested interests may take advantage of the RTI Act".

Section 8 of the RTI Act has a long list of exemptions - security matters or those, which constitute a breach of privilege, trade secrets, cabinet papers, etc. Similarly, Section 24 lists government organizations whose activities the Act cannot probe.

The CIC has interpreted the RTI Act to include a citizen's right to get copies / inspection of file notings containing advices and opinions given by various civil servants. The government, on the contrary, has argued that this right was never included in the Act and that it is now willing to confer a limited right with regard to social sector expenditure and projects only, and not with other areas of governance.

If merely the final decision is conveyed, the rationale and logic behind the decision may not become apparent. Any unfair influence or collateral considerations in decision-making will not be known. Governments are expected to act fairly and rationally. All actions must be informed by reason. Decisions must necessarily be in the public interest and not suffer the vice of arbitrariness.

In order to exercise the freedom of speech and expression effectively, you need an informed public opinion. The right to knowledge includes the right to information. The right to information thus flows out of freedom of speech and expression. The RTI Act, 2005 is not the repository of the right to information. Its repository is the constitutional right to free speech and expression. The RTI Act is merely an instrument that lays down the statutory procedure in the exercise of this right. (8)

Certain sections of the RTI Act pertaining to complaints and appeals need to be reviewed, as it is not clear how the Information Commission should treat complaint of non-compliance, among other issues. (10)

6. CONCLUSION

The campaign for an RTI Act was started by grass-root movements. The idea was to empower people with legislation and an administrative apparatus that would keep a check on the government.

An effective RTI Act will force a culture of transparency, which is mandatory for good governance. Transparency and public monitoring of governments' policies are essential to fight endemic corruption and ensure effective delivery mechanisms. This will be possible only when there is a sound RTI in action and it is strictly enforced. (7)

The Right to Information Act is not only about access to information in the public domain; it also, has the potential to bring about systemic changes in the functioning of government departments. (3)

7. REFERENCES

1. http://inpolicy.typepad.com/information policy/2007/09/international_r.html
2. http://rti.gov.in
3. *Bangalore Mirror*. Sep 9, 2007
4. *Bangalore Mirror*. Oct 12, 2007
5. *Bangalore Mirror*. Jan 19, 2008
6. *Sunday Vijay Times*, Bangalore. Aug 14, 2005
7. *The Hindu*, Bangalore. Jan 4, 2005
8. *The Hindu*, Bangalore. Aug 24, 2006
9. *The New Sunday Express*. May 21, 2006
10. *The Sunday Times of India*, Bangalore. Jun 4, 2006
11. *The Sunday Times of India*, Bangalore. Dec 23, 2007
12. *The Times of India, Bangalore*, Business Times. Aug 28, 2000
13. *The Times of India, Bangalore*. Aug 17, 2006

14. *The Times of India, Bangalore*. Sep 9, 2006
15. *The Times of India, Bangalore*. Sep 14, 2006
16. *The Times of India, Bangalore*. Oct 21, 2006
17. *The Times of India, Bangalore*. Nov 1, 2006
18. *The Times of India, Bangalore*. Dec 26, 2006
19. http://bangalorebuzz.bogspot.com/2006-09-01-archive.html (visited on 2007.01.22)

12

A FRESH LOOK AT THE PROVISION OF EDUCATION AND TRAINING FOR LIBRARY AND INFORMATION PROFESSIONALS IN INDIA IN 21ST CENTURY

R. Satyanarayana[1]

Explains the concept of a profession and its application to Library and Information Science. Mentions the ways in which the responsibilities of "Professionals" are changing in the context of present day society. States that the impact of information and communication technologies has been profound, raising new challenges and new dilemmas for "Information Professionals". Identifies the "Core skills" essential to the new breed of professionals. Points out that no one person in the future will be able to possess all the knowledge needed to provide users with the products and services they need. Emphasizes the fact that the "Information Professional" of the future is not going to be a person but a group (team). Discusses the point

1 Professor & Head (Retd.). Faculty of Library & Information Science, Indira Gandhi National Open University, New Delhi

that the apparent convergence of information handling processes engendered by the technology has led to suggestions of an associated convergence of disciplines. The term 'information professional' itself is an indicator of this process, providing an umbrella for a combination of skills formerly attributed to separate sectors of workforce. An integrated approach to formal professional education, as revealed in literature, has been briefly described while discussing the nature of education and training programmes necessary at different levels to effectively meet the challenges posed by the emergence of Information / Knowledge Society. Also, indicates the directions for change in Indian context.

0. INTRODUCTION

Our society is witnessing an era of unprecedented technological, social and economic changes. These changes have been particularly dramatic in the past two decades. These have implications for the library and information profession. The significant factors in this change have been:

- The new status of information as an asset and resource for organisational development and competitive advantage;
- The development of information and communication technologies, which has resulted in the exponential growth of information in electronic format and the emergence of end-user culture, which potentially bypasses the information professional as intermediary;
- The shift from the focus on the teacher teaching to learner learning, which heightens the importance of information resources and therefore impacts on the role of information professionals;
- Widening of participation in higher education both

for initial and life long learning; and

- The globalisation of society, which breaks down not only physical but also temporal barriers. A key characteristic of globalisation enables asynchronous exchanges anywhere and anytime.

It is obvious that within this highly dynamic environment, information professionals not only feel the pull of the situation described above but also the push of their own professional aspirations. These aspirations are traditionally explained as providing the right information to the right person at the right time and at an affordable price in a convenient format. In this context, information professionals need to be able to respond to the new challenges and therefore require professional education, which equips them with the necessary knowledge and skills.

Before discussing these aspects, it is necessary to discuss the criteria that distinguish a profession and examine whether these criteria are applicable to the library and information profession.

1. PROFESSION AND ITS NORMS

Francis Bacon (1613) once commented "I hold everyman a debtor to his 'profession', though each one of our debts is different" [3]. Our profession – be it that of a doctor, engineer, librarian or information scientist – has helped to make each of us what we are! Let us now try to understand what constitutes a profession and its essential norms. It may be mentioned here that the range of concerns and the plethora of viewpoints render any description of profession incomplete!

The dictionary tells us "any type of work which needs a separate training or a particular skill, often which involves a higher level education may be called a profession and cites examples of doctor, lawyer and engineer". On the other hand, Dale (2001)[3] defines a profession as "a calling requiring specialised knowledge and often long and intensive academic preparation". To be accorded societal recognition, it would appear that a number of criteria needed to be met. Some of which are:

- There must be an identifiable subject with reasonably clear boundaries, not immediately accessible to a lay person;
- There must be a long apprenticeship involving the learning of both theory and practice and the application of the latter;
- The application of the subject matter of this apprenticeship must be useful to the society;
- The profession must promulgate standards for the products or services that are produced and delivered to its members; and
- Members of the profession are individually responsible for the standards of their work and for their professional conduct but are overseen by a professional body, which has powers to ensure compliance.

1.1. Library and Information Profession

The application of the above listed criteria to library and information profession has been somewhat problematic because of the divergent attitudes of professional experts relating to its nomenclature and the disciplines associated with the profession. It may be mentioned here, that different names have been in use for the activities concerning the profession. Therefore, under the umbrella of 'Information Profession' come: Librarianship, Library Science, Documentation, Library and Information Science along with its variant Library and Information Studies and finally Information Science. Hence the problem that confronts us is "how to find out ways to define the subject matter as also its main focus and boundaries?"

There has been a long debate among the professional experts regarding Library Science and Information Science and nobody has, yet said, the last word relating to their boundaries and the subjects covered in their study and practice. However, there has been a general understanding among the majority of information professionals as to what these terms connote, which is reflected in the following explanation:

"Library Science, more accurately labelled librarianship, is a professional area of study designed to prepare individuals for careers as librarians. Librarians are primarily concerned with such tasks as evaluating, processing, storing, and retrieving information. Librarians also help library patrons use collections, software, and online public access catalogs (OPACS). Most graduate school programs in library science incorporate the study of information science in curriculum. Information science combines elements of librarianship with ideas and technologies from many other fields, including social sciences, computer science, mathematics, electrical engineering, linguistics, management, neuroscience, and information systems theory. Within the field of information science, information may be defined as the knowledge contained in the human brain and in all electronic and written records. Information science is the scientific study of that information: how it is created, transmitted, encoded, transformed, retrieved, measured, used and valued. Information scientists analyse, the many and various phenomena that affect any aspect of information. They are interested in studying such questions as the following: what is the effect of information on individuals and groups when it is presented in various formats? How publication dates, frequency of citation, productivity and prominence of authors affect the relevance of literature on a given subject? How do humans and computers interact? What is the reliability of receiving information from online databases and the Internet?

For the information scientist, therefore, the library is only one of several sites for information storage and usage. Information scientists may study information stored in archives, switching centers (systems that establish connections between electronic communications, such as e-mail), or institutions such as schools and business. Information scientists work in such places as medical centers, computing companies, university and corporate research institutes, and indexing companies. They are concerned with a wide range of activities, from creation of computer file structures to experimental tests of interactive communication between computers and humans". [21]

The above quote explains the essential aspects of library science and information science. In this context, it is worth noting the opinions expressed by Birger Hjorland [2000] in his paper entitled Library and Information Science: practice, theory and philosophical basis. This paper certainly throws light on information profession and its scope. Peter Brophy [7] discusses the professional norms concerning information profession and opines that much work is needed to redefine professionalism in the context of Information Society. Middleton [1994] dwells on the convergence of information professions and suggests that the boundaries between these professions have become much less distinct. According to him the term 'information professional' itself is an indicator of this process, providing an umbrella for a combination of skills formerly attributed to separate sectors of the work force.

1.2. Changing Roles of Information Professionals

For centuries, information handling has been the preserve

of a select group of appropriately trained individuals. Over time, the information profession has developed and refined its various roles as preserver, codifier, and deliverer of information. Its social mission has been supported by the development of a corpus of procedures, tools and techniques, and these in turn have helped to give the profession status and respectability. Until recently, the profession's strength stemmed from the fact that it operated as the society's information retailer. This position has begun to change as a result of accelerating developments in computing and communications technologies. Information skills are no longer the territory of information profession alone. Many professions are getting involved in building new information tools in the form of computer-based information systems. Information services have become de-institutionalised and moved away from libraries and information centres. In fact, improved personalised communication and workstation technology, as well as increasing availability of information delivered in electronic format directly to the end-user, are changing the current position and role of information professional in providing information to various categories of clients. In some instances, the re-engineering or redesigning of processes in organisations has been downscaling in importance of the information department.

As a consequence, we live in an environment of increasing complexity with regard to the range and quantity of information available. In this situation, the traditional approach of the information professional *as an intermediary* (finding and providing information sources) must change to one, which also integrates new information technologies for an organisation and assists end-users in the organisation to become more information independent. The information professional, in a new role, performs the creative tasks of information product development and product synthesis. The changes (retooling) taking place in the corporate environment are challenging the information professional to retool his or her skills to provide information solutions, not just information or information sources. [30]. There are several areas in which today's information professional can develop new skills and strategies in order to change, survive and continue to compete in the world of electronic information. Some of these areas are;

- *Information 'anxiety'* amongst corporate knowledge workers. Anxiety or uncertainty about what they (knowledge workers) don't know, and further, about what they don't know regarding the decision-making resources that are suitable to help them learn. The information professional can help workers to overcome this anxiety.
- *Intellectual Capital and Knowledge Management* Intellectual capital is now a days increasingly being referred to as the corporate asset. Using information resources to create a knowledge base to support the development of intellectual capital presents an important new strategic marketing opportunity for information professionals. They should seize the opportunity to help knowledge workers maximise the return on investment with decision-making information.
- *Information resource audit*: If correctly executed, an audit should be a strategic opportunity for information professionals to maximise the return on the investment of their organisation's intellectual capital. [30]

Also if information professionals are to compete successfully with members of other professions who are developing knowledge management skills, they will need to develop knowledge and skills in areas that business managers perceive to be information professional's weaknesses. For individual information professionals these areas might include business knowledge, business orientation, analytical skills, and an understanding of information technology and its use in designing and developing better information systems. It must be mentioned here that it is the evolution and growth of the Internet that is having profound effect on the thinking behind the future role of information professional. This discussion naturally leads us to the question of skills (traditional as well as new) associated with information professionals.

1.3. Information Skills

Information skills as a term is a broad one encompassing the ability to:

- Formulate and analyse information needs
- Identify and appraise likely sources
- Trace and locate resources
- Examine, select and reject them
- Interrogate sources
- Record and store what is relevant
- Interpret, analyse, synthesise and evaluate information
- Present and communicate it
- Evaluate personal strategies for handling information.

The problem is to actually identify what the 'core skills' of the information professional are? Are they different from the core skills of the traditional librarian, but now required in a new guise or required across a range of media and technologies? Do we require a brand new breed of information professionals? Much has been written about on all these questions and different opinions have been expressed on these aspects. Judith Eklin [15] opines that the following three categories constitute core skills:

- **Information handling skills:** cataloguing, indexing, general management and organisation of information, organisation of knowledge;
- **Training and facilitating skills:** helping people, of any age, back ground, specialism or need, to use libraries and information resources in any media, user support, user instruction;
- **Evaluation skills:** selection, critical evaluation and review; quality assurance of information; fitness for purpose, as needed in both traditional and digital library environments; and
- **Concern for the customer :** All these incorporate an understanding of information technology, as well as our personal transferable skills. In Judith Eklin's [15] opinion information professionals are at the gateway of new age, as mediators, guides, and navigators to more diverse media, technologies, and resources. They have a crucial role to play in the development and implementation of global information infrastructure. In order to keep a major role in the information chain across a spectrum of information opportunities, the information professionals will need:
    - High level information handling skills;
    - High level management and leadership skills;
    - Transferable skills, perhaps moving between sectors;
    - To be good communicators;
    - To be flexible and adaptable;

- To be innovative and imaginative; and
- The ability to be proactive.

It will be seen that the need to assist users to develop skills that will make them effective within information society provides a major challenge, especially as changes in technology and applications will almost certainly mean that skills will have to be updated regularly.

At this juncture, it may be observed that as we enter the knowledge-based society, no one person will be able to possess all the knowledge needed to provide users with the products and services needed. The 'information professionals' will be specialists in one or more of the following:

- *Information access*
- *User interface*
- *Technology / user interface*
- *Technology management*
- *Information / Software interface and*
- *Web interface*

2. EDUCATION AND TRAINING OF INFORMATION PROFESSIONALS

In the introductory part of this paper, mention has been made of the changes taking place in present day society and the factors contributing to these changes which impact information professional's life today. In this context, information professionals, to be able to respond to the new challenges require professional education, which provides them with the necessary knowledge and skills.

It is stated that to meet the changing needs the domain of information studies today has extended its scope to embrace not only the traditional sphere of published information associated with libraries but also information generated by organisations as output of their business activities. In the information service organisations, as opposed to libraries, the emphasis shifts from collection development and availability of a resource base, to the active communication of a resource, both internally generated as well as externally acquired to meet the user need and aid decision-making. Nowadays, via Web technology in particular, these types of information (such as internal reports, online databases etc.) often merged and are communicated seamlessly for PC user. New information specialisms such as records management, knowledge management, Web management and documentation control are in some contexts being consolidated and others being established to develop and control these new and highly dynamic environments.

Thus, information professionals in training need not only learn about and be able to use the new technologies as the elements of the working world today, they also need to understand them and their use potential in order to exploit them in fulfilling their professional role, because these new technologies are the technologies that are specific to information and communication. Also, these new technologies provide means of supporting learning at a distance where the separation between the teacher and the learner is as much temporal as physical. There remains the unchanging goal of university education, which the development of understanding that transcends the transmission of information and communication of knowledge. This requires the student to engage actively with the operational aspects of the subject matter and to articulate its theoretical aspects. [12]

2.1. Convergence of Information Professions: An Integrated Approach for Education

The apparent convergence of information handling

processes has led to suggestions of an associated convergence of disciplines. The term 'information professional' itself as cited as an indicator of this approach providing an umbrella for a combination of skills formally attributed to separate sectors of the information workforce. [26]

If such a combination is indeed a requirement, then they anticipate changing employment roles will be the resulting consequence. If these changes take place, there should be a common framework for formal education of information professionals. Michael Middleton [26] analyses and presents the views of some experts in this regard. In this context, a useful approach to the necessary framework is provided by Diener (1992) with a description of strategic, analytical and operational domains in which information management is carried out. He separately identifies the issues and principles that are the main concern of the strategic domain (standardisation, privacy, transborder data flows, retention, etc.), the research elements that are the main concern of the operational domain (system design, cataloguing, indexing, etc.). He opines that a curriculum prepared based on the domain framework may form a basis for an integrated approach for the education of information professionals of the future. This draws attention to the fact that one of these domains tends to be addressed by the educators in a particular discipline to the neglect of others. It must be mentioned here that despite the calls for the integration of multidisciplinary approaches, factors continue to operate against this. There is need to surmount ideological arguments over intellectual autonomy. Forgionne (1992), noting the fragmented approach in educational institutions where relevant material may be taught separately in business, computer science, library science, communications and engineering with consequent partial but not integrated information science education, sees the need for a concerted approach using a college structure.

Forgionne believes that this would bring the separate fields together in a college, commonly to impart information wisdom and knowledge attributes and characteristics; processes that successfully transfer information, knowledge and wisdom to the human mind; and concepts, methodologies and technologies that lead to effective utilisation of information, knowledge and wisdom.

In fact, Forgionne advocates field approach bringing together communication, computer engineering, computer science, information systems, software engineering, and library science in a college (under one umbrella) to address *Core concepts:* communication and information theory, computer hardware, software and programming, database development and management, modelling and problem solving, scientific research, design and method, systems theory, analysis and design, and management theory. As a particular example of the integrative approach, he opines instruction on database development and management could be imparted taking into consideration data structures as in computer science, file storage, retrieval and manipulation as in library science, and management of the database as in information systems.

Interestingly, this view of Forgionne is somewhat similar to Large's optimistic scenario (1993) in which he sees technologically literate information professionals involved in the design, production and evaluation of information systems. However, Large talks of graduates from library schools competing with, rather than coalescing with those from management studies, communication studies and computer science. [16]

Brittain (1989) discussing the manpower needs of

information industries in Britain observes evidence for a new type of 'information scientist' as information managers and information officers who are charged variously with identification, collection, collation and statistical analysis of data as part of management support, and therefore, students from library schools will find themselves in competition with business and management students for employment. [6]

It may be stated that subsuming of library school within information systems school or management studies or computer science schools may be about as palatable to the occupants, as the reverse. In other words, amalgamation of different disciplines under one umbrella and having an integrated approach for the education of information professionals of the future may be a difficult proposition though there are advantages to bringing these cognate parties together in college. Some of the advantages might be that library skills (acquisition, cataloguing, indexing, and reference) may be taught in a process-oriented rather than institution-oriented framework, and without being confined to one type of data (bibliographic). On the other hand, instruction in business data processing skills which may formerly have reduced all information to data for processing purposes may now be informed by the variation and utility of the information itself, with a consequent better sensitivity to different types of users.

2.1.1. Curriculum Content

One of the major tasks, which would be faced by educators, is to translate all the above aspects into a rational integrated curriculum. It may not be particularly difficult or problematic to state curriculum content for information professionals, if the content is kept in broad terms. For instance Unesco's modular curriculum in information studies identifies some areas like: information in its social and communication context, information users, quantitative methods, research methods, information sources, information storage and retrieval systems, information services, electronic data processing, telecommunications and networking, management of information systems and services, and economics and marketing of information. These areas may also be compared with the curriculum developed by the (former) Institute of Information Scientists in the U.K. and a new curriculum be designed which will be acceptable to all groups representing different sectors of information profession. The curriculum design process would certainly face difficulties to clearly define boundaries in different operational areas to a broader perspective with detailed interpretation and exposition of different areas. Such a curriculum design should not lose sight of the impact of ICT revolution.

It must be pointed out that the above discussion relates to the commonly accepted paradigm for information management. As such it is more of a conjecture than reality. The fact is that many educators of library and information science across the world are keen to expand their areas of concern to reflect the many facets of information handling skills to combat the challenges posed by the evolving information and knowledge-based society. Thus, changes in the names of library schools have become fairly routine matters in certain countries. For example, in U.K. eighteen university departments used to deliver undergraduate, post-graduate programmes in the past. The departments were collectively known as the "library schools"; but now only five of them maintain the word library in their title. In their individual institutions these schools may be found in faculties of humanities, social sciences, business, management and science, and may often have changed the home. Reflecting this diversity of affiliation, underpinned by the twin concepts of information and communication awards and diplomas are given both in arts and sciences.

The traditional combination in joint programmes of information studies with other academic subjects, especially from social sciences, is now being supplemented by courses that combine information and computer science, as for example, the Information and Computing degree offered by University College, London. The recognition of the need for information professionals to be proficient in the use of information technology (IT) has resulted in the inclusion of IT in all courses but in a way that requires learners to go beyond the acquisition of generic information technology skills. In this context, it may be mentioned that Micheline Beaulieu [28] believes that professional competencies extend beyond the definition of the level of technical competence and favours the set of eleven competencies developed by the special Libraries Association in United States. These eleven competencies can be grouped into three categories: [28]

1. *Technical competencies* covering the use of appropriate information technology to acquire, organise and disseminate information to create information products and the ability to identify and evaluate information resources.
2. *Social competencies* relating to provision of instruction and support for information users to meet their needs.
3. *Organisational competencies* in terms of specialised knowledge relevant to their employees, ability to develop, and manage information services and to undertake research into information management challenges and in general, greater involvement in achieving the objectives of the organisation.

This wide range of areas of competence can be found in

most information studies programmes in U.K. Of particular significance, however, is the approach accorded to the teaching of information technology, which needs to be studied not as an end in itself but also as a means to an end and an agent of change in the whole information process from creation through storage to retrieval.

The LIS education in USA is closely related to the technological advances in Information Science. Technological innovations have brought changes not only in the subjects taught, but also how they are taught. Programmes at all levels (i.e.) undergraduate, Masters and Ph. D have attempted to reinvent curricula to educate the "new" information professionals as per the consensus arrived at the 1996 Annual Meeting of ASIS at its session on "Planning Curricula for the Information Professionals of the 21st Century". In USA LIS Programmes are designed to prepare the students for a wide range of careers in all environments – Information Management, Systems Analysis and Design, Online Searching, Information Brokerage, Competitive Intelligence, Research Analysis, Network Management, Marketing Electronic Information Resources, Knowledge Management, Information Visualisation and Presentation and such other areas. The UC Berkeley School of Information Management and Systems curriculum model has grown fully into creating a new school addressing the emerging needs, problems and trends in the Information Science field.

In the case of Australia, the situation relating to education of library and information professionals presents a different picture. In Australia, education for information professionals is carried out in universities, which now include former institutes of technology and colleges of advanced education. The key professional bodies in Australia for influencing curriculum are the Australian Computer Society (ACS) and the Australian Library and Information Association (ALIA). The ALIA 'recognises' courses that are deemed to have complied with requirements in its education policy statements, these include curriculum content statements that require essential studies in ten areas. Only one of these areas specifically mentions libraries. The areas are:

- Communication process;
- Generation, flow and utilisation of information;
- Information users and their needs;
- Sources of information and their characteristics;
- Functions of libraries and other information agencies;
- Provision and management of information services;
- Acquisition and organisation of information sources;
- Information control and retrieval;
- Information technology; and
- Information dissemination.

It would seem that a course that is serious about producing information professionals should be able to be structured so that it can be recognised or accredited in some form by the professional bodies ALIA and ACS. This procedure has been followed within an undergraduate course at the University of Technology, Sydney, which provides for pathways within the course that may be followed to become member of the two professional bodies (ALIA and ACS). Kirk (1993) has commented on the underlying philosophy of this course, which defines factors common to information (identification of need, search design, retrieval, evaluation, analysis, synthesis, packaging, repackaging, dissemination, design and provision). These are taught with information being considered as both a tangible and intangible resource. [23]

There are other Australian courses that have been developed with a relatively interdisciplinary approach to information in mind. For example, Queensland University of Technology has an information management major in its Information Technology Course, which considers information management in some detail in each of the three domains of Diener. Similarly the Victoria College has established a multidisciplinary undergraduate course that combines information science and management studies.

There is, therefore, evidence that educational programmes in Australia have been moving from different disciplines in the information spectrum to explore and share a common ground. However, this experiment is limited to undergraduate courses. In fact, the integrated approach paradigm has not yet been tried in case of post-graduate courses.

Studies of developments in library education worldwide reflect similar problems. Information has now become much more commonly accessible through the Internet so that the curriculum designed must be increasingly global in perspective. Global developments in the information sector have to be taken into account in assessing the role of educational programmes in order to survive and stay competitive.

3. EDUCATION AND TRAINING OF INFORMATION PROFESSIONALS IN INDIA

In the preceding sections, the changing role of information professionals in the contemporary society and the impact of this on professional education programmes in some developed countries like U.K., USA and Australia have been discussed. What effort needs to be made in India to keep pace with the changes taking place world over in the information profession? The problem can be viewed from two angles; first the major areas of likely employment of new breed of information professionals must be assessed. This necessitates that a responsible body must undertake this research (survey) and come out with the manpower requirement for the next decade. After obtaining sufficient information relating to the markets – both traditional as well as emerging market for information professionals, the major areas of education and training required for the new type of information professionals must be decided upon. Till date, no such effort has been made in this direction. It is high time; we made a beginning in this direction.

As for the present, it has been well appreciated that "an expanding area of information work out side the libraries as traditionally understood creates the prospect of new opportunities" and the schools of Library and Information Science should adapt their programmes accordingly. Apart from speculative knowledge, no body is very sure as to what appropriate qualities and attributes are necessary and sufficient for the information professionals. This situation may prevail in India until the survey suggested is carried out and authoritative information is made available. The situation being what it is a discussion on the need for restructuring LIS Education in India is not out of place.

3.1. Present Situation

Currently about eighty-seven (87) universities offer Bachelors / Master's degree programmes in LIS, eleven (11) universities offer M. Phil, while thirty two (32) universities have provision for doctoral degree. Besides these, DRTC, Bangalore, and NISCAIR (National Institute of Science Communication and Information Resources), New Delhi offer specialised programmes in Information Science leading to the award of Associateship in Information Science. These two courses have been recognised by Govt. of India as equivalent to Masters Degree. In addition, there are Open universities, which offer LIS programmes through distance mode. In other words, we have nearly one hundred and fifteen (115) LIS schools and institutions offering education and training at six different levels: Certificate, Diploma, Undergraduate Degree, Masters Degree, M. Phil and Ph. D. [2]

3.1.1. Curriculum Design

Though library science departments attached to the universities have changed their names from Library Science to Library and Information Science with *predictable inclusion of or emphasis on* the word information, they, with few exceptions, still offer courses designed on traditional lines. The problem is how to design a meaningful curriculum, which could offer enough new aspects and also to ensure that it does not become unwieldy. It is prudent to split LIS course *into two parts*- one part solely covering library aspects, and the other part for information science outside library environments. This specialisation may be taken further, with existing individual schools unable to provide wide enough range of courses, and thus choosing to differentiate their curricula more strongly and specialise in some particular sectors like information access, business information systems and information technology. Information and communication technologies (ICT) have contributed to a complex higher education context and created need for new kind of library and information workers who are at the leading edge of the ICT revolution. In fact, IT has brought many changes into curricula of LIS programmes in most of the developed countries. Hence, there is clearly a need to initiate changes in the curriculum of LIS education and training programmes in India to catch up with the rest of the world. Unfortunately, the Curriculum Development Committee (CDC) constituted by the UDC has not done much in this direction. The CDC (1992) suggested a scheme of papers comprising core papers and electives. The six papers recommended by CDC are as follows:

Core Papers : (Bachelor's Degree Programme)

i) Library and Information Society;

ii) Library and Information Management;

iii) Library Classification: theory and practice;

iv) Library Cataloguing and subject Indexing: theory and practice;

v) Information Sources and Systems and

vi) Computer Applications in Libraries

Elective Courses: Under electives are listed different library systems (both general and special) and Information Systems like: Engineering and Technology Information System, Medical Librarianship, Agricultural Information System, Law Libraries, Non-book Materials, etc. numbering sixteen (16) in all.

Similarly the CDC suggested a scheme of papers comprising core and elective courses for the Masters Degree Programmes. They are as under:

Corc courses:

i) Information and Communication: Evolution and Development

ii) Library and Information Management: Sources and Services

iii) Computer Technology: Library Automation and Information Systems

iv) Information Processing and Retrieval

v) Research Methodology and

vi) Infometrics

Electives:

i) Comparative and International Librarianship
ii) Higher Education and Academic Library System
iii) Communication, Mass Media and Public Library
iv) Bibliographic Control
v) User Education and User Studies
vi) Education for LIS

Only broad areas have been suggested. Problems will certainly arise when detailed interpretation and exposition of the different areas are called for. The depth of content at which many of these subjects need to be taught is left to the individual schools. These will lead to non-uniformity in the LIS Programmes across the country.

The CDC must have clearly enunciated the general objectives of the courses offered at graduate and post-graduate levels. In fact, the objectives of the courses at the first level should be to train professionals for middle level managerial and operational positions who may constitute the bulk of the manpower required. Skill developments in operational routines, supervision and control of daily turnover of the work and smooth functioning, clear understanding of the contemporary role of libraries and the information systems in the present context particularly in the new information age, especially the shift in focus to include the following directions in addition to the basic functions:

- Shift from library *as an institution* to library as an information provider, and the librarian as skilled information specialist functioning in an information environment
- From using new technology for automation of library functions to utilising technology for the

enhancement of access to and delivery of information not physically available in the library

These are some of the important areas that may form the course contents at this level. On the other hand, the Masters level programmes should attempt preparing persons to hold higher level managerial positions, who would be involved in providing leadership, plan the activities and programmes of the information institutions and execute them, having close knowledge and understanding of user needs and requirements, develop user oriented innovative services and information solutions to help decision-making staff in organisations.

Persons who take up research leading to M.Phil and Ph. D. degree programmes, should contribute to problem solving, develop theoretical models, conduct basic and developmental research; in short, expand the horizons of the discipline involving themselves in practical situations to have a grasp of real life problems.

3.1.2. Course Models

Modular planning is a useful approach for designing course models. The essence of modular planning is to offer a number of courses for bachelor or other degree programmes, out of which a set of ten or twelve courses may be required to be completed to bc cligiblc for obtaining a degree. As far as possible these modules may be similar in structure and together constitute optimal requirement for the level (1st level or 2nd level) preparation. The time duration for each of those modules should be more or less the same. A student completes the required courses in two or more semesters, decided by the competent authority offering the programmes.

All the LIS schools need not necessarily follow the same combination of courses. The combination may be varied depending upon the demand. Also, new modules of different specialisations may be added to the existing modules depending on the need.

For example, titles of such courses that may be offered for the Bachelor's Degree programme:

- Role of Libraries in Modern Society
- Library and Information Systems
- Information Sources including Electronic Resources
- Collection Development
- Cataloguing: Theory and Practice inclusive of Internet Cataloguing
- Classification and Indexing: Theory and Practice including Metadata
- User Studies and User Education
- Management of Libraries
- Use of technology for automation of library functions and for the enhancement of information access and delivery
- Library Networking for information provision

In a similar manner different modules could be thought of for the Master's Degree programme covering, apart from other traditional modules,

- Electronic Publishing including Digitization
- Study of Networking including Inter and Intranets
- Setting up Web Sites
- Content Preparation
- IT Applications
- Multimedia
- Information Infrastructure: National and Global
- Electronic Commerce

- Knowledge Management
- Records Management
- Information Resource Management
- Electronic Delivery of LIS Programmes and similar others.

3.1.3. Methods of Instruction

In the previous sections of this paper, we discussed issues like curriculum contents as well as different course models to be followed in imparting education and training to the information professionals in India. In this connection one of the areas highlighted was the inclusion of information technology in the curriculum. Information technology (IT) needs to be studied as a means to an end, and as an agent of change in the whole information process from creation through storage to retrieval. A student, therefore, needs to understand and learn not only what technology is, needs to be able to use it, but also needs to understand its strengths and weaknesses. The student needs to study through the technology, as well as learn about the technology, but in a way, which allows him to disentangle the principle from the practice, the knowledge from the skill. It requires 'a holistic approach to learning with hands-*on experience*'. Also, the learning will not stop once formal studies are complete, because technologies will continue to develop and impact their work. Technology also has a greater role to play in the instruction methods. [4]

It may be mentioned here that the methods of communicating the curriculum contents to the students play a significant role in professional education. LIS schools in India normally impart professional education through classroom teaching. Student-teacher interaction is limited to questions and clarifications. In some schools, colloquia and seminar methods are encouraged as learning techniques. Project work and special lectures by invited visiting faculty supplement the formal classroom teaching. Not many schools have the resources (material as well as manpower) to employ innovative techniques. Use of Technology is almost non-existent in a majority of schools.

Therefore, it is imperative that LIS Schools should use some of the new methods mentioned below to impart education in an imaginative and innovative manner to sustain interest in learners. For example:

- Use of transparencies / slides / power point presentations
- Use of Web-based Online Training Courseware, wherever such courseware is available
- Internet-enabled Multimedia PCs with provision of LCD Projection Systems enabling students to have practical interactive sessions and
- Use of Audios and Video films produced in-house or produced by outside organisations like IGNOU and UGC's country wide class room programme

It must be mentioned here that there is hardly any audio or video programme commercially available at present in India. IGNOU has started preparing such kits. But, their quality and effectiveness are still to be assessed. UGC's countrywide programme also produces some videos. Preparation of audio and video kits is a highly specialised activity. Planning a programme for a specified time span on a particular topic, writing the script, selecting a suitable place to take shots on the themes, choosing the right type of voice for the purpose, presentation techniques, and the production – all these demand team work, time and money. IGNOU is attempting to perfect this new activity. It will be useful to call a national seminar on this subject in which different groups of specialists and professionals could participate and workout proper plan in this regard.

Another basic requirement, which should be considered seriously, is the human resources in the form of qualified teaching staff (lecturers' and professors with appropriate subject specialisation and experience). Of course, the staff should have access to important information resources and also facilities for continuous professional development and research.

In so far as the basic infrastructure is concerned, many LIS schools at present do not possess facilities in the form of computers and network infrastructure. Imparting training in the use of products and services of new information technologies necessitates establishment of dependable computer and network infrastructure in LIS schools. The minimum infrastructure necessary for a LIS school is indicated below.

- Internet-enabled Multimedia PCs are to be provided to students in the ratio of 1:2 (i.e. one computer to every two students) with recent (latest) configuration so that the systems can remain functional at least for a few years without upgradation;
- Multimedia laboratory having Internet-enabled PCs/VCRs/TV/LCD projection systems, CD ROM / DVD ROM Workstations, Laser Disk Drives, General Application and LIS Software packages.

4. PROVISION FOR CONTINUING PROFESSIONAL DEVELOPMENT

There is one more question, which needs our consideration. This concerns the professionals already working in the field, who too will need continuing professional development in integrating technologies into information management, but also learning how to learn, so that they can continue to move on as their professional activity demands. For this purpose they should further their skills via good quality continuing educational programmes, short courses, or postgraduate work that are suitably designed. In India such training opportunities are not available. Some work must be initiated in this direction.

In many fields, distance learning, as a means of both initial and continuing education has come to stay. The British Open University and the Indira Gandhi National Open University in India are playing a key role in showing what can be achieved through distance education. But this mode of study, to date, had a limited implementation and its potential can be fully exploited for the provision of continuing professional education for information professionals in India. It is not the question of totally changing from one system to a new one. A hybrid environment for learning comprising both traditional face-to-face and technology-based formats needs to be employed. This hybrid mix of resources could play a key role in learning for all, and especially for the information professionals who need to use them as the raw materials and tools in the profession. E-earning materials therefore have a major role to play in the education of information professionals. Also, it is claimed [12] that ICT learning is more efficient in terms of teacher time and therefore, more cost effective.

5. CONCLUSION

As we enter the Knowledge-based Society, specialisation becomes so intense that no one person will be able to possess all the knowledge required to provide users with the products and services they need. Therefore, the information professional of the future will not be *a single person* but *a group of persons* with different specialities.

No doubt the emerging information society requires professional approaches. On one hand, its technological structures require people who can act as information architects with all the skills and standards that such terms imply, while on the other the complexity of information organisation and use necessitates expert information advisers and teachers. These lead us to take a fresh look at the provision of education and training to the new breed of information professionals. In this context, attention is also drawn to the discourse, taking place on the convergence of different information related professions and the possibility of changing employment roles between different groups of workforce. The advent of Internet and consequently, the global information infrastructure necessitate a completely different approach to education and training of information professionals. Intensive thinking and planning is necessary for designing programmes with new content. For the digital environment, course contents should be completely different from the library-based traditional programmes. Details of such programmes, methods and techniques of delivering them particularly in the local context have been discussed in the paper..

6. REFERENCES

1. Adams, D. R. and Athey, J. H., eds. (1981) DPMA Model curriculum for undergraduate Computer Information Systems Education, DPMA, Park Ridge, U.S.
2. Association of Indian Universities (1997). Handbook on Library and Information Science. Delhi, The association;
3. Bacon, F. (1613). The elements of the common lawes of England. London, Assignes of I, More, Esq.
4. Beaulieu, M. (1998). "Developing the information professional: Whose responsibility? Educating and

developing the information professional for success", *Impact*, 1 (7), 107-112.

5. Beheshti. J. 'Computer programming in LIS education – a necessity'. *Education for Information*, 11 (2), 123-136.
6. Brittain, M., ed. (1989). Curriculum Development in Information Science to meet the needs of the Information Industries in the 1990s.The British Library, Wetherby. (BL LIR report 70).
7. Brophy, Peter, (2003). The role of the professional in the information society *In Hornby*, S., and Clarke, Zoe, eds. Challenge and change in the information society. London, Facet Publishing. 218-232.
8. Clausen, H. (1990). 'The future information professional: old wine in new bottles? Part one'. *Libri*, 44(4), 265-277.
9. Cooper, M. and Lunin, L. F., (1989). 'Education and training for information professional'. In Annual Review of Information Science and Technology, 24, 295-341.
10. Cronin, B., and Stiffler, M. (1993). 'The emergent market for information professionals – educational opportunities and implications'. *Library Trends*, 42(2), 257-276.
11. Dale, A. (2001). Despatches: Letters from the Corporanian War Zone: Letter 7- meeting the demands of chartered status. *J of Inf. Science*, 27(6), 4341.
12. Daniel, Sir John, (1999). "Distance learning in the era of networks, *ACU Bulletin of Current Documentation*, 138, 7-9.
13. Debons, A. etal. (1981). The Information Professional: survey of an emerging field. Dekker, N. Y.
14. Diener, R. A. V. (1992). 'Strategic, analytical and operational domains of information management. *Bulletin of American Society for Information Science*, 19(1), 18-19.
15. Eklin, Judith, (1997). Information Navigators: future

professionals? http:// www.cni.org/regconfs/1997/ uklon-content/repor~12html.

16. Forgionne, G. A., (1992). 'Streamlining information science research and education'. *Information and Management*, 23(3), 141-147.
17. Gorman, G. E (1999). The future of library science education, *Libri*, 49(1), 1-10.
18. Hart, T. L. and Summers, F. W. (2004). The Information Profession for the 21st Century. file://C:\Documents% 20and%20Settings\Ownetr\My%20Documents\The%20 Information...
19. Hjorland, B. (2000). Library and information science: practice theory and philosophical basis. *Information Processing and Management*, 36, 501-531.
20. India. UGC. Curriculum Development Committee (Chairman: P. N. Kaula) Report, 1992. New Delhi, The committee, 1992.
21. "Information Science" – Print View. (2001). In Online encyclopaedia. New York, Microsoft Corporation.
22. Jeng, I. H., (1993). 'From cataloguing to organisation of information; a paradigm for the core curriculum. *Journal of Education for Library and Information Science*, 34(2), 113-121.
23. Kirk, J. (1993). 'Information and information practice – implications for the education of information professionals', In Proc. Of the56th Annual Meeting of the ASIS, 30, 269-273.
24. Large, A. (1991). 'Curriculum development: some reflections on Unesco's role, *Journal of Education for Library and Information Science*, 32(1and2), 73-83.
25. Large, A. (1993). 'Information technology education for library and information studies – the challenge', *Canadian Journal of Information Science*, 18(1), 23-33.
26. Middleton, Michael, (1994). Differences in implementation of programs for education of information professionals with reference to models

developed by information associations. *FIDET Seminar Paper.*

27. Rajan, T. N. and Satyanarayana, R. (1990). Guidelines for Library and Information Science Education and Training, *Library Science*, 27(2), 81-89.
28. Special Libraries Association, (1996). "Competencies for special librarians", SLA, Washington. D. C.
29. U. C. Berkeley. School of Management and Systems. *In* Electronic format. http:/www.sims.edu/programs/overies.html
30. Van Brakel, Pieter. Education and Training for Information Professionals in the face of the Internet and World Wide Web. 43p.

13

MANPOWER DEVELOPMENT FOR TECHNICAL LIBRARIES: AN INDIAN PERSPECTIVE

A. Amudhavalli[1]

Library and information professionals have to play a new role in the rapidly changing information environment. This paper addresses two critical issues: Information professionals' work profile and the role of Library & Information Science Schools.

New technologies are greatly impacting the society and are proving to be change agents in many sectors. Libraries and librarianship are no exception to this. There has been a paradigm shift in libraries and librarianship with the advent of new information technology. Information handling is becoming increasingly complex and this has implications for - Libraries and Information Centers (LIC), Library and Information Science Schools (LISS) and Library & Information Professionals (LIP). Given the rapid growth of information, information sources, technological advances and changing user demands, LIP, LIC and LISS need to respond quickly and position

1 Professor & Head, Dept. of Information Science, University of Madras, Chennai.

themselves to provide a useful and relevant service. LIP need to anticipate, innovate and excel in whatever they do. One needs to be alert and continuously review the environment, anticipate changes innovate and provide services and products that are useful and relevant. LIC must look at how they can continue to help users as they have always done in the past and also look at opportunities that will add value. These will depend to a significant extent on the nature and quality of manpower being trained by LIS schools. Most LIS schools in the country have structured their programmes in such a way as to have contents carrying about 72-75 credits. In this paper it is proposed to examine briefly the manpower requirements of technical libraries.

1. ISSUES

Different kinds of libraries are functioning in India: national libraries, academic libraries, the scientific and technical libraries, libraries attached to various ministries and departments of the governments at the national and state levels, and public libraries. Owing to a variety of historical factors scientific and technical libraries are more developed compared to other libraries. However, this is also the sector where substantial changes have occurred as a direct result of impact of technology and the growing importance of information as an economic factor. It is important:

- That necessary and relevant administrative and technical changes are initiated to make libraries more service-oriented;
- To take stock of actual need of the Library and Information users;
- To consider both preservation and access as vital components of library and information service;

- To promote resource sharing and networking of libraries;
- To focus on the marketing of information and library services;
- To mobilize resources - money, material and information.

This paper raises certain issues related to the relevance and methods of human resource development vis-à-vis Indian scientific and technical LIC. In the present situation, it is pertinent to raise the following queries:

- What it means to be '*professional*' in the library and information field, particularly in Scientific and Technical Libraries?
- What are the attitudes and performance of LIP in Scientific and Technical Libraries?
- What do these LIP need to know - skills and competence of professionals in the work place?
- Is something wrong with the programmes of library schools?
- What kind of education should be available to professionals?
- What are the measures to develop the required manpower?

It is the people who make the difference to any system and hence the need to identify and develop high caliber staff. They will ensure better performance and maximize the potential of technologies, facilities, locations, and partnerships to provide value added services. There is, thus, a compelling need for a systematic and deliberate planning process to develop not just the collection and services, but more importantly the human resource. They act as mediators between users and technology by assisting them to tap the vast amount of information in digital form. Hence the LIC and LIP need to redefine their job functions. Each of these is discussed in some detail in the following paragraphs, followed by a few suggestions for manpower development.

2. DISCUSSION

1. Today, the term 'Library and Information Professionals' has a different meaning, as the roles of this workforce are being re-examined. In an adjectival sense the term has come to imply competence and élan in the workplace. Increasingly we find the members of the group moving into different roles related to those investigating the properties and behavior of information, the forces governing the forces of information, and the means of processing information for optimum availability, accessibility and usability. The scientific and technical LIPs handle that body of knowledge and content relating to the origination, collection, organization, storage, retrieval, analysis, synthesis, consolidation, repackaging, transformation, interpretation, transmission, and utilization of information.
2. The general impressions about LIPs in technical LIC are that they actively organize and address issues involved in acquiring the knowledge and skills to maintain adequate levels of competence in the library workplace. However, current changes warrant certain competence and skills, particularly involving technology. This challenge makes an LIP to probably feel at least once, that "I never learned about that in school". LIPs ought to adopt, adapt and continue to function in a constantly changing information world and instill in themselves an active acknowledgement that learning is lifelong, and to

be good at it is a chief source of personal/ professional empowerment.

3. Emphasis has to be placed in developing the skills in both LIPs and also the end-users. For the profession, there is a need to move away from traditional operating philosophy and look at the new roles LIP can play. For instance, they can help organize electronic information sources by creating information maps, help in Web publishing, and play a greater role in teaching / helping users to navigate and search for information. LIPs need to learn to write for the electronic media—this skill comes in useful when packaging and disseminating information electronically. Users thus need to be trained and information search skills inculcated to ensure they are equipped with the appropriate skills. Users need to be also taught to evaluate sources of information.

4. Organizations hear these statements from their members and are concerned that courses in LISS may not be teaching up- to- date skills to prepare new information professionals for their jobs. LISS though is a key enabler to prepare and produce LIP suitable for the workplace, the simple truth is, everything cannot be taught within the classroom and LISS has numerous limitations. Adaptability and accountability are expected of the trained professional entrants to fit into the demanding current job descriptions. For those LIP graduated from LISS, 10 or 15 years ago—or even 5 or 6 years ago—and who today visit LISS, would certainly find changes in the curricula and academic credits.

5. While a wide range of training programmes - workshops, intensive training, short term and long term courses, specialized theme or task- oriented programs – are being conducted as in-house

programmes or by other agencies, these efforts, particularly, continuing education programmes are not effective for two reasons. Firstly many of the programmes aimed at updating the LIP lack clarity. Secondly the professionals who attend these programmes generally lack motivation.

6. Nearly every school has made curricular changes in the last few years, ranging from a total revamping of the curriculum to minor tinkering. Education and training of LIP have to be fine-tuned to provide with sufficient numbers of new wave library technicians to meet the needs of this decade. Scholarships may be offered to enhance not only the prestige of the profession but to create a core group of high caliber staff with executive and professional leadership. This has to be set in place to lead the transformation of the current library service.

Effective coordination and constant interaction among the working professionals, LIS schools, professional organizations and employers can alone stand as a support to ensure that LIP are keeping up with the knowledge and skills in the field to meet the changes and challenges in the electronic environment

3. CONSPECTUS

The new millennium will open up unprecedented opportunities for information professionals. Employers will look for a work force, which can take on different roles and responsibilities, as and when, required. Hence, the LICs are in need of competent professionals with sophisticated knowledge and skills, and there is an increasing need for education and training. Tomorrow's information professionals will be knowledge navigators instead of information collectors. In the Indian situation, the new generation of LIP will have to face these challenges and risks to remain in the information business in all sectors. Inter-changeability and capabilities to adjust from one sector to the other will be the biggest challenge for Indian LIPs. India is on the threshold of major changes, which will be possible only if a worthwhile and modern information system is set up with the help of right infrastructure managed by right people. In this context, the three key enablers, namely., LIP, LIC and LISS should consider the following factors:

- Understanding the global and national changes and the challenges;
- Creating a conducive working environment
  - Willingness to change and learn new techniques and technologies.
  - Accountability and credibility in the role and responsibilities
- Utilizing the traditional expertise and applying them effectively in the new situations by understanding the actual requirements
- Continuous upgrading of the curricula and adoption of innovative teaching methods in the teaching-learning process.

Peter Drucker once said, "*Elephants have a hard time adapting. Cockroaches outlive everything.*" If the LIP has to be relevant in the emerging environment, it is time that information professionals seriously consider the implications of the changes discussed above.

4. REFERENCES

1. Abell, Angela. Skills for the 21st Century: editorial, *Journal of Librarianship and Information Science*, 30(4) December 1998 pp.211-214.
2. Aguti, J. N. (1998) The Challenges of virtual campus in a developing country. Paper read at the International

Conference on Communication in the third Millennium: Which Way, Africa, Makerere.

3. Berghahl, B. (1989). IFLA's Programme Advancement of Librarianship in the Third World ALP: A proposal for the Future. Stockholm: Swedish Library Association, 41p.

4. Henderson, F. (1992) Relationship with users in Information Technology in Special Libraries Margaret Britting (Ed.). London: Rutledge, pp 99- 106.

5. Indian Library Association (1999) National Seminar on Challenges before the University Libraries in India in the 21st Century, Vadodara, ILA, Delhi.

6. Indian Library Association (1999) Library Vision 2010: Indian Libraries and Librarianship in Retrospect and Prospect: 45th ILA Conference, Hisar, ILA, Delhi.

7. Neill, J.R. (1991) The Marginalized Workforce: Africa's Library and Information Profession. *Afri. J. Lib. Arch & Inf. Sc.* Vol. 1 no. 1. pp 9-18.

8. World Information Report 1997/98, Paris: UNESCO, 1997.

14

EDUCATION OF NEW INFORMATION PROFESSIONALS IN THE ELECTRONIC / DIGITAL ENVIRONMENT

S. Seetharama[1]

0. PREAMBLE

I had the good fortune and privilege to listen to Prof. S. Parthasarathy's lectures on "Information Systems: their design and evaluation", when I was a student at DRTC about four decades ago (1964, to be precise). His command over the subject and the simple language and style used for communication was simply great and drew immense admiration from all of us. He was and is indeed a great teacher.

Prof. Parthasarathy was one of the trusted lieutenants/ disciples of Dr. S.R. Ranganathan and I still remember his glowing tributes when he spoke about Prof. Parthasarathy. All through the many years I have known

* Professor & Head (Retd.), DRTC, Indian Statistical Institute, Bangalore-560 059 **Contact :** 17, Vardarajulu Naidu Street, Egmore, Chennai-600008

him, I was stuck by his sincerity, dedication and commitment to work, which is exemplary. His range of knowledge and work are indeed very wide and varied, and in each one of the areas that he has worked on he has made a lasting impression and impact, whether it be planning of information systems, information policy issues, library education, library standards, library management, etc. to name a few. He is an active participant in conferences, seminars, workshops and his incisive questions and comments are looked forward to by one and all.

Professor Parthasarathy is a gem of person. He is simple, gentle, humble, unassuming and a non-controversial person who is highly committed to the cause of the Library and Information Science profession. I strongly believe that he is one of those who have contributed a lot to the development of libraries and the profession in India in his own, simple characteristic style. He is through and through, a true Karma Yogi.

I offer my salutations to him and wish that he continues to make available his expertise and services to the Library and Information Science profession for many more years to come.

1. INTRODUCTION

In recent times, the words "Information and Revolution" coupled with the third popular term '*Globalization*' have brought about a sea change in our lives fuelling the belief that "we are living in a world of one, ever freer, modern and universal ... culture with an increasingly and beneficially unified political system". This has been further strengthened by the juggernaut of information technology consisting of computers, laser beams, optical fibers and cyber wave in the present millennium. This transition of the society from an economy based primarily on manufacturing to one that is predominantly based on information and the application of information and communication technologies (ICT) has profound implications, shaking the very foundations of traditional librarianship. This largely has been "due to the paradigmatic shift of the library as a place ... towards the information to which it can provide access", a natural consequence of the digital icon replacing the icon of books in modern times. This situation appears to have strengthened further with the arrival of Internet. In other words, the kind of work traditionally performed by librarians and information professionals is different in kind and degree from the work required in a hypertext, networked, digital environment wherein one should manage virtual information flows in intelligent, learning, networked organisations. Hence, education for Library and Information Science (LIS) is no longer only technical, but must include consideration of new cognitive, social and situational processes. Further, quality should be built into LIS education programmes if one has to tackle issues of internationalization, globalization, multi and inter-disciplinarity, as well as preparing the graduates for a career. Internationalization is an issue in the education for 'New Information Professional (NIP) because of their fluid and mobile lives, and the multi-national companies that they might work for. NIPs, therefore need transportable and internationally recognized qualifications which make accreditation an issue. We are not educating for a homogenous domestic market anymore. Attracting the right type of students to LIS courses and ensuring that they get employment after graduation is critical (Myburgh, 2005).

In other words, quality LIS education defined as: 'the development of human potential through a continuously supportive process which stimulates and empowers individuals to acquire all the knowledge, values, skills and understanding they will require throughout their life times and to apply them with confidence, creativity and enjoyment in all roles, circumstances, and environment' is the need of the hour.

In this regard, the approaches that LIS schools should adopt to encourage quality are quality assurance, quality control and quality improvement.

2. EMERGENT TRENDS

2.1. Changing World of Information

There is a distinct, visible change in the world of education partly because society is changing into one in which knowledge work becomes even more important and partly because of ICTs, which are transforming our economics. In the context of visions for the future of education, Thornburg (1997) has made the following observations.

- The digital divide is real, and the financial have-nots are also the information have-nots. Hence, it is essential that access to powerful information technologies is provided in every classroom, library, and other places;
- Information, worldwide, is doubling every two years and much of the information one has today is useless and, even worse, inaccurate. This, makes the challenge harder - as to how does one find needed information which is accurate and relevant;
- Collapse of the information float, as the time lag between discovery and application is rapidly shrinking;
- The communication revolution has shrunk the world to our desktops;
- Computers continue to increase in power while dropping in cost; and

- The web has taken the world by storm and its impact on education is likely to be profound as it is being used in novel ways to allow students access to the latest breakthroughs in scientific discovery i.e., the web has democratized the publishing of information in ways unanticipated even a few years ago.

Consequently, a complete rethinking of education must take place with focus on new competencies and every learner must master the "Three 'C's: Communication Collaboration, and Creative problem-solving. As a matter of fact one of the challenges facing education today is to go beyond technological literacy to technological fluency. Therefore education, including LIS education, must focus on technological fluency among students and prepare them for the kinds of jobs available today and in the years to come".

2.2. Changing Learning Situation Trends

Twigg and Miloff (1998) analyzed the changing learning situation in USA, which, perhaps, is true of India and have observed the following trends:

- Student intake in Library Schools is still growing;
- Different types of students are seeking education - women, older students, ethnic minoritics, etc. – thereby, creating need for accommodating different learning styles, customization and attractive learning routes;
- Increasingly, work and study are combined leading to a need for more flexible learning arrangements - like distance education;
- Trend towards lifelong learning leading to an emphasis on "learning to learn";
- Education is under constant budget pressure necessitating a more efficient and effective education;

- Teaching staff are exhibiting job-hopping behaviour; and
- Many dropouts in the current education system.

Therefore, they envisage a 'Global Learning Infrastructure', where learning environments of the future will be:

- Student-centered;
- Interactive and Dynamic;
- Enabling students to determine their own learning routes;
- Enabling team approach to solving real world problems; and
- Emphasizing competencies like information literacy to support lifelong learning.

In other words, students would adopt active learning styles implying that they don't limit only to resources supplied by instructors and develop their competencies continuously.

2.3. Changes in LIS Education

To begin with LIS education was practice-oriented as can be seen from the fact that Dewey was not interested in the theoretical underpinnings of the profession, but rather with its practice. This set the tone for LIS education programmes in those days, and, probably, this explains why the focus in our LIS education programmes was not on information and knowledge, but its containers. Consequently, the aims of LIS education was to provide trained manpower to manage different types of libraries and information centers, which over a period of time changed in tune with the times resulting in the design and development of appropriate tools and techniques. In this context, IFLA's (2000) position that "traditional LIS education programmes — have focused on developing physical collection of books and other materials in library buildings staffed by people who have learned to select, acquire, organize, retrieve and circulate these materials .... (but) to-day, the emphasis is on the individual practitioner and the concentration is on information provision in a variety of contexts" is quite relevant. But the application of ICT has revolutionized the whole concept of libraries, the system of information storage and retrieval and ways to access information – suggesting a need for redefining the objectives of LIS education. In effect, the LIS education programmes should impart information handling skills, training and facilitating skills, evaluation skills, and most important, concern for the user. In other words, multidisciplinary knowledge is required if information professionals have to survive. But, for this to happen the "librarian mindset" should change and a new paradigm for professional LIS education should be developed to guide the profession through times of low funding, virtuality, commodification, globalization, diversification and mobilization. In other words, professional LIS education needs to be broad-based cross-sectoral.

3. CORE SKILLS OF FUTURE INFORMATION PROFESSIONALS

While emphasizing that individuals need to be flexible, adaptable to change and open-minded to continue to educate themselves and be educated throughout life, personally and professionally – lifelong learning has a professional as well as personal dimension —, Elkin has identified the following core skills of information professionals:

- **Information Handling Skills:** Cataloguing, Indexing, Management and Organization of information, Organization of knowledge;

- **Training and Facilitating Skills:** Helping people of any age, background, specialism or need; to use libraries and information resources in any media; user support; user instruction;
- **Evaluation Skills:** Selection; critical evaluation and review; quality assurance of information; fitness for purpose; as needed in both traditional and digital library environments; and not least,
- **Concern for the Customer / User:** Alison Scammell (1997) based on an analysis of compiled skills criteria of Institute of Information Scientists and the Special Libraries Association and the results of a 1997 survey of information professionals, has summarized below the information skills and competencies:
- Professional Information Skills:
  - Identifying, anticipating and analyzing user and organizational information needs
  - Technological skills
  - Subject expertise
  - Knowledge of disparate information resources and how to access / integrate them
  - Familiarity with research methods
  - Ability to evaluate information
  - Ability to organize and store information for effective retrieval
  - Ability to add value to information: presentation, editorial and publication skills
  - Knowledge of delivery mechanisms and means of disseminating information
  - Training, education and consultancy skills
  - Knowledge management

  - Knowledge of legal, economic and political aspects of information
- Management Skills:
  - Understanding the organizational culture
  - Strategic Planning
  - Financial Management
  - Human Resources Management
  - Project Management
  - Change Management
  - Communication Skills
  - Marketing Skills
  - Vision and Creativity
  - Liaison and Negotiating skills

A similar line of thinking can be seen in a research report of Oxbrow and Abell (1999) who have listed key skills and attributes which information professionals, especially at senior level, should possess: Business Management skills; Team skills; Human Resource skills; Knowledge Management skills; Information Management skills; Personal Attributes that include strategic thinking, image, creativity, interpersonal — influential, diplomatic, persuasive, engendering trust, approachable, confident, involvement — interest, curiosity, motivation, high levels of responsibility and willingness to accept accountability.

Perhaps, as Stewart (1995) puts it, information / knowledge manager must be "part librarian, part entrepreneur and part cruise ship social director".

The implication of identifying the competencies / core skills of future information professionals is that they be translated into course work in LIS education programmes designed and developed by library schools.

4. CURRICULUM FOR LIS EDUCATION PROGRAMMES

Since many information professionals seek employment not only in libraries but also in many new information related jobs in multi-national companies and a variety of settings it is imperative that curricula should be appropriate and should attract young recruits to fill new types of jobs, and provide choices and flexibility in scheduling that appeal to students, both those pursuing a first career and those changing careers (Tenopir, 2002).

In the context of curricular change, KALIPER Report identified the following six trends:

- LIS curricula are addressing broad-based information environments and information problems. Most schools now offer LIS education that prepares students for jobs in other environments and other situations.
- A distinct core of skills and commitment has taken shape that is predominantly user-centered. Faculty and approach may come from multidisciplinary areas, but a focus on understanding users and meeting their needs distinguishes LIS curricula.
- LIS schools and programs are increasing their investment and infusion of IT into curricula. LIS schools integrate the use of IT into all aspects of the LIS curricula.
- LIS schools are experimenting with specialization within the curriculum areas like archives, school media, medical librarianship, or records management.
- Instruction is offered in different formats, providing students with flexibility, including distance education, variant scheduling, and collaborative courses with other departments or other universities.

- Curricula are expanding, into related degrees at the undergraduate, master's and doctoral levels. New undergraduate programs are growing especially rapidly.

The above six trends can be seen even in the Indian LIS education scene. However, with the focus on the library as the location of the profession resulting in an undue emphasis on the tasks performed within such a place, LIS education programmes in India are largely library-centered rather than information-centered.

Commenting on revised curricula being prepared, Aversa says that students will become much more "technologically astute than in the past" particularly in the areas of networking, Internet issues, design of information products and services, and electronic publishing.

Spink and Cool in 1999 recommended "an expansion of traditional LIS and Computer Science curricula to encompass a more general digital libraries track". The curricular areas and suggested topics for library education in a digital environment are given below:

- Theoretical and Historical Foundations: History of libraries; Human information behaviour; Information retrieval theory; Development of digital collections and Digital libraries.
- Technical Infrastructure of the Digital Library: Information retrieval engines; Data base and construction of digital libraries; Distributed collection; Multi-media formats and applications; Interoperability; Network technology; Web applications in digital libraries; Interface design; Communication protocols; Query languages.
- Knowledge Organisation in Digital Libraries: Metadata; Indexing; Classification; Database integration; Document formats.

- Collection Development and Maintenance: Digital Archives; Digital conversion technology; Digital preservation.
- Information Access and Utilization of Digital Libraries: Users and uses of digital libraries; Usability and evaluation research; Information behavior in digital libraries.
- Social, Economic and Policy Issues: Electronic publishing; Scholarly communication; Copyright issues and intellectual property rights in digital libraries; Cost of building digital libraries; Funding for digital libraries.
- Professional Issues: Roles and responsibilities of the digital librarian; Management of digital libraries; Bibliographic instruction.

On the other hand, IFLA and the Computer Curricula report prepared jointly by the Association for Computing Machinery (ACM) and IEEE have identified 14 areas of knowledge in Computer Science, and 10 core elements for LIS as shown in the Table below:

Library and Information Science	Computer Science
Information Environment, Information Policy and Ethics, History of the field	Discrete Structures
Information Generation, Communication and Use	Programming Fundamentals
Assessing Information Needs and Designing Responsive Services	Algorithms and Complexity
Information Transfer Process	Architecture and Organisation
Organisation, Retrieval, Preservation, and Conservation of Information	Operating Systems
Research, Analysis and	Net-centric Computing

Interpretation of Information	
Application of ICT to Library and Information Products and Services	Programming Languages
Information Resource Management and Knowledge Management	Human Computer Interaction
Management of Information Agencies	Graphics and Visual Computing
Quantitative and Qualitative Evaluation of Outcomes of Information and Library Use	Intelligent Systems
	Information Management
	Social and Professional Issues
	Software Engineering
	Computational Science

Though it has been recognized and realized that the curricula need to be modified in view of the impact of IT, most LIS educational programs both in India and internationally have responded in a piecemeal manner, by simply adding various courses to the existing curricula such as Web design, Records management, Database construction, Systems analysis and design, Database fundamentals, Human computer interaction, etc. in order to increase job opportunities for information professionals. David Braybrooke and Charles Lindblom described this approach as "*Disjointed Incrementalism*". This increased the workload for students and gave an impression that LIS education was in chaos with no real core LIS disciplinary knowledge. Hence, this type of disjointed incrementalism should be avoided.

The question then is – how can LIS schools do all things for all students through their educational programmes. This, perhaps, is the real challenge for LIS education.

To overcome this challenge, collaboration among library

schools in organizing different types of LIS education programmes is essential; perhaps, a step in the right direction is to identify centers of excellence from among the library schools and make them responsible for designing and organizing appropriate LIS education programmes to suit all markets. In addition, concepts like active learning styles, life-long learning should be encouraged among the information professionals.

In India, the curricular models for LIS education have largely been traditional - training potential information professionals for working in traditional libraries. However, in recent times, the Curriculum Development Committee of UGC have framed a modular, curriculum for a two-year integrated master's degree in Library and Information Science with a panel of experts taking into consideration the traditional and modern practices, skills and techniques required both in traditional and digital environment not to forget the hybrid environments. It is hoped that the course contents will prepare the information professionals to play a proactive role in coping with new technology and information explosion on the one hand, and to make them as change agents, facilitators and guides with appropriate information empowerment.

5. CONCLUDING REMARKS

In order to provide quality LIS education to turn them into good quality information professionals, one should consider adopting the following strategies:

- Reinvent the role of information professionals from collectors / integrators of information to researchers / analysts, creating a new role adjacent to the existing role but not losing the traditional skills.
- Change our (librarian) mindset from working in a

traditional library (building) environment to a hypertext, networked, digital environment i.e. shift from document management perspective to an information management perspective, which locates users, technology, and information professionals within a socially constructed, complex context.

- Focus on information and knowledge and not its containers!
- Recognize that shelf life of any qualification is about five years and adopt life-long learning, thereby facilitating continued professional development.
- In LIS education programme (content) design:
  - Disjointed incrementalism is not desirable
  - Too much focus on specific information resources and how to use them to be avoided
  - Emphasis on information management
  - Social issues, such as, access, information's contribution to social uplift, role of information policies in organisations and countries, relationship between society and technology is vital for a professional and international perspective
  - Fluency of information systems and technologies, with awareness that such technologies are not a surrogate for professional activities, but support and expand them
  - Program should focus more on general practices and principles in a wider range of information environments and with a larger number of document formats
  - Interaction between information, society and

humans should be examined as well as human interaction with information systems

- Should impart information handling skills, training and facilitating skills, evaluation skills, and most important, concern for the customer/ user
- Best library practices should be included
- Should be:
  * Fostering global competencies among students
  * Inculcating value system
  * Promoting use of technology, particularly ICT
  * Institutionalizing quest for excellence
- Should concentrate on digital libraries as they are natural complements to digital learning environments, as they are able to integrate web information with more formal literature for which licenses on electronic versions are arranged with publishers, and facilitate time and place independent information services for students, needed especially, if active learning styles become common place (however, today's courses are self-contained and assessment is based on whether or not a student is able to reproduce text / notes prescribed / prepared by the teacher!). In this context, digital portfolios can be used as new tools for student assessment.

To conclude, it is not quantity but quality of information professionals, which is important and our endeavour as educators should be to produce quality information professionals who are people-oriented, content-oriented, customer-oriented, and proactive (not reactive) in the information society. For this purpose, we need to:

- Dedicate ourselves to developing quality human resources
- Recognize teaching as a unifying activity
- Nurture integrity, creativity and academic freedom
- Retain a willingness to experiment with new paradigm

6. BIBLIOGRAPHICAL REFERENCES

1. Aversa (E). ALISE viewpoint. **Quoted in** Tenopir (C). Educating tomorrow's information professional's today. *Searcher.* Vol. 10(7); Jul-Aug 2002.
2. Braybrooke (D) and Lindblom (C). 1963 **Quoted in** Neill (SD). Dilemmas in the study of information: exploring the boundaries of information science. New York. 1992, Greenwood.
3. Elkin (J). Information navigators. http://www.ukoln.ac.uk/sciences/paper S/bk/bliro78/content/ authour
4. IFLA. Guidelines for professional library/information educational programmes 2000. http://www.ifla.org/VII/s23/bulletin/gaidelines.htm
5. Kaliper Advisory Committee. Educating library and information science professionals for a New Century: The Kaliper report. Executive summary. July 2000.
6. Myburgh (S). Education directions for new information professionals. *Australian Lib. J.* Vol. 52(3); 2004.
7. Oxbrow (N) and Abell (A). Investigation of underpinning skills for knowledge management: Training implications. 1999 London, TFPL.
8. Scammell (A). The role of the special librarian in the electronic era. **In** Scammell (A), *Ed.* Handbook of Special Librarianship, Ed. 1. 1997, ASLIB, London.
9. Seetharama (S). Quality frameworks in library and information science education: An overview. Keynote

address at the conference on "Quality Assessment and Quality Indicators for LIS Education". Nov. 2006, Nagpur University, Nagpur.

10. Spink (A) and Cool (C). Education for digital libraries. *D-Lib. Magazine*. Vol. 5(5); May 1999.
11. Stewart (T). Mapping corporate brainpower. *Fortune*. Vol. 30 Oct 1995; p.246-248.
12. Thornburg (DD). 2020 visions for the future of education. 15 April 1997. http://www.tcpd.org
13. Tenopir (C). Educating tomorrow's information professionals today. *Searcher*. Vol. 10(7); Jul-Aug 2002.
14. Twigg (C) and Miloff (M). The global learning infrastructure. In Tapscott (D) and others. Blueprint to the digital economy 1998. McGraw-Hill.

15

A QUANTITATIVE STUDY OF SOFTWARE LITERATURE IN INDIA WITH COMPARISION TO WORLD LITERATURE

Bibhuti Bhusan Sahoo[1]
I K Ravichandra Rao[2]

Data on "software literature from two bibliographic databases, COMPENDEX & INSPEC have been collected. A scientometric analysis is carried out to study the contribution of different countries. The data show that the growth rates for developing countries are more than the growth rates for developed countries. An attempt was also made to identify an appropriate growth model to explain the growth of literature in Software Studies. The Pareto curves drawn to identify high productive countries in the area show that over a period of time number of countries are involved in R&D activities. A close relation between economic indicators like GDP, Per capita, S&T budget allocations and number of publications is seen in developing countries.

1 Central Library, Indian Institute of Technology, Delhi 110 016. E-mail: bibhuti.sahoo@gmail.com

2 Professor and Head, Documentation Research and Training Centre, Indian statistical Institute, 8th Mile, Mysore Road, Bangalore 560 059. E-mail: ikrrao@hotmail.com

1. INTRODUCTION

Scientometric studies can assist in the analysis and formulation of science and technology policy by mapping changes in research activities, providing thematic and strategic analysis of relative position of research communities; sketching profiles of activities and performance of countries and institutions. This study is concerned with quantitative analysis of software literature, related to India. The bibliographic databases COMPENDX, INSPEC and Indian Science Abstracts have been used for the purpose of collecting data. A number of different software packages were used for processing and analyzing the data.

India is now regarded as a software giant. Ramamritham (7) has discussed some of the factors contributing to India's domination in IT sector, especially in the software market. They are:

- A large pool of technical manpower (both software and hardware engineers)
- High reliability and rapid delivery of goods & services
- High growth rate of software industry in the recent past, and
- High-class academic institutions & chain of R&D centres

Considering all these, a quantitative study of the research output in software was undertaken.

1.1 Software Research in India

Ramamritham (7) has given a detailed account of computer science research in India which includes both software and hardware research. Intensive Computer Science (CS) research in India started in the mid-80s triggered by the establishment of post-graduate programmes in many institutions. However, its history goes back to 1950's. Indian Statistical Institute (ISI) carried out research in 1940's and 1950's and built a 2nd generation computer in collaboration with Jadavpur University. The All India Council for Technical Education (AICTE) and a number of Governmenet departments are funding research in Computer Science. Besides, a number of higher education institutions such as the IITs, ISI, IISc, TIFR and the Institute for Mathematical Sciences (MatScience), etc., research laboratories and industry-sponsored laboratories are also engaged in research in the area.

1.2 Research Publications

While many researchers do publish in journals and conferences, the chosen forums are usually not the ones with a high profile. For instance, very few Indian researchers even attempt to publish in "transaction journals". Several Indian journals are available for computer scientists to publish their work. The Computer Society of India publishes the Journal of Computer Science and Informatics. Another journal, Sadhana, is published by the Indian Academy of Sciences. The IISc publishes its own journal. Both Sadhana and the IISc Journal cater to a wide variety of engineering disciplines, including computer science. There are other journals, such as the one published by the Institution of Engineers.

For a researcher in India, attending a conference in Europe or the U.S. is a costly affair. This is cited as yet another reason for the poor visibility of Indian research. However, Indian researchers participate in several conferences in India to present their work. If one were to measure research productivity and interest purely by the number of conferences held in India, it is quite impressive. Many of these are sponsored by international organizations such as the IEEE and IFAC. These are devoted to VLSI design, parallel processing (IWPP), theory (FSTTCS), software engineering (CONSEG), databases (COMAD, CISMOD), and communication networks (Networks). While these international conferences do attract a number of researchers from abroad, most of them are non- resident Indians. One exception is the theory-oriented FSTTCS, an Indian conference with perhaps the longest history. Many from outside India, especially, Europe, attend it. Its proceedings are published by Springer-Verlag.

2. OBJECTIVES OF THE STUDY

This paper presents a quantitative analysis of software literature, with an emphasis on research carried out in India. The main objectives are to:

a. Study the overall contribution of different countries over a period of time.

b. Study India's research output and compare it with that of other countries

c. Study any correlation between number of publications and economic indicators among different countries.

d. Study the growth of literature in Software related topics

3. RESEARCH OUTPUT IF INDIA – 1989 TO 2003

The total number of Indian publications between 1989 and 2003 is 10,163 – the annual average being 677.53. The growth rate of India's research publications is 16.83%. India is in the 15th position in research publications in software studies in the 15 years from 1989 to 2003 (Table 1.)

Table 1. Total Number of publications in different countries (1989-2003)

Sl. No	Country / publications	Total	Cumulative total	%	Cumulative %
1	USA	312676	312676	35.51	35.51
2	Japan	66747	379423	7.58	43.1
3	UK	59114	438537	6.71	49.8
4	China	50781	489318	5.77	55.6
5	Germany	45701	535019	5.19	60.8
6	Canada	34454	569473	3.91	64.7
7	France	33943	603416	3.85	68.5
8	Italy	27819	631235	3.16	71.7
9	South Korea	19642	650877	2.23	73.9
10	Taiwan	19612	670489	2.23	76.1
11	Australia	17652	688141	2	78.1
12	Netherland	13557	701698	1.54	79.7
13	Spain	12879	714577	1.46	81.1
14	Russia	10858	725435	1.23	82.4
15	India	10163	735598	1.15	83.5
16	Sweden	8858	744456	1.01	84.5
17	Singapore	8684	753140	0.99	85.5
18	Switzerland	7837	760977	0.89	86.4
19	Hong Kong	7709	768686	0.88	87.3
20	Brazil	7184	775870	0.82	8.81
21	Israel	6936	782806	0.79	88.9
22	Belgium	6762	789568	0.77	89.7
23	Finland	6458	796026	0.73	90.4
24	Greece	6062	802088	0.69	91.1
25	Poland	5851	807939	0.66	91.7
26	Austria	5008	812947	0.57	92.3
27	Denmark	3763	816710	0.43	92.7
28	Portugal	3646	820356	0.41	93.2
29	Turkey	3247	823603	0.37	93.6
30	Norway	3029	826632	0.34	93.9
31	Hungary	2709	829341	0.31	94.2

32	Mexico	2414	831755	0.27	94.4
33	Czech	2239	833994	0.25	94.7
34	New Zealand	2168	836162	0.25	94.9
35	South Africa	2005	838167	0.23	95.2
36	Ukraine	1963	840130	0.22	95.4
37	Slovenia	1952	842082	0.22	95.6
38	Egypt	1858	843940	0.21	95.8
39	Ireland	1810	845750	0.21	96
40	Yugoslavia	1561	847311	0.18	96.2
41	Saudi Arabia	1433	848744	0.16	96.4
42	Romania	1396	850140	0.16	96.5
43	Argentina	1207	851347	0.14	96.7
44	Iran	1164	852511	0.13	96.8
45	Malaysia	1076	853587	0.12	96.9
46	Thailand	1051	854638	0.12	97
47	Bulgaria	926	855564	0.11	97.2
48	Others	25092	880656	2.85	1

3.1 Institution, State and City- wise Analysis

Research institutions of CSIR, DRDO and other research laboratories sponsored by government, contributed maximum number of papers in these 15 years. Engineering colleges also contributed a number of publications, suggesting that they are also involved in research. However, their (about 87 engineering colleges) contribution is only 949 publications. Seventy universities contributed 1,481 papers, with an average of 21 articles per institution over a period of 15 years. IISC alone published (970) as many publications as all of the engineering colleges put together. The IITs published 3,191 publications. Indian Statistical Institute published 333 papers. IIMs published 58 papers. Interestingly, some of the universities like Jadavpur University (210), Anna University, Chennai (157), University of Roorkee, Roorkee (101) have each published more than 100 papers in the 15 years. One hundred and thirteen research organizations, including CSIR, DRDO, etc published about 1,614 articles. Indian Space Research Organization from 6 locations (Bangalore, Ahmedabad, Dehradun, Sriharikota, Kharagpur and Trivandrum) published only 169 research publications from 1989 to 2003. NIT, Rourkela; Bengal Engineering College, West Bengal; PSG College of Technology, Coimbatore; NIT, Tiruchirapalli; Shri GS ITS, Indore; Centre for Advanced Technology, Indore published 65, 62, 61, 43, 41 papers respectively in the 15 years. Other organizations like BARC, Mumbai; TIFR, Mumbai; BHU, Varanasi; NAL, Bangalore; NCL, Pune published 168, 86, 63, 53 and 40 publications respectively from 1989-2003. Only a few private companies contributed towards research; fifty-two companies together published only 443 papers. The IT companies like Texas Instruments published about 53 articles, where other private companies hardly have any publications. Among other software companies, Infosys technology Pvt Ltd published 40 articles in 15 years at an average number of publications less than 3 per year. Motorola India Electronics Ltd., Bangalore published 23 articles in 15 years. Tata Consultancy Services from 8 locations (Bangalore, Kolkata, Chennai, Hyderabad, Pune, Mumbai, New Delhi, Trivandrum) published 38 research papers in 15 years.

Among the states, Karnataka has published the maximum number of publications (1,796 publications). West Bengal, Tamil Nadu, Maharastra, and New Delhi published 1,587, 1,460, 1,375 and 1,092 articles respectively during 1989-2003. Rest of the states together published only 2005; i.e., 71.88% of the articles were published by the top five states. In city-wise analysis, we have observed that the Bangalore has published a maximum number of articles – 1,679. Chennai with 1,167 publications followed Bangalore. New Delhi, Kolkatta, Kharagpur, Kanpur and Hyderabad published 1,089,1,028, 810, 615, 531 and 357 publications respectively. These cities together account for 80.5% of the publications.

Table 2. Research output of India: number of publications in the software

Year (1)	Number of Publications (2)
1989	521
1990	422
1991	394
1992	260
1993	399
1994	510
1995	612
1996	588
1997	770
1998	619
1999	828
2000	853
2001	895
2002	956
2003	1536
Total	**10,163**

The Table 4 lists the top ten journals chosen by Indian researchers during 1989 - 2003. IETE Technical Review and IETE Journal of Research (both published by Institution of Electronics and Telecommunication Engineers, India) published 230 and 132 articles respectively. Computers and Structures by Elsevier Science Ltd., UK have published 122 articles and it is 3rd in the list. Indian researchers published their articles in 1,328 journals (both from India and abroad.) Of the top 10 journals, 5 are published from India. Out of 1,328 journals, only 152 journals have published more than 10 articles each by Indian researchers. The journal Computer

Table 3. Research Publications by different types of Organizations (1989 – 2003)

Type of organization	Total
Research Institutes	1614
Universities	1481
IISC	970
Engineering colleges	949
IIT, Chennai	794
IIT, Kharagpur	615
IIT, New Delhi	607
IIT, Mumbai	566
IIT, Kanpur	523
Private Companies	443
ISI	333
ISRO	169
Govt depts.	66
IIMs	58
Others	952

Science and Informatics published by the Computer Society of India published 61 papers in software studies. At the global level, the journal Electronics Letter published maximum number of articles in software studies. However, it has only 48 Indian articles in 15 years. Indian researchers publish papers in journals devoted to physics, chemistry, etc. indicating the interdisciplinary nature of software studies.

3.2 Subject-wise Analysis

The subject-wise analysis was carried out using the descriptors assigned by the database publisher. Table 5 indicates the area of research for COMPENDEX database for 10 years from 1994 to 2003. There is a clear increase in research publications in computer programming, data processing, databases systems, and artificial intelligence and computer applications. Since1998, research in

Table 4. Distribution of journals in Software Studies in India for 15 years

Title	Total
IETE Technical Review (India)	230
IETE Journal of Research (India)	132
Proceedings of SPIE (USA)	122
Computers and Structures (UK)	113
Pattern Recognition Letters (Netherlands)	96
Sadhana Academy Proceedings in Engineering Sciences (India)	90
Pattern Recognition (UK)	87
Defence Science Journal (India)	77
International Journal of Remote Sensing (UK)	74
Pramana Journal of Physics (India)	67

application of software has increased and a similar increase is noticed in the "others" category. Interestingly, the analysis reveals that there is hardly any paper in the area of "operating systems" by Indian researchers. The major area of research is "computer application", followed by artificial intelligence, data processing, and programming. It is possible that Indian researchers are developing software, useful to many fields.

3.3 Distribution by Document types and Languages

Indian researchers prefer to publish articles in journals rather than in conference proceedings. The percentage of articles published in journals varies from 64% in 1989 to 95%, in 2003. On an average, the percentage of articles published in journals is about 73% as against only 26% in conference proceedings. The average percentage of articles published as chapters in books and monographs is as low as 0.2%. Not many patents are listed; it could be that COMPENDX and INSPEC do not cover Indian patents in their database!

Indian researchers publish mostly in English. Only one

Table 5. Subject-wise Analysis

Software keywords (1)	2003 (2)	2002 (3)	2001 (4)	2000 (5)	1999 (6)	1998 (7)	1997 (8)	1996 (9)	1995 (10)	1994 (11)	Total (12)
723.1 (Computer Programming)	194	106	99	97	101	50	95	84	138	144	1108
723.2 (Data Processing)	351	148	180	159	147	115	165	114	147	133	1659
723.3 (Database Systems)	77	36	34	28	18	16	23	24	12	17	285
723.4 (Artificial Intelligence)	298	142	109	122	130	95	123	117	118	76	1330
723.5 (Computer Applications)	830	486	492	448	443	331	367	303	292	191	4183
Others	1159	568	584	502	527	409	444	360	379	333	5265

publication each has been published in French and German in 15 years. The preferred language of publication at the international level is also English. The average percentage of publications in English language is about 94%, in 15 years. It increased from 92.2% to 97.5% between 1989 and 2003. Further it has been observed that the average percentage of publications in Chinese language is only about 1%. However, the share of the Chinese increased substantially in the 15 years from 0.4% to 5% in 2002 indicating a huge growth in research activities by Chinese researchers!

Articles in Japanese languages also increased and the average is 1% in 15 years. No literature in Hindi or any other Indian languages was found. All other languages including European languages contributed only 4%.

4. COUNTRY-WISE ANALYSIS

Many in the past studied the distribution of literature over countries. For example, Lal and Ray (4) observed that USA is a leading contributor (26.02%) of the research papers followed by Australia (17.89%) and Netherlands (8.94%) in the area of Horticulture. Among 25 countries, India published only 2.44% of the total research publications in the field of horticulture. Miquel and others (5) have identified a publication pattern for nations that reflects its interest and potential in 18 disciplines and compared the publication patterns of 48 nations by descriptive multivariate analysis. They observed that USA published a maximum number of articles – 2.3 million articles; it corresponds to about a third (33%) of the total and that is 5 to 10 times greater than of its closest peers (Japan, England, USSR, FRG, France & Canada). India was in the 9th position. Parmar et.al (6) analyzed the Library Automation related bibliographical records in the *INSPEC* (1969 to July 2004). They observed that, the literature grows approximately linearly with a growth of about 600 items per year, since 1984. The USA is the predominant publishing country in the area of Library Automation related literature. The USA contributed 54% of the literature and the first 7 countries — USA, UK, Germany, Netherlands, Australia, India and Hungary — contributed 90% of the total publications. There are numerous such studies. The present study is centered on software. Table1 gives the number of publications by different countries. In Table 1, we may observe that:

- India's contribution is only 1.15% (10,163) of the total publications. However, India's contribution remains more or less constant – between 1.1% and 1.5% from 1989 to 2003.
- USA has contributed about 35.5% (3,12,676 of the research papers
- Japan, China and Canada contributed 7.58% (66,747), 5.77% (50,781) and 3.9% (34,454) respectively.
- Contribution of European countries (including Russia) is about 31.4% (2,77,278).
- Contribution of Mexico, Brazil and Argentina amounts to 1.2% (10,805).
- Asia's (excluding Japan, China and India) contribution is 8.5% (75,341).
- Israel contributed less than a percent (6,936).
- Other countries together contributed 5.1% (45,628).

Software research Publications have declined from 48.8% to 30.7%, 8.1% to 5.2%, 4.8% to 4.7% and 4.8 % to 3.8% in USA, UK, Germany, Canada, respectively. It may be due to the involvement of more countries in software research. Software research Publications have increased from 6.1% to 7.1%, 2.9% to 3.3%, 1.8% to 11.2%, 0.8% to 2.5%, 0.5% to 1.9%, 0.3% to 3.1% and 1.20% to 1.7% in Japan, Italy, China, Taiwan, Spain, South Korea and Australia respectively. In other countrics, the change is marginal.

Research output in the field of software studies is growing in the developing and less developed countries. The over all percentage of contributions in software studies is decreasing in developed countries as compared to developing countries. China's research contribution has grown from 1.8% in 1989 to11.2% in 2003. It shows that the average growth rate of developing counties is more than the growth rate in developed countries. We can thus say that research in countries like China, South Korea, Taiwan, and Singapore is growing.

The Pareto curves in Figure 1 have been drawn to identify the most productive countries. The top twelve countries have published 80% of the total number of publications.

Table 6. Percentiles of the Software literature (among top 70 countries)

Year	No. of countries accounting for following percentage of contribution					
	50%	60%	70%	80%	90%	95%
(1)	(2)	(3)	(4)	(5)	(6)	(7)
1989	1	2	4	7	20	48
1990	1	2	4	7	21	48
1991	1	3	5	9	22	48
1992	2	3	6	10	23	48
1993	1	3	6	10	20	48
1994	2	4	6	12	23	41
1995	2	4	7	12	24	43
1996	3	5	7	13	24	38
1997	3	5	8	13	24	38
1998	3	5	8	13	23	39
1999	3	5	8	13	23	36
2000	3	5	9	13	23	36
2001	4	5	9	13	22	30
2002	4	5	8	12	22	28
2003	4	5	8	13	22	31

While in 1989, the first nine countries published 80% of the articles; in 2003 it took thirteen counties to publish 80% of the articles. It shows the involvement of more countries in research in software studies.

Further, we note that China has the highest growth rate; South Korea and Taiwan too have higher growth rates. In Europe, Germany had the high growth rate. India's growth rate of software literature is quite high, particularly when compared to USA, UK and Canada.

Table 6 shows the number of countries accounting for a specified percentage of articles from 1989 – 2001; it also gives the data on the number of countries having different percentiles. Further in recent times, there are more countries in the least productive group, particularly at the 95th percentile – less number of countries in the most productive group (say, 95th percentile).

5. DISTRIBUTION OF JOURNALS OVER COUNTRIES

An attempt has been made here to study the journals, from different countries, preferred by Indian researchers. Table 7 gives the preferences of Indian researchers in the field of software. Indian researchers have published their articles in 1,392 journals, of which 1,286 are foreign periodicals, which amount to 92.42% of total number of journals.

Only 7.58% of journals have been published from India. The favorable journals by the Indian researchers are journals from USA, UK, and the Netherlands, which constitute 32.82%, 30.10% and 15.72% respectively.

6. DISTRIBUTION OF LITERATURE AND GROWTH RATES

Table 8 presents the data on distribution of articles (in journals and conferences) for both India and world for

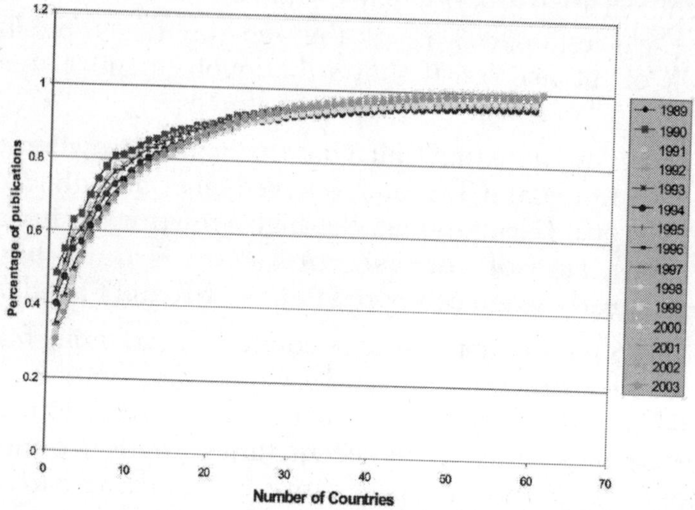

Fig. 3: Pareto Curves

Table 7. Percentage of journals from different countries

Countries (1)	% of contribution (2)
USA	32.82%
UK	30.10%
Netherlands	15.72%
India	7.58%
Switzerland	3.79%
Germany	2.58%
France	1.60%
Canada	0.81%
Singapore	0.76%
China	0.59%
Australia	0.56%
Japan	0.42%
Thailand	0.36%
Denmark	0.31%
Others	1.99%

the period 1989-2003. Significant fluctuations can be seen in the growth of articles. As "software studies" is an applied subject, the research in this field does not show a continuous growth.

Table 8. Distribution of Articles for Both World and India

Year (1)	India (2)	World (3)
1989	521	46491
1990	422	50414
1991	394	47802
1992	260	32538
1993	399	34899
1994	510	47595
1995	612	54850
1996	588	63081
1997	770	83960
1998	619	67554
1999	828	72612
2000	853	83024
2001	895	87583
2002	956	84137
2003	1536	113653

The average growth rate of Indian literature is 11% where as it is 8% for world literature. However, the compound growth rates are 8.0288% and 6.5932% for Indian and World literature respectively. For the world literature it has been observed that there is a decrease between 1990 and 1992. After 1993 the growth rate has increased except for 1998 and 2002. The growth rates present a mixed picture.

The nature of growth makes it difficult to fit models like exponential and power model. So we have chosen other two models, logistic model and the Gompertz model.

Table 10 shows the average growth rates for the first 17

Table 9. Growth rates of literature

Year (1)	India (2)	World (3)
1990	-19	8.43
1991	-6.63	-5.18
1992	-34.01	-31.93
1993	53.46	7.26
1994	27.81	36.37
1995	20	15.24
1996	-3.92	15
1997	30.95	33.09
1998	-19.61	-19.54
1999	33.76	7.48
2000	3.02	14.34
2001	4.92	5.49
2002	6.81	-3.93
2003	60.67	35.08

countries for 15 years. Growth rates for China, South Korea, Singapore and Spain are more than 20%; for most of the other countries, it is around 10%.

7. RELATION BETWEEN NUMBER OF PUBLICATIONS AND ECONOMIC INDICATORS

Researchers have developed several indicators to analyze the research output of a country and relate them to economic indicators. There are three categories of indicators: input indicators, output indicators and innovation indicators. Input indicators include outlays on R&D, Gross Domestic Expenditure on R&D, and indicators related to R&D personnel. The output indicators evaluate the results of the investment and allocation of resources. Three types of indicators are used, including one related to publications known as bibliometric indicator. The other output indicators are

Table 10. Growth rates (in percentage) of Software Literature for the period 1990-2003

Country (1)	Average growth rate (2)
USA	5.2
Japan	9.9
UK	6.4
China	27.1
Germany	9.4
Canada	7.4
Canada	7.4
France	9.4
Italy	9.8
South Korea	74.8
Taiwan	17.8
Australia	12.1
Netherlands	8.7
Spain	20.2
Russia	13.2
India	11.3
Sweden	11.5
Singapore	22.6

related to patents, the Technology Balance of Payments, etc. The indicators related to patents give information on the cumulative knowledge and its integration in the R&D fields.

India's IT export services are valued at more than $9.5 billion dollars per year, which is more than the combined software exports of the next five leading countries - Canada, Ireland, Israel, the Philippines and South Africa. These numbers are echoed in terms of number of engineers actively employed in software development and exports. Further, the revenue generated through software export has direct impact on GDP.

The current study focuses on identifying relationship between GDP and the number of publications. Hart and Summerfeld (1) in 1998 studied the relationship between GDP and the number of publications in chemical engineering. Based on the GDP for the five English-speaking countries; they observed that the GDP is linearly correlated with the chemical engineering literature over a period of 26 years. i.e., higher the GDP, higher the publications. Inonu (2) in 2003 compared the number of publications per million people with that for the GDP for different countries. In order to compare, he has arranged the countries according to the number of publications per million people and then compared with that for the gross domestic product per capita. He ranked the countries according to the publication per million person and GDP per capita and he observed that the two lists are not equal. In other words, his results are quite opposite to that of Hart and Summerfeld's results. Kishida and Matsui (3) in 1997 examined the correlation among the number of published monographs, GDP, population and the number of people attaining a university education. A regression model that incorporates GDP as explanatory variables explains well the variation of the number of monographs by countries; however, for their data, R^2 (= 0.77) is very low, indicating a low correlation between these two variables. Rousseau and Rousseau (8) in 1997 described a tool known as data envelopment analysis (DEA) to construct relative scientific and technological indicators of different countries. Inputs to their model include gross domestic product among other quantities, while patents comprise the one of the outputs. Thus, using the input-output analysis, the efficiency of countries is assessed.

In this study, the GDP data has been collected from International Energy Annual 2002. The GDP data have been compared with the number of publications —

correlation coefficients were computed. The results are given in Table 11.

Table 11. Correlation Coefficients between GDP and Publications

Year (1)	Corr. Coefft. (2)	Year (1)	Corr. Coefft (2)	Year (1)	Corr. Coefft (2)
1989	0.8556	1994	0.8793	1999	0.9388
1990	0.8490	1995	0.8878	2000	0.9347
1991	0.8536	1996	0.9013	2001	0.9235
1992	0.8529	1997	0.9089	2002	0.9190
1993	0.8711	1998	0.9203	2003	0.9495

In Table 11, we see that the correlation coefficient is more than 0.85 for the years 1989 to 2003 and it is continuously increasing over a period of time; t-test suggests that we may have to reject the hypothesis, that H_0 r = 0; i.e. there exists a linear relationship between the number of publications and the GDP — higher the GDP, higher the number of publications to some extent! Correlation coefficients were also computed for each of the countries, to study whether there exists a relationship between the number of publications and the GDP over a period of time or not. It may be noted from Table 12 that for most of the advanced countries, the correlation coefficient is very low; only for 18 countries, the correlation coefficient is more than 0.90.

Among the developed countries, seven countries have correlation coefficient less than 0.80, indicating that GDP has little impact on R&D publications in software literature

8. CONCLUDING REMARKS

The contribution of India's research output in software studies is about 1.15% only of total research publications. The average number of articles per year by Indian

Table 12. Correlation coefficients (r) between GDP and Number of Publications for different countries.

r (1)	*Countries* (2)	*r* (3)	*r* (1)	*Countries* (2)	*r* (3)	*r* (1)	*Countries* (2)	*r* (3)
>0.95	Spain	0.9846		Japan	0.9227		Malaysia	0.8126
	Taiwan	0.9722		Hong Kong	0.9032		Canada	0.8005
	Brazil	0.9598		Norway	0.9012	<0.80	Yugoslavia	0.784
	Finland	0.9551	0.80-0.90	India	0.8994		UK	0.7816
	Greece	0.9549		France	0.893		Czech	0.77
	Sweden	0.9544		Netherlands	0.8915		Hungary	0.7517
	Egypt	0.9512		Belgium	0.891		USA	0.7253
0.9-0.95	Portugal	0.9466	0.80-0.90	Israel	0.8812		Saudi Arabia	0.7114
	New Zealand	0.9384		Turkey	0.8744		Thailand	0.6691
	Italy	0.9366		Switzerland	0.8692		South Africa	0.6685
	Denmark	0.9326		Mexico	0.8667		Argentina	0.5566
	Ireland	0.9306		Australia	0.8574		Ukraine	0.4586
	South Korea	0.9284		Iran	0.8385		Romania	-0.0099
	China	0.9267		Slovenia	0.8268		Canada	0.8005
	Poland	0.9264		Germany	0.8139			

researchers is about 677.53. Research institutes include various laboratories like CSIR laboratories, DRDO and other government laboratories that contributed maximum number of papers, during the period. The number of articles published by universities and engineering colleges is quite low. Indian Institute of Science is the leader with maximum number of publications (970 articles!). Very few private companies appear to do research. Bangalore, the IT capital of India is dominating the scenario of software publications in India. 92% of journals chosen by Indian researchers are foreign journals; only 7.58% of journals are from India. The favored journals are journals from USA, UK, and Netherlands with US journals accounting for 27.63% of articles published by Indian researchers.

IETE Technical Review (published by Institution of Electronics and Telecommunication Engineers, India) is the most preferred Indian journal. It has been observed that about 33.20% (in 1992) to 34.23% (in 2001) of articles are published in Non-SCI journals by Indian researchers. The major areas of research are computer application, artificial intelligence, data processing, programming, database management systems (DBMS), data handling techniques, distributed systems software, software engineering techniques, etc. Indian researchers prefer to publish articles in journals rather than in conference proceedings. The language used by Indian researcher is only English whereas for the world literature in addition to the English language some other languages like Chinese and Japanese are also preferred.

The average growth rate of Indian literature is 11% as against world average of 8%. The compound growth rates are 8.0288% and 6.5932% for Indian and World literature respectively. Pareto curves show that the number of countries involved in R&D activities in the most productive group is increasing. The percentage of contributions of developed countries is decreasing whereas the percentage of contributions of developing countries is increasing. It shows that there is an increase in the awareness of the need for research and development in software in developing countries

The relation between the GDP and number of publications show that there exists a linear relationship between these indicators. For most of the advanced or developed countries, correlation coefficient (for GDP vs. number of publications) is very low; only for 20 countries, the correlation coefficient is more than 0.90. For the developing countries the correlation is significant – thus indicating that higher the GDP higher the number of publications.

9. REFERENCES

1. Hart, P.W. and Sommerfeld, J.T. "Relationship between growth in gross domestic product (GDP) and growth in the chemical engineering literature in five different countries." *Scientometrics* 42.3 (1998): 299-311.
2. Inonu, Erdal. "The influence of cultural factors on scientific production." *Scientometrics*, 56.1 (2003), 137-146.
3. Kishida, Kazuaki and Matsui, Sachiko. "International publication pattern in Social sciences: a quantitative analysis of the IBSS files." *Scientometrics* 40.2 (1997): 277-298
4. Lal, Arjun and Ray, P.K. "Pattern of research contribution in leading horticultural journals of the world: a comparative study." *IASLIC Bulletin* 36.3 (1991): 95-102.
5. Miquel, J.F., et al. "World science in 18 disciplinary areas: comparative evaluation of the publication patterns of 48 countries over the period of 1981-1992." *Scientometrics* 33.2 (1995): 149-167.

6. Parmar, Arvind, et al. Highlights of Library Automation related documents in the INSPEC. <http://eprints.rclis.org/archive/00002525/01/parmar-08-11-04.pdf>.

7. Ramamritam, Krithi. "R&D at Indian Computer Science Establishments." 5th November 1995. <http://www.fas.org/nuke/guide/india/ agency/krithi1.html>.

8. Rousseau, S and Rousseau R. "Data envelopment analysis as a tool for constructing scientometrics indicators." *Scientometrics*, 40.1 (1997) 45-56.

16

RELATIONSHIPS IN MULTI-LINGUAL THESAURI IN HUMANITIES : ISSUES AND CASE STUDY

A. Neelameghan[1]
K.S. Raghavan[2]

Examines certain issues related to multilingual thesauri for culture-specific domains based on a case study of a bilingual Tamil-English thesaurus being developed for the domain, 'Tamil studies' of the Sangam Period.

1. CONCEPTUAL RELATIONSHIPS AND KNOWLEDGE ORGANIZATION

Librarians have addressed issues of information storage and retrieval for more than 150 years. The tools and techniques that have been developed by them have been reasonably effective in handling library materials in *print-on-paper* format. While in recent years, there have been

1 Professor & Head (Retd.), DRTC, ISI, Bangalore 560059. Contact: 216, 4th Main Road, 16th Cross Road, Malleswaram, Bangalore 560055, India. E mail: anm2002@vsnl.net

2 Professor, Documentation Research and Training Centre, Indian Statistical Institute, Mysore Road, 8th Mile, Bangalore 560059. E-mail: raghavan@drtc.isibang.ac.in; ksragav@hotmail.com

deliberations on the future of traditional tools in the context of networked resources and the nature of information retrieval on the Web, concurrently within the Web community there has been a growing interest in vocabulary-based techniques. Harpring (1999) gives an overview of the Getty's vocabularies with examples of their use in Web retrieval interfaces and collection management systems. Ontologies incorporating thesauri or related semantic models underpin several ongoing projects aimed at design of more effective information retrieval systems for the digital environment. An examination of the relevant literature suggests that several types of knowledge organization tools are being considered - classification schemes, taxonomies, thesauri, ontologies, concept maps, semantic maps, lexicons (Termnet, Framenet), etc - to assist knowledge organization (KO) in the Web environment. Looked at from a general and broad viewpoint, all these tools are based on implicit conceptual relationships between the concepts represented by the terms or codes used in the vocabulary. 'Relationship' is an abstraction belonging to or characteristic of two entities or parts together (WordNet 2.0) and in tools for knowledge organization, we use terms / codes to represent these entities. As early as in 1964, the Ellsinore Conference came out with the following definition of classification: "*By classification is meant any method creating relations, generic or other, between individual semantic units regardless of the degree of hierarchy contained in the system*". Looked at from this perspective, all the tools referred to above involve classificatory processes. In fact determination of similarity, closeness, or degree of *association* between semantic units (concepts) is at the core of all systems of knowledge representation and organization. A relation exists between two concepts when some meaning is implied between them. Identification and categorization of relationships, therefore, plays an important role in all information processes, more so in knowledge organization and information retrieval.

Since the middle of the 20th Century, information retrieval thesauri are being widely used in information systems for knowledge representation of both documents as well as end users' queries. These tools differ from conventional language thesauri in terms of the nature and extent of relations between concepts that are intended to be represented and displayed. A language thesaurus is generally restricted to displaying synonymy (and near-synonymy), antonymy and is designed to assist users in the choice of an appropriate term for an idea. An information retrieval thesaurus, on the other hand, by its very purpose requires display of a range of relationships to support vocabulary management in information systems and facilitate meaningful and effective navigation between related terms (Narrower, Broader and other Related terms) by users during the information retrieval process to achieve optimal recall and precision outputs.

2. CATEGORIES OF RELATIONSHIPS

Traditionally information retrieval thesauri have recognized two primary types of relationships between concepts, namely:

- Hierarchical Relations
  - Genus-Species / Class inclusion relation (also refereed to as taxonomic, subsumptive, and '*IS A*' relation)
  - Partitive Relation / Whole-Part relation (in so far as they apply to living systems and geographical areas)
- Non-Hierarchical Associative Relations or Lateral Relations (LR)

Another type of relation widely recognized by thesauri is the Equivalence relation. Equivalence relations are relations between verbal representations of concepts and are generally language-dependent. The growth of information resources in different languages and the resulting growth of multilingual databases have generated a need for tools that facilitate cross language retrieval. Multilingual tools for KO, such as, multilingual thesauri, are finding wider applications and becoming increasingly more useful as diverse groups "from different cultural and linguistic backgrounds seek access to diverse pieces of information" (Jorna and Davies, 2001) and information professionals have to work with information sources and users with diverse language and cultural backgrounds. The proposed IFLA Guidelines for Multilingual Thesauri is a clear indication of this growing interest.

In the actual interpretation and application of the categories of relationships referred to above for building thesauri, however, there are wide variations. The terminology employed to label the relationships (BT, NT and RT) suggests that these have evolved in the context of building thesauri in the fields of science and technology. Generally in the sciences and in technology, the connotation of terms and their scope are clearly defined and are, more or less, universally accepted; hierarchical relations between concepts are also fairly clearly defined and are generally amenable for categorization into BTs and NTs. The problems of establishing and defining relationships between concepts in the humanities, and to a lesser extent in the social sciences, are of a different order. Several additional issues also arise in the context of a multilingual thesaurus for a culture-specific domain. This paper examines some of the typical issues and problems that arise in building a bilingual / multi-lingual thesaurus for a culture-specific area. Some possible approaches to address these issues are discussed.

3. OBJECTIVES OF THE PAPER

In an earlier paper issues related to the development of an online multi-lingual multi-faith thesaurus, F-THES, covering the subject of Religious Mysticism has been reported (Neelameghan and Raghavan, 2005). More recently a project aimed at building a bilingual (Tamil and English) thesaurus on Tamil studies to support the digital library being developed by the Central Institute of Indian Languages, Mysore has been undertaken. While the time-line for the thesaurus is terminology of the Sangam period[1] and earlier, in reality, this does not restrict the coverage of the thesaurus, as there are indeed a large number of works of later periods that comment on, analyze, evaluate or make comparisons of, works of the classical periods. In terms of subject coverage practically all subjects are covered. Another paper presents the major structural issues in building this thesaurus (Neelameghan and Raghavan, 2007). In this paper we examine in some detail some issues specific to the building of the thesaurus in progress:

Given the situation that there is no information retrieval thesaurus covering the subject of Tamil Studies either in English or Tamil, the thesaurus had to be built using a 'bottom up' approach starting with Tamil terms. The approach was to collect a broad set of relevant candidate terms in Tamil using several print-on-paper and electronic sources. In building the thesaurus, it was found necessary to adopt a stratified approach. In other words the domain of Tamil Studies was visualized as comprising of several disciplines and collection of candidate terms for inclusion in the thesaurus proceeded separately for each discipline. This was considered the best course of action to have

1 Many historians refer to the Tamil literature from ca. 300 B.C. to 300 A.D. as Sangam literature; Sangams were Tamil academies, which enabled poets and authors to gather periodically to publish their work (*Wikipedia*).

adequate control over the process of building the thesaurus, even though it was realized that integrating records for terms in different disciplines could raise problems. Initial examination of the literature of Tamil Studies suggested that the literature pertained to the following major areas:

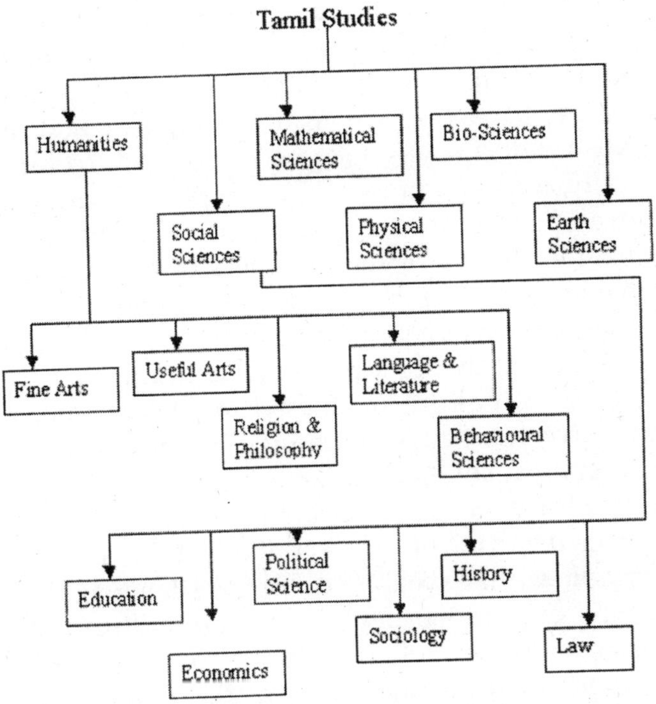

Fig. 1 : An overview of the Disciplines / Sub-disciplines

At present about 100000 Tamil terms have been identified and basic thesaurus records for all these have been created. The terms for inclusion in the thesaurus were gathered from available 'print-on-paper' as well as electronic sources. One of the most useful sources has been the *Tamil Lexicon* of the University of Madras – an edition of which has been made available on the Web by the University of Chicago.

4. SEMANTIC RELATIONS

Reference has already been made to the fact that conceptual relationships between terms in the Humanities are not as precisely defined as in the physical or life sciences. In addition to this general issue, building a multilingual thesaurus for a culture-specific domain raises certain issues that are related to the nature of the respective culture-specific domains. Concepts encountered in and associated with culture-specific domains in particular are abstract in nature and rarely can we relate these concepts to concrete referents. Secondly, a large number of concepts encountered in culture-specific domains are those that have some meaning in the life of the members of the community belonging to the culture. These have implications for a multilingual thesaurus. A language is a product of, and reflects the culture of the particular community. In other words, it is the culture and lifestyle prevalent among the members of a particular community that necessitates and results in the formation of lexemes / expressions (words / terms) for concepts associated with that culture and lifestyle. It is therefore very likely that, unless the communities that speak two different languages share the same culture, certain concepts in culture-specific domains may have verbal expressions only in a particular language. In building this multilingual thesaurus therefore, it was indeed very difficult to find exact equivalent concepts in the English language. The notion of '*equivalence relation*' which is widely used in thesauri had to be extended to include both equivalent terms in the source language (Synonyms in Tamil for Tamil terms) and terms in English denoting near equivalent / similar concepts. The second major issue, also related to the notion of '*equivalence relation*', that had to be addressed was the occurrence of several different terms in Tamil with closely similar meanings / connotations; it was important to decide on how to handle this situation and to understand the implications for the bilingual thesaurus. A few examples are given below to illustrate the nature of this problem. Searches for two Tamil words, 'tAmarai' (தாமரை) and 'kamalam' (கமலம்) (which are synonymous) and their English equivalent, ***'lotus'*** were carried out in the online *Tamil Lexicon (http://dsal.uchicago.edu/dictionaries/tamil-lex/).* The search retrieved all the records in which the input string occurred either as an independent word or embedded in a larger word. The number of records retrieved for each of these searches was indeed very large as seen from the table below:

Search Term	No. of Records
TAmarai(தாமரை)	327 Entries with *tAmarai* as entry word or in the explanation
Kamalam (கமலம்)	36 entries with *kamalam* as entry word or in the explanation
Lotus(லொாதுஸ்)	309 entries with Lotus as entry word or in the explanation

It was thought that an examination of the records retrieved would help identify features that are characteristic of the language and the subject domain that are relevant to building bilingual and multilingual thesauri. In the following paragraphs some of these are examined. For the purpose of identifying the range of issues that need to be addressed, all the 327 retrieved records for ***'tAmarai'*** were examined. Barring a certain number of records in which the word was employed to demonstrate usage of some other term not semantically related to it, more than 200 records were for terms, which were semantically related to ***'tAmarai'***. The words that were not semantically related to ***'tAmarai'*** were ignored and a detailed examination of all the remaining words was carried out. An attempt was made to define the relation between ***'tAmarai'*** and each of these words and group the terms on the basis of the relation. The standard set of relationships normally employed by all thesauri was used for categorization; i.e. the terms were grouped as Synonyms (equivalent terms), Broader terms (BTs), Narrower Terms (NTs) and Related Terms (RTs). The Table (*see Appendix 1*) groups all the terms under these broad categories. It is relevant here to mention some of the guidelines that have been adopted in categorizing the relationships:

- Terms representing types of lotus (varieties of lotus) as also terms representing parts of the lotus plant have both been treated as narrower terms;
- In reality a part may be part of any level (order). For example, the following hierarchy represents the relationships obtaining between the concepts.

  TAmarai (lotus)

  MirunLam (Stalk of the Lotus)

  TmaraimuL (thorny portion of the stalk of the lotus)

While terms representing parts of a lower level will be appropriately labeled as NT1, NT2, NT3, etc, in the actual thesaurus, this has not been shown in the table (Appendix 1).

An examination of the table reveals the nature of the issues that need to be addressed in building this bilingual thesaurus:

i) There are a large number of synonyms in Tamil (this is probably true of other Indian languages also). Synonyms in the form of variant forms of spelling also appear to be in wide use in the Tamil language. 82 of the over 200 words were synonyms to '***tAmarai***'.

ii) A large number of RTs (laterally related terms) also

appear to characterize the Tamil language. There were as many 80 RTs to ***'tAmarai'***

iii) For most of the terms related to a descriptor, there was no single equivalent word / term in English. This may suggest the need for using phrases / compound terms in English to denote many of the concepts encountered

iv) Many of the terms that are related to ***'tAmarai'*** (as synonyms, NTs and RTs) were found to be homographs with multiple connotations. This creates certain problems especially if a related term is employed as the descriptor to denote some other concept. The importance of employing appropriate role operators (individualizing elements) to clearly indicate the connotation of a term cannot be over emphasized.

An examination of the large number of RTs suggested that the term ***'tAmarai'*** has been used to represent four broad ideas / concepts:

- Lotus as a plant
- Lotus as a flower
- Lotus as a shape (Entities in the shape of a lotus)
- Lotus-like properties (E.g., soft like lotus petals)

It must be mentioned here that in this case study ***'tAmarai'*** (along with ***kamalam,*** a synonym for ***'tAmarai'*** and the English equivalent, **'*lotus*'**) has been used as an example to identify the nature of problems and issues that are likely to arise in building a multi-lingual thesaurus for culture-specific domains, especially involving Indian languages. The issues raised are representative of the problems common to most Indian languages. These issues need to be addressed and appropriate guidelines developed. Besides, there are also issues related to transliteration, etc which have not been discussed in this paper.

5. REFERENCES

1. Harpring, P. (1999) "How forcible are the right words: overview of applications and interfaces incorporating the Getty vocabularies". Proceedings of Museums and the Web 1999, Archives and Museum Informatics. http://www.archimuse.com/mw99/papers/harpring/harpring.html
2. Jorna, Kerstin and Davies, Sylvie (2001). Multilingual thesauri for the modern world – no ideal solution? *Journal of Documentation*, 57(2); 284-295
3. Neelameghan, A. and Raghavan, K.S. (2005). An online multi-lingual, multi-faith thesaurus: a progress report on F-THES. Webology, 2(4) http://www.webology.ir/2005]v2n4/a19.html
4. Neelameghan, A. and Raghavan, K.S. (2007). Online Bilingual Thesaurus for Subjects in the Humanities: A case Study / (**In**: [Proceedings]: ICSD 2007: International Conference on Semantic Web and Digital Libraries / edited by A.R.D. Prasad and Devika P. Madalli. – Bangalore: DRTC, 2007. p. 489- 505)

APPENDIX - 1

Note: All the words are rendered in the transliterated form and not in the Tamil script

Synonyms

Term	Nature of Relation with '*tAmarai*'	Meaning / additional connotations, if any
tāmarai		1. Lotus, Nelumbium speciosum 2. Array of an army in the form of a lotus 3. A large number; 4. Ringworm;
arattam	Synonym	1. Lotus; 2. Red substance; 3. Affection; 4. Tilaka on the forehead; 5. Gold 6. Bee's wax
ampucam	Synonym	
ampuyam	Synonym	
ampōcam	Synonym	
ampōrukam	Synonym	
aravintam	Synonym	
iramāppiriyam	Synonym	
iravikāntam	Synonym	1. Lotus 2. Sun-stone
iracackūyam	Synonym	1. Lotus; 2. Sacrifice performed by a victorious monarch attended by his vanquished tributary princes
iracīvam	Synonym	
iRumpu	Synonym	1. Lotus 2. Shrub, bush; 3. Hill, mountain; 4.. Thicket 5. Malabar glorylily. 6. Wonder;
iRumpūtu	Synonym	1. Lotus 2. Magnanimity 3.Mountain; 4. Shrub, bush; 5. Shoot, sprout; 6. Amazement
kańcam	Synonym	1. Lotus 2. Water
katirppāri (Wife of Sun)	Synonym	
kantōtam	Synonym	

kamalam	Synonym	1. Lotus 2. Water 3. A large number 4. Circular salver, like a full-blown lotus 5. Faceted diamond
kazhukkāNi	Synonym	1. Lotus; 2. Stout man with out common sense, thick head, dullard; 3. Indian kino tree; 4. Pestle
kaRkam	Synonym	1. Lotus 2. Mahwa flower
kucēcayam	Synonym	
kōkayam	Synonym	
caccaTam	Synonym	
catataLam	Synonym	
caracicam	Synonym	
carōrukam	Synonym	1. Lotus 2. A hell
calakarangkam	Synonym	
calacam	Synonym	1. Lotus 2. Pearl 3. Green moss
calarukam	Synonym	
cāracam	Synonym	1. Lotus. 2. Common crane. 3. White heron
cītaLam	Synonym	
cūkam	Synonym	
cūzhtāzhai	Synonym	
tammi	Synonym	
taruTam	Synonym	
tāmpirai	Synonym	
tēvanam	Synonym	1. Lotus 2. Gambling
tōTakam	Synonym	1. Lotus 2. Pustule, blister
tōyacam	Synonym	
natīcam	Synonym	
naLam	Synonym	
naLinam	Synonym	1. Lotus. 2. Water
nālikam	Synonym	1. Lotus 2. Buffalo
nīracam	Synonym	
nīrōrukam	Synonym	
nēLi	Synonym	

pangkērukam	Synonym	
pangkayam	Synonym	1. Lotus, as mud-born; 2. A lotus-shaped weapon 3. Heron
pangkērukam	Synonym	
patumam	Synonym	1. Lotus. 2. Lotus-shaped section of a crown 3. (NTya.) A hand-pose; 4. Ten million crores 5. The 15th nakshatra 6. A hell; 7. Curls of hair on the shoulders of a horse;
paRpam	Synonym	1. Lotus 2. A very large number 3.A PurNa
pānirukam	Synonym	
panmini (padmini)	Synonym	1. The first of the four classes of women. 2. Lotus
pātōcam	Synonym	
puTakam	Synonym	1. Lotus 2. Cup or vessel formed by stitching leaves;
puNTarikam	Synonym	1. Lotus 2. Male elephant of the South-East, one of aSTa-tik-kajam, 3. Tiger; 4. Beetle; bee;
makōRpalam	Synonym	
matanālayam	Synonym	1. Lotus 2.Pudendum muliebre
markkaTāciyam	Synonym	
miriNāLam	Synonym	
miruNāli	Synonym	
muNTakam	Synonym	1. Lotus 2. Thorn bush 3. Fragrant screw-pine. 4. Thorn 5. Water thorn. 6. Indian night shade 7. Jagged jujube 8. Sweet toddy 9 Jaggery from palmyra
muLari	Synonym	1. Lotus; 2. Ten million crores. Brahma's world; 4. Bramble 5. Jungle; 6. Thorny twig, used by birds in building nests; 7. Firewood 8. Sacrificial fuel; 9. Fire; 10. Firebrand; 11. Fever; 12. Subtlety
mauval	Synonym	1. Lotus. 2. Arabian jasmine. 3. Wild jasmine
tāmaraippoo	Synonym	

puTkaram	Synonym	1. Lotus flower 2. Water3. A celebrated place of pilgrimage.. 4. Sky, heaven 5. Cyrus crane, Grus antigone 6. Tip of an elephant's proboscis; 7. Sword-blade; 8. Sheath of a sword; 9 Arrow; 10. Battle, war; 11. Drum-head; 13. A musical instrument; 14. Mouth of a vessel; 15. Union; 16. A disease; 17. A medicinal pill; 18. Arabian costume. 19. Intoxication; 20. A kind of snake; 21. A treatise on dancing; 22. Share, part; 23. Fullness; 24. Star; 25. Cave; 26. Common kite.
vanacam	Synonym	
vanacōpanam	Synonym	
vanarukam	Synonym	
vāricātam	Synonym	
vāriyuRpavam	Synonym	
vārirukam	Synonym	
viNTukam	Synonym	1. Lotus. 2. Fetid cassia
vicapuTpam	Synonym	
appucam	Synonym	1. Lotus 2. Chank 3. Water cadamba
ampucanmam	Synonym	
amputam	Synonym	
ampunēcam	Synonym	
ampurōkiNi	Synonym	
arkkapantu	Synonym	
āciyapattiram	Synonym	
āymalar	Synonym	
irāmappiriyam	Synonym	
kavāram	Synonym	
cirukam	Synonym	1. Lotus 2. Wind; 3 Dart;
Alli (Water Lily)	Synonym	1. Lotus. 2. White water lily. 3. *Nymphaea lotus* 4. Inner flower petals, 5. Filament of a stamen 6. Lily seeds; 7. Iron-wood tree. 8. New root, shoot

Broader and Narrower Terms

pū	BT	Flower
karNikai; karuNikai	NT - Part	Pericarp of the lotus
nava-taLam	NT – Part	Tender Lotus leaf
kaNNikai	NT (Part)	Pericarp of the lotus
koTTai	NT (Part)	1. Pericarp of the lotus flower 2. Testicles; 3. Seed of any kind not enclosed in chaff or husk, nut, stone, kernel; 4. Fruit-bud of the jack; very small green pumpkin 5. Large rounded form, as in writing; 6. A gold ornament for women's hair; 7. Castor-plant. 8. Knob of wooden sandals; 9. Knots made of warp threads at the end of a cloth, as ornament, etc 10. Warp threads at the end of a cloth hanging loosely and not made into knots; 11. Head of a pole used as a prop; 12. An ornament for elephant 13. Base of a hand spindle 14. Rolls of cotton prepared for spinning; 15. Plug or tent of cloth to widen the ear-holes for jewels 16. A kind of ear-ornament for women 17. Pad for the head in carrying a load; 18. Small round pillow, cushion
tāmaraikkāy	NT (Part)	
tāmaraimaNi	NT (Part)	1. Lotus-seed 2. A rosary of lotus-seeds
tāmaraivaLaiyam	NT (Part)	
naLinīrukam	NT (Part)	Lotus stalk
picam	NT (part)	Fibre of the lotus; lotus-stalk
pītarākam	NT (part)	1. Lotus filament; 2. Gold colour
pokuTTu	NT (Part)	1. Pericarp of the lotus or common caung flower 2 Bubble formed in turbid water . 3. Mountain, hill
miruNālam	NT (part)	Lotus fibre
mirunāLam	NT (Part)	Stalk of the lotus
mukuLam	NT (part)	1. Lotus-stalk; 2. Bud 3. NTya.: A gesture

		with one hand in which all the fingers are held upright with the tips joined 4. (YMga.) A squatting posture in which the two legs are joined to form a horizontal circle; 5 Medulla oblongata, hindmost segment of the brain
muñcaram	NT (part)	Lotus root
varāTakam	NT (Part)	Seed-pod of the lotus
valayam; vaLaiyam	NT (Part)	1. Involute petal of a lotus 2. Discus; 3. Sea; 4. Zone of earth; 5. Bracelet; armlet; 6 Circle, ring 7. Surrounding region; 8. Tank, pool; 9. Plot, garden plot; 10 Garden; 11. Limit, ambit
valūkam	NT (Part)	The root of the lotus plant
Vicam; viTam	NT (part)	1. Lotus fibre; 2. Mineral poison 3. Anything injurious or pernicious 4. Scorpion; 5. Inflammation from a bite, sting or prick; 6. Outer skin of dried ginger; 7. Nepal aconite. 8. Water 9.; Poison
vīcakōcam	NT (part)	1. Pericarp of the lotus 2. Seed.
aLimpakam	NT (part)	1. Pollen of lotus flower 2. Frog;. 3. South Indian Mahua; 4. Cuckoo;
karāTam	NT (part)	Tuber of the lotus plant
cavarikkoTTai	NT (part)	Pericarp of the lotus
patumavīcam	NT (Part)	Lotus Seed
tāmaraimuL	NT (Part)	1 Thorny portion of lotus-stalk 2. Lichen
tāmarainūl	NT (Part)	Lotus fibre
tāmaraivaRRal	NT (Part)	Dried root of the lotus
vaccirakam	NT-Part	Pericarp of the lotus
patumavīcam	NT (Part)	Lotus Seed
purimuRukku	**NT - ???**	**Un-blown Lotus**
aRpakantam	NT - Variety	Red Lotus
urōcani	NT - Variety	Red Lotus
erimalar	NT - Variety	1. Red lotus 2. Flower of the Indian Coral tree

Irattakamalam)	NT (Variety)	1. Lotus 2 Red Indian water-lily
Irattacantiyakam	NT (Variety)	
IrattamaNDalam	NT (Variety)	1. Red Lotus 2. Purple Indian water lily
cengkamalam	NT (Variety)	Red Lotus
centāmarai	NT (Variety)	Red Lotus
cōmākkiyam	NT (Variety)	Red Lotus
tāmaracam	NT (Variety)	1. Red lotus. 2 Gold 3. Copper
vannivaNNam	NT (Variety)	1. Red lotus. 2. Red Indian water lily.
viccam	NT (Variety)	
veNTāmarai	NT (Variety)	White lotus
aRpapatumam	NT (Variety)	Red-lotus
kaTaRRāmarai	NT (Variety)	A Kind of lotus

Related Terms

Term	RT Type	Meaning
ākācattāmarai	RT	Seedless nelumbo
allittāmarai	RT	Red water-lily
koTiccittāmarai	RT	
kuLittāmarai	RT	Rootless nelumbo, floating in tanks and ditches
nīlattāmarai	RT	Blue nelumbo
ōrilaittāmarai	RT	A small plant
ōritazhttāmarai	RT	A pasture weed; small plant with its lateral petals so close together at the base as to appear like a single undivided petal, *Ionidium suffruticosum*
pangkayappaTu	RT	Lotus Pond
puTkarini	RT – Normal Place of occurrence	1. Lotus tank; 2. Sacred tank near a temple
nilattāmarai	RT	Rose
tāmaraicciRaki	RT	A kind of teal in lotus-tanks

poTTuttāmarai	RT	Indian lotus croton
vaTTattāmarai	RT	Indian Lotus Croton
azaru (Mire)	RT – Normal Place of occurrence	
kamalavaippu	RT – Normal Place of occurrence	*Lotus Pool*
kōpattiram	RT - Product	Fibre obtained from lotus stalk
puTakini	RT - product	1. Cluster of lotus flowers 2. Lotus-pond
naLinātcamālai	RT – Product	Necklace of lotus seeds
itayakamalam	RT (Figure of speech)	Lotus-shaped heart
kakanāravintam	RT (Figure of speech)	1. Lotus, which flowers in the sky, as a thing that is non-existent; 2. Seed Moss, *Sida humilis*;
ākācattāmarai	RT (Figure of speech)	1. That which is absolutely non-existent, as an aerial lotus 2. Seed moss. 3 A weed, *Pistia stratiotes*
kamalavaruttanai	RT (Figure of speech)	Gesture with both hands signifying obeisance, consisting in folding one's hands so as to resemble a lotus bud
koTiñci	RT (Figure of speech)	Ornamental staff in the form of a lotus, fixed in front of the seat in a chariot and held by the hand as support
kiNkiNivāyccey-tal	RT (Figure of speech)	To open slightly, as the mouth of a tinkling bell
cennāppōtār	RT (Figure of speech)	The poet TiruvaLLuvar, as having beautiful lotus-like tongue
caraNāravintam	RT (Figure of speech)	Lotus-like feet
tāmarangkāy	RT (Figure of speech)	The liver, as resembling the pericarp of a lotus
pātakamalam	RT (Figure of speech)	Lotus-like foot
pātatāmarai	RT (Figure of speech)	Lotus-like foot

malaraTi	RT (Figure of speech)	Foot of a divine or great personage, as lotus-like
mukāmpuyam	RT (Figure of speech)	Lotus-like face
patumaviyūkam	RT – Association	Array of an army in the form of a lotus
ampuyanūlnāNān	RT – Association	Kama
Kamalavūkrti	RT – Association	*One who rides on a lotus*
patmavari	RT – Association	The lowermost tier of a temple shaped in the form of the petals of a lotus flower
kōkanatan	RT – Association	*Brahma*
calacalōcanan	RT – Association	*Vishnu (*as having lotus-like eyes)
cengkamalavalli	RT – Association	Lakshm+, as the creeper dwelling on red lotus
cuvātiTTānam	RT – Association	A *cakra* or mystic centre in the body, described as a six-petalled lotus, situated above *mkltram* and below the navel
cūriyamaNTalam	RT – Association	Mystic circles in the body regarded as lotus flowers and assigned in worship to *jńna, kriy, icch□akti* of the deity under the respective emblems of the sun, moon and fire
vicutti	RT – Association	A mystic circle or *cakra* in the body, conceived as a sixteen-petalled lotus situated at the root of the tongue above *ankatam*
mūlātāram	RT – Association	A *cakkiram* or nerve-plexus in the body, described as a four-petalled lotus, situated between the base of the sexual organ and the anus
kamalālayan	RT – Association	*Brahma*

kōkanatai	RT – Association	*Lakshmi*
malarōn	RT – Association	*Brahma*
muLarippāvai	RT – Association	Lakshmi
muNTakācanai	RT – Association	Lakshmi
kūviram	RT – Association	Ornamental stake in the form of a lotus-bud fixed in front of the seat in a chariot and held by the hand for support
naLini	RT – Association	1. Lakshmi 2. Lotus tank
pañcapāNam	RT – Association	The five arrows of Kma, viz., *tmarai malar (arrow with Lotus Flower, etc)*
pangkayaccelvi	RT – Association	Lakshmi
pangkayan	RT – Association	1. Brahm, as lotus-born 2. Sun, as Lord of the lotus
patumācanan	RT – Association	Brahma
patumācani	RT – Association	Lakshmi
patumanāpan	RT – Association	Vishnu
patumapantu	RT – Association	1. The Sun. 2. Bee
patumayōni	RT – Association	Brahma
pauTTikam	RT – Association	1. Cow dung gathered on a lotus-leaf before it falls to the ground. 2. A ceremony
pōtinan	RT – Association	Brahma as seated on a Lotus
puvvattāmarai	RT – Association	Lotus from the navel of Vishnu

tāmaraicciRaki	RT – Association	A kind teal found in louts pools
tāmaraikkaNNan	RT – Association	Vishnu - Lotus-eyed
tāmarainanpan	RT – Association	Sun
tāmarainātan	RT – Association	Sun, as the lord of lotus
tāmaraippīTikai	RT – Association	A raised stone-slab with lotus-petals carved on the sides and Buddha's feet on the top
tāmaraiyācanan	RT – Association	Brahma (one who is seated on lotus)
tāmaraiyācanan	RT – Association	Brahma
tāmaraiyāL	RT – Association	Lakshmi, as seated on lotus
tāmaraiyāL	RT – Association	Lakshmi
tāmaraimukai	RT – Association	An ornamental staff in the form of a lotus
tāmaraimoTTu	RT – Association	A VaiSHNava caste mark resembling a lotus-bud
tāmaraiyilai	RT – Association	A VaiSHNava caste mark resembling a lotus leaf
tutturu	RT – Association	An ornament like the pericarp of a lotus
pañcanīrāñcanam	RT – Association	Worship of an idol in five ways, viz., waving of lamp, lotus, cloth and leaf, and then falling prostrate before it
patumakōcikam	RT – Association	A gesture with one hand in which the fingers are so held as to appear like the calyx of a lotus
patumapīTam	RT – Association	Seat in the shape of a lotus
hēmāravintaparima La niyāyam	RT – Association	Nyāya in illustration of an excellence of one kind co-existing with an excellence of another kind, as a lotus

		made of gold having the fragrance of the lotus
tēvatāmarai	RT – Association	A treasure of Kub–ra
patumarēkai	RT – Association	Lotus-mark on the palm of the hand, believed to indicate one's good fortune

17

CLASSIFIED CATALOGUE CODE TODAY

B K Sen[1]

Ranganathan's Canon of Context enshrined in the Classified Catalogue Code (CCC) states 'that the [cataloguing] rules should be amended from time to time to keep step with changes in the Context' The advent of information technology brought about a sea change in the realm of cataloguing, following which MARC and ISBD format came into existence and AACR was revised to accommodate the aforesaid format. CCC did not respond to changes endangering its own survival. The change in the context has made the situation ripe for the emergence of Canon of Universality, which Ranganathan did not think of. To revive the Code, it needs to be thoroughly revised keeping in view the changed context.

Keywords: Cataloguing; Classified Catalogue Code; Canon of Universality.

1 Scientist & Head (Retd.), Training Division, National Institute for Science Communication & Information Resources (CSIR), New Delhi.
Contact : 80, Shivalik Apartments, Alaknanda, New Delhi - 110019, E-mail : bksen@airtelmail.in

1. CLASSIFIED CATALOGUE CODE–ORIGIN AND DEVELOPMENT

Classified Catalogue Code (CCC) made its first appearance in 1934. Thereafter till 1964 four more editions came out in the years 1945, 1951, 1958 and 1964. The Code continuously evolved during the period and witnessed the formulation of nine canons, viz., Canon of Ascertainability, Canon of Prepotence, Canon of Individualization, Canon of Sought-Heading, Canon of Context, Canon of Permanence, Canon of Currency, Canon of Consistence, and Canon of Recall Value. Apart from these canons, CCC's foundation was based on the Five Laws of Library Science, Laws of Interpretation, Law of Impartiality, Law of Symmetry, Law of Parsimony, Principle of Local Variation, and Principle of Osmosis[1][1,2].

The generation of class index entries for a document based entirely on its class number was developed by Ranganathan. This system of indexing was called chain indexing. It required the document to be classified minutely so that all the elements covered in the document will first of all get reflected in the class number, then in the subject index. This was to ensure meeting of all possible subject approaches to a document. The chain procedure became the bridge between classification and cataloguing.

The rules for style of writing, alphabetization and the rules for cataloguing single-volume simple book, composite book, multi-volume book, and periodical publication were framed during the period. This apart, rules were also framed for entries in union catalogue of books, union catalogue of periodical publications, national

1 The use of capital letters in this paragraph is according to Ranganathan's style, which does not always obey the accepted rules of capitalization.

bibliography, indexing periodical, and abstracting periodical.

Ranganathan framed different cataloguing rules for different forms of publications, and did not think of a single format like *Common Communication Format* (CCF) that can embrace all forms of publications. Ranganathan enumerated non-book materials that were prevalent till early 1960s, but did not frame rules for their cataloguing.

Ranganathan used CCC for cataloguing books of the libraries of University of Madras, Banaras Hindu University and University of Delhi. Many other libraries of the country also followed CCC. The use of CCC outside India was negligible.

2. CHANGE IN CONTEXT

The Canon of Context states 'that the [cataloguing] rules should be amended from time to time to keep step with changes in the Context' [3]. In the realm of cataloguing how this change came into being is described below in brief.

Prior to 1960s, *Anglo-American Code* (AA Code) published in 1908, and *ALA cataloguing rules for author and title entries* (ALA Code) published in 1949 were generally used in the West especially UK and USA. Both the codes were having obvious shortcomings and were facing criticism, at times quite severe. To remedy the situation and to develop one international code, IFLA held in 1961, the International Conference on Cataloguing Principles in Paris. The Conference generated a set of broad guidelines / rules that paved the way for evolving an international catalogue code. Subsequently, the American Library Association, the Canadian Library Association, the Library Association, and the Library of Congress jointly developed the code, which was published in 1967 under the title *Anglo-American cataloguing rules* (AACR). AACR was brought out in two different versions – the North American text and the British text, though the differences between the two were not major [4]. This is one scenario. The development that really brought about the *change in context* is the happy union of several factors described below.

In 1960s computers were making inroads in almost every sphere of human activity, libraries being no exception. In 1960 itself the Library of Congress (LC) dreamt of computerizing its catalogue and appointed a committee under the chairmanship of Dr W K Gilbert to study the feasibility of automation of various activities of the library [5]. Gilbert submitted his report in 1963 that signaled green for the computerization of library activities not only in LC but in the world as a whole and simultaneously heralded the dawn of IT era in librarianship.

Following the Gilbert report, LC went ahead with the programme of machine-readable catalogue (MARC) and MARC I format originated in 1966. IFLA brought out UNIMARC in 1967 [6].

Attempts by LC to develop MARC format led others also to develop their own formats suitable to their needs. British National Bibliography started the UK MARC project. At this juncture, the realization dawned that formats will have to take care of the exchange of bibliographic records amongst libraries meaning thereby that a great degree of compatibility among formats will have to be ensured. This resulted in

- The revision of the MARC format developed by the Library of Congress;
- The revision of the AACR;
- The development of International Standard Bibliographic Description (ISBD).

All these activities gave birth to ISBD (M) in 1974 and

other versions in subsequent years; the second edition of *Anglo-American Cataloguing Rules* (AACR II) incorporating the rules of ISBD (M) in 1978; UNIMARC (2nd ed. 1980); ISO standard (ISO 2709) titled *Format for Bibliographic Information Interchange on Magnetic Tape* in 1981; and *Common Communication Format* (CCF) in 1984.

The advent of Internet and World Wide Web at this juncture brought about a revolution in the arena of communication and converted our planet into a global village. The library activities were affected heavily demanding a new vision for depicting the library and information scenario. The networking of libraries resulted by the aforesaid development made the concept of an isolated library catalogue almost obsolete. A library catalogue now is a part of a huge catalogue of networked libraries, sometimes a part of a global catalogue.

All the aforesaid developments brought about a sea change in the sphere of cataloguing and demanded a new canon, not thought of by Ranganathan, the **canon of universality**.

3. CANON OF UNIVERVERSALITY

This canon emerges as an offshoot of the change in context. It may be stated as follows: **A cataloguing code should be universal in scope and application.** The word 'universal' in the statement connotes that

(a) The code should provide rules for

- (i) Cataloguing of all forms of documents, e.g. books, non-book materials, etc
- (ii) Cataloguing of documents in all languages;
- (iii) Producing catalogues in all languages;
- (iv) Cataloguing of documents recorded in all

media, e.g. print media, micro media, magnetic media, optical media, Internet, etc

(b) The code should be applicable in all libraries, e.g. small, medium and big; general and special; government and non-government, etc.

(c) The code should be applicable in all countries;

(d) The code should be applicable both for manual as well as computerized cataloguing;

(e) The code should conform to an internationally accepted bibliographic format such as ISBD.

Most of the statements in the Canon are self-explanatory. Some statements need some explanation, which is given below.

Statement a (ii) – Most libraries are multilingual. Cataloguing of all books may be done in the favoured language. In that case the catalogue code should provide rules for transliteration from all languages to the favoured language. If an internationally accepted standard is available for transliteration that may be followed. For example, British standard may be followed for transliteration of Russian characters. The code should make a specific mention about it. Transliteration without diacritical marks is to be preferred since many diacritical marks are not available in software packages used for typing.

Statement a (iii) - For producing catalogues in all languages, in certain cases specific rules are to be framed. For example, while cataloguing *Gitanjali* in English language, the name of the author is usually written as Tagore, Rabindranath. The same cannot be done in a Bengali catalogue since Bengali users will generally look under Rabindranath Thakur in the Bengali catalogue.

Statement a (iv) - The medium (optical, magnetic, etc) in which the document is available is to be mentioned.

Statement d - The code should be same for manual and computerized cataloguing.

4. CONCLUSION

In the world of living organisms, an organism that fails to adapt itself to the changed situation perishes. The same is true in the case of catalogue codes as well. Ranganathan in his Canon of Context hinted that. There is no denying the fact that CCC has failed to keep step with the change in context. As a result, libraries that were following CCC opted for AACR II during automation. At present, libraries are no more preferring CCC as the Code has not yet been updated keeping in view the changed situation. Chain procedure, the unique method of indexing devised by Ranganathan attracted the attention of the world, and was used by BNB for quite sometime. Because of some shortcomings, BNB stopped its use and developed PRECIS. DRTC developed POPSI to remove the shortcomings of chain procedure. Somehow POPSI failed to be a popular system of indexing. In such a situation the future of CCC does not look bright today.

To revive CCC it needs to be thoroughly revised in view of the changed context by recasting the existing canons, abolishing restrictions on the number of authors or collaborators to be included in the catalogue entry, including all items figuring in CCF and UNIMARC and generating a unified format for all kinds of documents.

5. REFERENCES

1. Ranganathan S R. *Classified Catalogue Code with additional rules for Dictionary Catalogue Code.* 5th ed. Bombay: Asia Publishing House, 1964. Pts B and C.
2. Girja Kumar, Krishan Kumar. *Theory of cataloguing.* 3rd rev ed. Delhi: Vikas, 1981.

3. Ranganathan, S R. Op cit: p 47
4. Girja Kumar, Krishan Kumar. Op cit: p122-123.
5. Gilbert, W K. Automation in Library of Congress. Washington (DC): Library of Congress, 1963.
6. Hopkinson, A. MARC developments in United Kingdom. Infotheca 2003 (March). Viewed on Internet <www.unilib.bg.ac.yu/en/e-sources/infotheca/1-2003/hopkinson2.php>

18

CHANGE: A PRECURSOR OF KNOWLEDGE

G. J. Narayana[1]

Change occurs in a time-space framework. The study of change, its causes and effects is a precursor of knowledge. Change appears in different modes and causes different effects. Science, sociology and economic development are presented as parts of sectoral change. Of particular interest is revolutionary change, which results in a change of our "world view". The relationship between change and knowledge, change and experience are discussed. Touches upon the role of reflectivity in shaping an individual's perception of reality and its role in shaping ones response to change.

1. INTRODUCTION

One of the important characteristics of time and space is their un-detachable association with change, which in turn impacts on the creation and utilization of knowledge. In nature, change is caused by the interaction of matter and energy in a time-space envelope. In human affairs, a

• Scientist (Retd.), Aeronautical Development Establishment, DRDO, Bangalore - 660 017. **Contact :** #1270, MRHB Colony, Govindaraja Nagar, Bangalore - 560 079. Ph. : 23303598, E-mail : gjnarayana@gmail.com

change occurs when an individual interacts with other individuals or with the environment in a time and space embrace. Nothing is permanent in the universe. Living organisms, and non-living objects of this earth and that of a far away galaxy, and the particles inside matter - all undergo change, but the difference is in the nature, magnitude, frequency and duration of change over time and space. A change can take place in less than a second or may take billions of years and may happen in micro-space or at the order of galactic space depending upon the item. What has change to do with knowledge? The study of change, its causes and effects is a precursor of knowledge. If there are no changes taking place in the universe, human life and society, and if everything is constant all the time and allover space then there would be no growth of knowledge. Webster's dictionary lists several meanings to the word "change", but a constant feature underlying these meanings in the context of action or phenomena is the meaning of "*different*" or "*to make different*" and the synonyms given are *alter, modify,* and *vary* (Webster's 1993). These dictionary meanings miss the factors of time and space, which are inseparable parts of change.

A more satisfactory technical explanation is that a change occurs in an existing order or system whenever there is:

a) A break followed by variation or difference in the functioning of a system or behaviour over time

b) A modification, however imperceptible it may be, in an existing mode of functioning.

c) A disruption affecting continuity, orderliness, regularity, harmony or equilibrium of a system.

A change is always with reference to an existing state of functioning giving place to a different order and is contingent on time and space. From the study of change taking place in animate and inanimate universe and its impact knowledge is extracted. Gained knowledge when applied as an input may lead to further change creating a cycle of change: knowledge— change—knowledge—change—. Thus, change in the universe bound by time and space is an in exhaustive source of new knowledge.

2. CHARACTERISTICS OF CHANGE

Changes are of three types, namely:

a) A change that occurs with certain regularity and having ascertainable time and space interval, e.g. orbital movement of the earth around the sun is a change of position and time in relation to the sun occurring with certain regularity. The earth takes 365/366 days for one complete orbit, and this forms a basis for measurement of time and invention of calendar.

b) A change as above but with minor deviation from the normal or predicted behaviour of the system, e.g. menstrual cycle in women.

c) A change that occurs randomly, e.g. transfer of power to the people of India by the British in 1947 is a change of great consequences to India, Great Britain and the world. This change is also instrumental in shaping knowledge on India in the post-independent era brought about by a time/space divide. Prediction of Sir Winston Churchill, the War-time prime minister of Britain and many others that transfer of power to Indians will lead to disintegration of the country has not only been belied but the nation has become a leading democracy in the world with a strong economy, which exemplifies a property of predicted knowledge. Another example is an abrupt change caused by the abandonment of a regularly followed practice of greeting one's beloved before going to bed, which is a sure sign of an emerging conflict – a subject of study in social psychology.

The significance and effects of each type of change varies from one knowledge domain to another. There are easily discernable qualitative differences between changes occurring in inanimate world and those occurring in the organic and social world of man, the latter is invariably affective and value laden in nature.

3. PHENOMENA OF CHANGE

In the natural world we live in, the pre-change state of matter or phenomenon undergoing change, other than physical and dynamical system, will either be destroyed or modified giving place to a different matter or different phenomenon. Destruction and new creation occurs, if it is a chemical change and modification if it is a physical change. In either case the original state of the matter or phenomena cease to exist, except in temporary changes. In the emotional and social worlds change takes on a complex form as human events and actions are linked to the larger dynamics of social, economic, political and psychological forces, which are conditioned by time and place. A change could be a one-time event, or a set of successive events or intermittent events. After a change, the body undergoing the change can be reconstructed, at least theoretically, but outside its original special-temporal framework of the past. The effects of the reconstructed change- good or bad, can neither carry the original experience nor can they be retrieved—a changed organic relationship can be restored to its pre-change state, a new political system can be reversed to its earlier form but outside the original timeframe. In impersonal systems of organizations, effects of change may have a cascading effect spread across time and space, for example- a change in the corporate taxation policy may effect even the smallest household; a change in the socially sanctioned marriage norms may affect the whole community and the off springs of such a marriage.

Controlling Change : Effects of change in a system and its environment may vary from inconsequential to that of extreme impact- positive or negative, including the very survival of the system. This raises the question whether change can be controlled? The answer is both yes and no. A change is caused either by forces of nature or from actions of man. A change brought about by social actors and organized activities is amenable to control, at least theoretically, as they are the results of human initiation; and therefore can be started, stopped or directed to follow an intended path. Precisely because of the self-initiated nature of change, mankind has advanced to the stage of post-modernism. On the other hand, of the changes caused by forces of nature some can be controlled or prevented from taking place and some cannot. For example, dams are built across natural flow of water in rivers to irrigate lands, generate power, and control floods. But many a change caused by nature such as, movement of planets, stars and galaxies, earthquakes and eruption of volcanoes are beyond the control of man. What is possible is to address the harmful effects of uncontrollable change through precautionary actions and also derive benefits from change, wherever nature allows. Change has great impact on the quality, magnitude and the direction of growth of knowledge and its utilization. In fact, large segments of change that are taking place in human affairs are the result of planned changes utilizing existing knowledge that help in the birth of new knowledge, with time and space acting as midwives.

Critical-time, Critical-space and Critical-knowledge: All human affairs and actions of nature move along time and space with certain momentum. When this momentum is disturbed by actions of human agents or by nature, to bring it back to normalcy or overcome the adverse effects of the change, if any or to achieve an intended goal often necessitates certain counter-action. The selection of time and place of execution of intended action plays a critical role in determining the outcome; which in many cases may not have severe repercussions. But, there are many situations where the choice of time and space/place of action makes all the difference between life and death, success and failure. In such cases, time and space/place take the characteristic of criticality; for example, in a delicate neurosurgical brain operation the operational time and space become critical; another example is the criticality of time element in a missile attack. In the case of a heart attack, the first one hour - it is called "golden hour" - is critical to the survival of the patient. Similar to time and space, knowledge too has a dimension of criticality. In the case of knowledge, the most difficult part is ascertaining what knowledge and information is critical to a particular action or situation and when. A special feature of knowledge and information, unlike in most other fields, is that any item of knowledge or information has the potential to become critical. For example, in the interpretation of legal texts, certain words and phrases carry critical effect. Unaware of the requisite critical knowledge, a medical man can cause the death of a patient instead of curing him.

Identification of critical-time, critical-space and critical-knowledge in any action is one of subjective assessment. Accurate identification of items and parameters that impart criticality and also their proper assessment affects the outcome of action. No action in nature or human affairs takes place until the system reaches the critical point - a volcano will not erupt until the internal dynamics of the earth below reaches the critical point. It is not that in every incident of change critical-time, critical-space and critical- knowledge are *sine qua non.* Many of the events and actions occurring in the daily world are so routine and ordinary, they do not involve critical-time, critical-space and critical knowledge. In research, in quality assessment, in cost control, in *Critical Path Method*- a management technique and in a large number of events affecting life and living, criticalness of events account for radical change.

In business, industry and in many individual human activities a change generally creates either a challenge or an opportunity to the parties concerned. Dealing with challenge or opportunity often involves application of knowledge/information. A laissez-faire culture reacts to the change on the basis of feedback, whereas an aggressive and creative individual or organization tries to change the environment for its benefit following a feed-forward approach. Whatever be the approach, knowledge/information form a critical resource. It is the strategy marked by vision and organizational culture that decides how knowledge resource is utilized to achieve the all-important competitive edge. But strategies and tactics are also functions of time and space. Having designed the right strategy based on sound knowledge is not of much use unless appropriate time/space factors are built into the execution framework

4. SECTORAL CHANGE

The word "change" taken alone means difference and is in some way related to time and space. To know and understand change beyond its fundamental characteristics of difference and time-space relationship, one has to consider the context of change. The relevant field, subject or knowledge domain with which the particular change is associated provides the context. Study of change, in a way forms a sector study. As examples, change in three sectors- science, sociology and economics are treated here.

Science: The universe is not static. Things in nature are constantly undergoing changes- small or large, slow or fast, observable or hidden. Discovering the nature of change occurring in the physical universe is the object of science. A scientific interpretation of change is that the natural world seems to be undergoing progressive non-cyclic change within which is woven countless number of cyclic processes. From cyclic changes, constant in their frequency ratios, one can measure stages of progressive change. Our time concept implies both a going-on change of the world and a presence of equivalent units of time for measuring any process of change. There is also a contrary view that the origin of time rests on the existence of causal relationship among all physical events (Schlegel, 1967). The characteristics of change in inanimate physical world differ from that of organic world, and both differ from that of human world. The theory of change in the physical sciences is to account for happenings in the physical universe with forces of nature acting as the agents of change (Meadows, 1971 p.1). Change in physical technologies are methods and designs for transferring matter, energy, and information from one state into another in pursuit of a goal or goals (Beinhocker, 2006). Within science there is a separate branch of study- "dynamic systems", whose objective is to describe how natural systems change over time.

Dynamic Systems: A basic tenet of science is that the principles of nature can be expressed in terms of mathematics and physical events can be predicted and designed with mathematical certainty. The natural world consists of different systems made of parts such as particles, atoms, molecules, planets and stars, which move around different paths governed by the equations describing motion. The mathematical study of long-term behaviour in systems that evolve in time, usually under unchanging times is named *dynamic systems* (Hasselblatt and Kotak, 2002).

The principal idea behind dynamic systems is to describe how a system changes over time. Dynamic systems involve a space, time and a time evolution law. The space part is set with structures, whose elements represent possible states of the system. The time part may take discrete or continuous form, and reversible or irreversible state; and the time evolution law, in general settings, is a rule that allow us to determine the state of the system at each moment of time *t* from its states at all previous times (Kotak and Hasselblatt, 1995). Even a continuous-time system can be made to appear like discrete-time system. The study of dynamic systems is the study of long-term asymptotic behaviour, and especially that of its qualitative aspects, which require direct methods that do not relay on prior explicit calculation of solutions. Seeking probabilistic solutions is a part of dynamic systems study, since finding the relation between determinism and probability is a central mission of dynamic systems (Hasselblatt and Kotak, 2003).

The discipline of dynamic systems evolved from classical mechanics and celestial mechanics founded largely on the works of Galileo and Newton. Later the field extended its boundary by including problems drawn from mathematics, electricity, magnetism, thermodynamics, other natural sciences and from the biological world. The phenomenon of change occurring in the world of nature is not limited to dynamic systems alone, but also includes those innumerable changes taking place as individual and independent items also form the topics of scientific enquiry. Besides the field of science, a vast portion of the world of change is accounted by human agents acting through historical, social, economic, political and other types of percepts exhibiting characteristics that are specific to them. Knowledge domain of change is very vast and touches upon every aspect of human life.

It is said that mathematics is the queen of all sciences; if it is so then statistics is the handmaiden of all sciences. Change research depends heavily on observations of the phenomena in all its facets over time. Observations and experimentation yield large amounts of data. Collection, organization, analysis and interpretation of data, which is the function of statistics, help us understand change phenomena and also predict the future course of a change.

Social Change: Social change is the significant alteration of social structures - that is of patterns of social action and interaction (Moore, 1968, p.366). No society remains static all the time. But, from the very early period of social history of man stability has not only been the social ideal but also the normal social condition. In Western societies, at least for the last three hundred years, change is accepted not only as inevitable, but also desirable (La Piere, 1965). Oriental societies, including India are no exception to the stability motto, and in fact the feudal system of societies that prevailed till recently had all the reasons to oppose change.

Process of Social Change: All socially significant changes occur through time, under the conditions prevailing at a given period of time. Special processes and relationships of the period are central to social life and that centrality manifests itself at numerous conceptual levels- from mundane to higher but basic levels of abstraction, where special processes and patterns serve as useful indicators of technological and organizational adaptation of human groups to their natural and social environment (Frisbie and Kasarda, 1988). This means that social change is a product of time, space and social- historical environment of the period represented by the prevailing state of social, political, economic and technological knowledge.

Prior to modernism (and globalization), social change appeared in two modes- revolution and reform. The mid-twentieth century saw the appearance of a third mode of change prompted by social forums and "progressive groups" acting as "pockets of resistance". The resistance came from heterogeneous groups made up of citizens organizations, ecological movements, feminist groups, human rights activists and many more (Rioufol, 2004). Invariably, the pockets of resistance mode will have an inbuilt ideological tilt or limited agendas, the success of which depends to some extent on the tactical use of information to spread their cause and influence people in favor of their cause.

Economic Change: Fundamentally economics is all about creating wealth and its distribution, and this basic truth has not changed much. What has changed is the complexity surrounding the process of creating wealth in a competitive world, particularly due to the severe impact of rapidly changing technological and social environment and changing value systems. Industrialization is seen as the key process of creating wealth and industrialization is generally equated with progress or development, particularly in the context of developing countries. Bert Hoselitz observes that economic development, especially if it involves industrialization, implies "a rapid, and in a sense, revolutionary process which, if it is to take root in a society, must penetrate widely and deeply and hence affects social structural and cultural facets of a society. In other words, economic development consists not merely in a change of production techniques, but also, in the last resort, in a reorientation of social norms and values" (Hoselitz, 1995).

Information: *A Key Factor in Development:* Development and developmental transformation of society involve a change in the way people think and act and the societies function - a change in norms, expectations, and institutions. In this new interpretation of development, change is not only accepted but also promoted and routinized. In the knowledge-based economics it is ultimately the information and knowledge of one's own resources, institutions, social and economic organizations, and reforms that will form the engines of development. Any asymmetry in information leads to an equilibrium in which resources are less efficiently allocated. Information flow in the system has a bearing on development. A weak information flow is both due to and results in poor institutional arrangements. Because information is imperfect in developing countries including India, markets work imperfectly. Any under investment in the production and dissemination of knowledge, in the transfer and adaptation of new technology will retard the process of developmental transformation. It is for the governments of developing countries to remove the existing bottlenecks, namely- lack of information, lack of a way to convert information into knowledge, lack of capacity to analyze and lack of capacity to policy design (Lakshmanasamy, 2003).

5. REVOLUTIONARY CHANGE

Change works in different modes- gradual, abrupt, small-scale, large-scale, visible, hidden, discrete, continuous, cyclic, revolutionary and many more, whose measure is relative and often subjective. As against revolutionary change is evolutionary change, where things happen gradually under the influence of evolutionary forces created by nature as well as man. Creation of knowledge has followed both evolutionary and revolutionary styles. Because of its pervasive nature and extreme impact, revolutionary change has been the subject of many studies. Revolutionary change has enormous impact on the creation of knowledge.

The theoretical base of a revolution is always the creation of a few extraordinary minds supported by a small number of foundational knowledge texts. In the physical science it is the works of Galileo Galilee and Sir Isaac Newton on mechanics, Max Plank on quantum physics, Albert Einstein on relativity; in the biological science decoding of DNA structure by James D. Watson and Francis Crick, and in political science Karl Marx on capitalism are standard examples of such texts. Theoretical works, always small in number, become the intellectual foundation of a revolution. Once a revolution finds its first acceptance at least by a few, who matter, there will be a rush of further research, and the knowledge in that field moves forward. It is followed by a mushroom like growth of knowledge in the particular field attracting several participants from the same and related fields of study contributing and sustaining the revolution. The development of knowledge in the new area will continue until another revolution in some other field begins attracting attention or the existing paradigm has exhausted its potential for growth or is replaced by a new paradigm.

Some criticism of and opposition to any revolution and its rationale, at least in the beginning, is normal, given the intellectual and psychological traits of man. Hence, the repository of knowledge on revolution will also comprise of opposing theories. Following sectoral approach, revolutionary change representing three knowledge domains—natural science, sociology and economics are considered here.

Scientific revolutions are "non-cumulative developmental episodes in which an older paradigm is replaced in whole or in part by an incompatible new one..." (Khun, 970, p.92). A paradigm represents the entire constellation of beliefs, values, techniques, laws, theories, instrumentation etc. shared by the members of a given scientific community. Khun reasons out that scientific revolutions occur when an existing paradigm cease to function adequately in the exploration of an aspect of nature to which that paradigm itself had previously led the way. A scientific revolution changes our world-view of science. Such revolutions impact on the world of scientific knowledge and gives a new direction of growth and contributes towards knowledge revolution.

Social revolutions are rapid and their impact is pervasive to the whole society affecting its state and class structure in fundamental ways. It is a bottom up phenomena caused by the oppressed and deprived strata of society. Social revolutions combine two coincidences of social structural change with class upheaval and the coincidence of political and social transformation. A unique feature of social revolutions is that the basic changes in social and in political structure occur together in a mutually reinforcing fashion with class struggle playing a predominant role (Skocpol, 1979). Social revolutions in India has an additional dimension of cast and in most Islamic societies that of religion.. The cause of all social revolutions may be traced to large scale social and power imbalances in the structure of a society caused by factors such as race, language, gender, education and sharing of power. A society's inability or unwillingness to share equally educational (particularly professional and job-oriented), economic and political opportunities with the backward and discriminated sections of society constitutes the most important cause of social revolutions. In other words, the main cause of social upheaval may be identified with the distribution of social, political and material knowledge in society.

Land, labour, capital and organization are the four factors of production, which go into creation of wealth. Any large-scale rapid change in the mode of use of any of these factors of production in an economy results in an economic revolution. Though not expressed explicitly, knowledge and information are included under organization, and they act decisively in economic revolution. .

Information Revolution : When a change radically alters an existing order of things and replaces it by a new order that is incompatible with the earlier is termed a revolution. In politics, the change relates to the system of ruling, in sociology it is the social and cultural order and in science it is the scientific order constituting a paradigm. The revolution may be total or affecting only a major segment of the existing order. Information too has seen a few revolutions. The causal agent of the first information revolution was the invention of spoken language, which was followed by a supplementary revolution caused by the invention of writing. The world of information had to wait for a couple of millenniums to see the next revolution brought about by the invention of printing. The most recent and all pervasive information revolution is only two decades old and is caused by information technology- coming together of computer and communication technologies which created internet, the World Wide Web and the mobile phone. Cybernetics and artificial intelligence have played an important role in the information revolution. The impact of information revolution is clearly seen in e-governance and in the "New Economy". In the new economy the myriad of wealth-creating systems is nothing else but communication devices that do not directly handle matter, but instead facilitate the movements of bits of information in *cyberspace* and not place (Kefalas, 2003, p.377). It seems another information revolution is not too far off.

Unlike most other types of revolutions, information revolutions are the results of technological inventions, such as printing and the internet and their major effects have been on the instant spread of knowledge, its intensive use and raising of human spirit. Any revolution in any of the major disciplines impacts on the growth and application of knowledge.

6. KNOWLEDGE AND CHANGE

Change is a universal phenomenon and knowledge is a human phenomenon. Change and knowledge are closely inter-linked, and both exist and operate in a time and space enclosure. While change is a phenomenon of action, knowledge is a phenomenon of awareness or representation. Change is a prime source of knowledge, and knowledge when applied under right conditions leads to change. Occurrence of change and phenomenon of knowledge are bound to a particular activity or field. Thus we have political change, economic change, change in colour, age and knowledge of physics, of heredity, history, management, sports, taboos and so on.

To understand the impact of change on knowledge one needs to examine: a) the nature of change and its dynamics, b) the knowledge domain pertaining to the change and c) the cognitive working mechanism of the brain. Examination of the knowledge research methodology, relationship with other knowledge domains and areas of application of its findings. Nether science nor philosophy have so far been able to fully decode the mental process and more specifically the process of how sense input is actually transformed into awareness. Knowledge is considered by many to exist in two forms- tacit knowledge formed and stored in human meory and information, the external form of knowledge. The problem of awareness raises several questions for which we do not have definite answers yet. Some of the questions are: a) Does knowledge creation process involve change. If items of thought constituting a concept of knowledge exist independently and continue to do so then the change becomes only an integrating process; b) How an existing item of knowledge changes into new knowledge over time and space? c) What happens to the original item of knowledge that has given place to the new item of knowledge? d) Is the pre-change unit of knowledge destroyed in the change process or still retained in memory? Since one can recall and remember an item of knowledge in its pre-change state, it is reasonable to conclude that no destruction takes place. Regarding information there are no such problems. The pre-change state information continues to exist as long as it is recorded and stored either in an oral form or in a physical medium. If pre-state change events and phenomena enable one to interpret and draw useful conclusions, then such a knowledge becomes a part of historical process.

Individuals and Change : Every human life is a string of changes occurring from the stage of conception till death within the structure of time and space flow. The string of changes is made-up of several categories such as-physical organic, psychological, religious, social, economic, material and may others. Change appears in two forms: changes that are common to the entire human species and those that are unique to an individual. Examples of the former are ageing, feelings of pain and pleasure; and examples for the latter are quality and intensity of pain and pleasure felt, and one's degree of understanding a given situation. The environment of change is made-up of factors dictated by nature and the ones created by man in the form of social, cultural, economic and other practices. The process of socialization is intended to equip an individual to face the effects of change. Experience, education, organization and knowledge are among the main actors that prepare an individual to cope-up with the changes and also effect changes to achieve desired goals in life.

Experience : Experience, according to dictionary meaning (relevant to this topic) is something personally undergone, or lived through; direct observation of or participation in events; the act or process of perceiving; knowledge, skill or practice derived from direct observation of or practical participation in events; practical wisdom resulting from what one has encountered, undergone, or lived through (Webster's, 1993). Our understanding the reality of a thing or event and formulating our response to it, if called for, is directly influenced by experience. When confronted with a change, our mind enables us to compare it with our previous experiences and draw suitable conclusions. A major portion of change affecting individuals is accounted by the relationships the individual has with other individuals, groups and institutions. Cooperation, conflict, support, rights and responsibilities flow from the relationships depending on the type of relationship. Assessment of the nature and effects of change combined with knowledge form a critical input for devising our response to a change. The act of human perception of change involves an inter-play of context and situation, in which experience plays an active role. "Contexts are frameworks of meaning, and situations are the dynamic environments within which interpretive processes unfold, become ratified, change and solidify" (Cool, 2002, p.8). Contexts and situations are relational factors that participate in the process of perceiving reality and in the formation of one's information-seeking behaviour. Study of information-seeking behaviour has practical imprecations for information science. Our perception of a change or situation and the formation of our response to the change is a part reflective act of mind based on experience, human organism (i.e. an individuals personality composed by physiological, psychological and other mental abilities) and knowledge. The reflective phenomena is an ongoing process of the mind.

Reflectivity : Reflectivity, according to Anthony Giddens, a renowned sociologist, refers to the reflexive monitoring of action intrinsic to all human activity. In modern social life social practices are constantly examined and re-formed in the light of incoming information about those very practices, thus constitutively altering their character (Giddens, 1990, 1991). The role of reflectivity in the formation of our perception, and in the formulation of our response to change is negligible in changes happening in the natural physical world not involving human actors as participants. Where human actors are participants in the acts of change then in the formation of our knowledge about the change "the apprehension of meaning will be an act of the *whole* personality including the specifically social sector of the mind; indeed, it is not absurd to claim that the specifically social sector of the mind will have a larger say in the matter than either the sensual apparatus or the formal intellect" (Stark, 1958, p.15).

Initiation to Knowledge World : Growth in organisms is a process of change. From the time of conception of a child to its birth, growth, decline and death are all different stages of a change process- in other words, an aging process. As a child grows up its behaviour formation, recognition of objects in the environment and acquiring knowledge of the external world constitute a part of temporal phenomena. Physical growth and mental growth are interrelated. A new born baby's cry for feed or attention is an instinctive act, where as a toddler's mumbling for food or attention is linked to awareness process involving perception and language. The stage of physical change or age tells when the brain is ready for schooling, the range and depth of curriculum it can process (part of socialization process). The chronological stage of biological and mental changes are universal, but the rate of change varies from person to person. The study of age related mental changes in humans form a part of developmental psychology, cognitive psychology and educational theories. The effects of time, space/ place on change involving human agents are influenced by cultural and geographic factors. Cognitive aging relates mental abilities to age. Measure of variability in speed of performance serves as an indicator of cognitive aging (Fultsch, 2005). Time serves as a standard in measuring performance of time dependent changes.

7. CLOSURE

Change has a past, a present and a future and so is knowledge. We know (though not fully) how change has affected man in the past , how it is affecting in the present. How it is going to shape the future of mankind remains a matter of conjecture. In today's world, changes are occurring so fast and their effects are so widespread and intense it is difficult for any one to predict precisely what the future holds for humanity. However, the vision of the future drawn by Rifkin in the context of information seems within the realm of reality. He sees that "in our nanosecond culture everything changes so fast that it is necessary to construct a cosmology in which change itself is honored as the only timeless truth. By reinterpreting nature as the evolution of information, humanity achieves this end. Nature is no longer seen as a set of restrains, but rather as process of 'creative advance'. Knowledge gathering is now information gathering, and information gathering is the processing of changing conditions over time. With this linguistic metamorphosis, the door is opened to a thorough reinterpretation of existence as pure process devoid of any kind of ultimate, unchanging frame of reference" (Rifkin, 1998, p.220).

8. REFERENCES

1. Beinhocker, Eric D. The Origin of Wealth. Boston, Harvard University Press, 2006.
2. Cool, Collen. The Concept of situation in information Science. *Annual Review of Information Science and Technology*, 35: 5-42, 2002. P.8.
3. Frisbie, W. Parker and Kasarda, John D. Special Process. Pp. 629-666. In Smelser, Neil J. Ed.

Handbook of Sociology. Newburg Park (Calif.), Sage Publications, 1988.

4. Fultsch, David F. et al. Inconsistency in Response Time as an Indicator of Cognitive Aging. Pp. 33-58. In Duncan, John; Phillips, Louise and McLeod, Peter. Eds. Measuring the Mind: Speed, Control, and Age. Oxford, Oxford University Press, 2005.
5. Giddens, Anthony. The Consequences of Modernity. Stanford (Calif.), Stanford University Press, 1990.
6. Giddens, Anthony, Modernity and Self-Identity. Stanford (Calif.), Stanford University Press, 1991.
7. Hasselblatt, B. and Kotak, A. Handbook of Dynamical Systems. Vol. 1A. Amsterdam, Elsevier, 2002.
8. Hoselitz, Bert F. Non-Economic Barriers to Economic Development. Pp.17-27. In Corbridge, Stuart. Ed. Development Studies: A Reader. London, Arnold, 1995.
9. Kefalas, Asterios G. Cybernetics. In Bidgoli, Hossein. Ed.
10. Encyclopaedia of Information Systems. Vol. 1. Pp. 365-378. San Diego (Calif.), Academic Press, 2003.
11. Kotak, Anatole and Hasselblatt, Boris. Introduction to the Modern Theory of Dynamical Systems. Cambridge (U.K.), Cambridge University Press, 1995.
12. Khun, Thomas S. The Structure of Scientific Revolutions, Ed.2. Chicago, University of Chicago Press, 1970.
13. La Piere, Richard T. Social Change. Tokyo, McGraw-Hill, 1965. (International Student Edition).
14. Lakshmanasamy, T. New Information, new institutions and economic development. *The Asian Economic Review* 45: 425-439, Dec. 2003.
15. Meadows, Paul. The Many Faces of Change: Explorations in the Theory of Social Change. Cambridge (Mass.), Schenkman, 1971. P.1.
16. Moore, Wilbert E. Social Change. In Sills, David L. Ed. International Encyclopaedia of the Social

Sciences, Vol. 14. Pp. 365-375. The Macmillan and The Free Press, 1968.

17. Rifkin, Jeremy. The Biotech Century: Harnessing the Gene. New York, Jeremy P. Tarcher (Putnam), 1998.
18. Rioufol, Veronique. Approaches to Social Change in Social Forums: Snapshots of Recompositions in Progress. *International Social Science Journal* 56: 551-563, Dec. 2004.
19. Schlegel, Richard. Time and Physical Process, Pp. 37-48. In Moore, Wilbert E. and Cook, Robert M. Readings on Social Change. Engelwood Cliffs (NJ.), Prentice-Hall, 1967.
20. Skocpol, Theda. States and Social Revolutions: A Comparative Analysis of France, Russia and China. Cambridge (U.K.), Cambridge University Press, 1979.
21. Stark, W. The Sociology of Knowledge: An Essay in Aid of a Deeper Understanding of the History of Ideas. London, Routledge & Kegan Paul, 1958. (Reprint 1971). P.15.
22. Webster's Third New International Dictionary of the English Language. Unabridged. Cologne, Konemann Verlagsgesellschaft, 1993.

19

GHANA RAGA PANCHARATNA KRITIS OF SRI TYAGARAJA: A MODEL OF FUSION OF LYRICS, MUSIC AND RHYTHM: AN ANALYTICAL STUDY

T.N. Rajan[1]

Describes the characteristic features of the Panchratna Kiritis of Sri Tyagaraja, which are as hailed as his outstanding compositions, as a new model of fusion of lyrics, music and rhythm. Explains the motivations for composing these tana varna kritis, in svara-sahritya mode and the choice to set them in the Ghana ragas. Briefly highlights the salient features of the five kritis of Nata, Gowla, Arabhi, Varali and Sri ragams.

1. INTRODUCTION

Musical forms acquired a central place in classical carnatic music with the advent of Sri Tyagaraja (1767-1847), which contributed to its development very

1 C-343, East-end Apts. Mayurvihar Ph. 1 Ext. Delhi 110 096; Ph.011-22742362

substantially and significantly. During the time of Sri Tyagaraja and earlier, musical compositions were heavy and elaborate with emphasis on manodharma singita (imaginative and improvised music). Their presentations lasted for hours or even days. However, these forms had to change with the passage of time to more concretized and condensed simpler forms. Padams, kirtanas, kritis and such others were the emerging new forms. These forms appealing both to the head and heart, made a tremendous impact on the rasikas (listeners). These simpler forms, composed with lyrical poetic beauty, capturing effectively and portraying the nuances of a raga, structured in a simple rhythmic pattern, rendered in medium tempo, introduced a new trend in the composition of musical forms. Scholars opine that these new musical forms, have preserved our music for us today saving the extensive art being lost to us by its prodigiousness. Tyagaraja stands foremost with his marvelous contributions in this renaissance.

Raghavan has very vividly and picturesquely portrayed the volume and variety of the productions of Sri Tyagaraja, their sweeping breadth, depth and versatility in Spiritual heritage of Tyagaraja. He writes: Tyagaraja's "powerful genius comprehended the several and varied excellences of all, the early masters, the giants that went before him, and his brilliant contemporaries. In sheer volume of output, he essays in the direction of Purandaradasa and Kshetragna; in devotion, religious fervour, reformatory zeal and spiritual realization, his songs approach those of Purandaradasa; when we think of him singing in anguish to his Rama, we find in him a second Ramdas of Bhadrachala; in his lyrical moods, he takes a page off Kshetragna; in his *Pancharatnas* and some of his heavier compositions, he treads the path of the earlier *Prabandha-karas* and later *Varna-karas*; turning out pieces now and then in the language of the gods, he seems to beckon his contemporary Dikshitar; when he sings of Mother Tripurasundari, it appears as if Syama Sastri of Tanjore was soujourning at Tiruvotriyur; and he could sustain himself through the task of a dramatic composition like Narayana Tirtha or Merattur Venkatarama Bhagavatar and pay his homage to a *sampradaya* sanctified by Jayadeva."

2. PANCHARATNA KRITIS (FIVE GEMS)

Among the hundreds of kritis and kirtanas of Sri Tyagaraja, the reputed Pancharanta kritis, sung in groups at his aradana festivals all over the world, are everlasting monuments of his creative genius. They are composed in the Ghana ragas Nata, Gaula, Arabhi, Varali and Sri, all of them set to Adi Talam. These matchless pieces are a class by themselves. "There is nothing to surpass them from the point of view of richness of musical conception or the flowing character of their sahitya (lyrics). His talent for conceiving melodies of variegated beauty, inter-woven with phrases of sparkling designs is seen clearly in these pieces." (Sambamorthy: Great Masters, p.38).

In the succeeding sections, an analysis is made of the characteristic features of these five gems to highlight their excellence and the fine fusion of lyrics (sahitya), music (sangita) and rhythm (laya).

The compositions of Tyagaraja are generally studied in three periods. In the first thirty years of his life, most of his compositions were devotional (divyanama) kirtanas. During the next thirty years, he reached exalting heights both in music and spiritual attainments. It was during this period of his life, the panchratna kritis were composed. In the third period, he was a fully realized soul, during which some of his art music forms of outstanding merits were composed.

3. MOTIVATIONS FOR A NEW VARIETY

It is said that Sri Tyagaraja was motivated to compose these unique set of kritis for two reasons. The contemporary musicians of lesser caliber being familiar only with the heavy music of the times could not measure up to the requisite level of competence to appreciate the brilliant new varieties of compositions of Sri Tyagaraja. Out of jealousy and peevishness they made flippant remarks that Sri Tyagaraja had composed only light verse music without any depth. Sri Tyagaraja might have been inclined to ignore these observations of his contemporaries; nonetheless, it was sufficient inducement for him to come out with some extraordinary pieces to offset these criticisms. The second reason was that some of his own disciples expressed a wish that their guru should compose kritis, which would help them to practice and advance their musical skills further. Responding to these, Sri Tyagaraja conceived the pancharatna kritis, which have no parallel either before him or after. Not only the new set of kritis fulfilled the needs of his disciples, noteworthy for their lyrical beauty and music, but they also took the critics of the time by storm.

4. CHOICE OF GHANA RAGAS

Sri Tyagaraja chose the Ghana ragas for his new model of pancharatna kritis for their intrinsic value for practice and also for their special spiritual significance. There was the conviction that Vedic samhitas and sangita samparadaya were ways for spiritual salvation. In fact, sangita was considered as an upa Veda.

Ghanam is a method of practice to recite Vedic chanting, devised by Vedic acharyas, (ganapatigals) to render them with the correct intonation and also to understand and remember their meanings. Similar to this chanting practice, tanam, is a method of learning for students of music to grasp the raga nuances, and to understand the lyrical contents of compositions. In tanams, raga expositions are elaborated through syllables in a rhythmic pattern using the expression 'Anantam Tvam'. This is a branch of manodharma sangita of creative music. This is usually presented in modern music concerts in Ragam, Tanam and Pallavi (RTP). Tanams follow after raga alapana (elaborate and extensive exposition of the chosen raga). Pallavi stands for Pada Laya Vinyasam, a highly organized manodharma sangita set to intricate talas and also rendering them in different tempos.

Explaining the term 'tanam', Nageswara Rao and John Barlow, noted musicologists, say, "The word Tanam is related to the Sanskrit 'Anantam Tvam' meaning 'endless thou art'. The endlessness reflects that manner of reciting a chant, which involves the breaking of a text (Anantam Tvam) into syllables and the subsequent reordering of them in all combinations, both as a means of obtaining mastery over the sound system of the chant and of acquiring insight into the truths behind the text. This technique is also known as Ghanam which gives a second related meaning to this term." (Sadagopan, p.29-30)

Ghana ragas are those whose melodic individuality is well revealed through tana style of exposition. Nata, Gaula, Arabhi, Varali and Sri are the best examples of such ragas, which are eminently suitable for tanams.

In veena the tana style of playing and Gamaka prayogas (graces which embellish the beauty of svaras) are very special. Sri Tyagaraja was an expert vainika also. He used to practice kritis in the tana style. With this additional skill, he preferred the tana style of composing for his panchratnas. Therefore Sri Tyagaraja chose deliberately these Ghana ragas to compose the panchratana kritis to aid his students to advance in their knowledge and skills in practical music. However, high degree of technical skill is required to render them.

Besides these reasons for selecting the Ghana ragas for the pancharatna kritis, a technical aspect, viz. the subtle relationhip of the rishaba svaras that are seen in these five ragas is another reason. To quote again Nageswara Rao and John Barlow to explain this technical point, "The five ragas are in a state of equilibrium as suggested by the following scheme:

1	NATA	3	ARABHI
	|		|
	|	4	VARALI
2	GAULA		|
		5	SRI

The balance pivots around the changing character of the note Rishaba (Ri) (2nd degree of the scale i.e. Chatusruti Rishaba). Thus the Ri of Nata is high (sharp) pointing and striving upwards (to highlight the aesthetic beauty of the raga), while the Low (flat) Ri of Gaula falls back to the tonic (Sadjam, the first degree of Sa, identified as Guala Ri to indicate its uniqueness). Arabhi balances the ascension and depression with its median Ri (natural Chatusruti Ri). The Ri of Varali lies in the shadow of more powerful Ga (third degree). It is a point lightly touched upon in the fall from that flat Ga. Sri raga raises the Ri to its natural position and presents it in its simplest, purest form, an unvaried tone freed now from the curves and implied directionality which it carried in previous Ragas. This tonal purity is the melody Correlate of Silence, as the Silence resolves the rhythmic movement, so the natural, un-ornamental Ri resolves in stillness the striving of the tonal movement." (Sadagopan, p. 30)

5. Unique Features of the Pancharatnas

Some unique features of the panchratnas, which distinguish them from all the other compositions of Sri Tyagaraja are:

- The kritis are composed in tana varna form. However they are distinctively different from the conventional tana varnas. (The characteristic features of Tana varnas are explained in the Notes Section).
- The charanams of these kritis are composed in svara-sahitya pattern i.e. the lyrics are spelled out in svara notation which gives a standardized structural form, easy and attractive to render. Therefore they tend to be appropriate for group singing. It is to be noted here that entirely due to this particular characteristic feature, the original version of the compositions, as conceived by the composer, has been preserved without any improvisation, distortion or changes.
- Each of the kritis has a theme. The raga bhavas of the kritis express the emotional contents of lyrics exquisitely, establishing a fusion of the lyrics and music. These are monumental examples of how such feelings like rapture, self-introspection, prudence, admiration, sustained joy and humility could be delineated with telling effect. These kritis also reveal Sri Tyagaraja's depth of learning and gifts in Sanskrit and Telugu.
- Just as the lyrics and music are fused in a masterly manner, the rhythmic aspects are striking and match equally the quality of the lyrics and music. As the kritis are in svara -sahitya pattern, they are amenable for depth analysis and research, particularly, by percussionists. As is the normal practice of composing tana varnas with combinations of 3, 4, 5, 7, 9 svaras for every cycle of the tala, Sri Tyagaraja has composed these varna-mode kritis in his own inimitable style. The way in which he has handled this technique is unique, brilliant and majestic.

- All the kritis are in Adi Tala i.e. chatusra laghu triputa tala. Four svaras for each of the eight counts of the Adi tala cycle. This structuring of the rhythm gives a racy style, which is not only beautifully modulated but also highly attractive. The Adi tala provides an ideal length in each cycle for svara grouping.
- The kritis are set to madhyama kala (middle tempo), which has a striking effect on the listener, except the kriti in Varali which is in vilamba kala (slow tempo) which is befitting the theme of the kriti describing the Rupa Mahima of Sri Rama. For each kriti, there is a unique tempo (kala pramana) and should be adhered to very strictly; if not the beauty of the structure would be lost. Again, as a tana varna permits singing them in all the tree tempos, these kritis cannot be sung in all the three tempos (trikalas); if attempted, the entire kriti will get totally distorted.
- The sarva laghu (modular structure of the tala) i.e. the rhythmic movement of the rendering of the kritis, is captivating. The pauses provided at appropriate places in the kritis and the sarva laghu flow bear ample evidence to the composer's divine gift.
- The starting points of the kritis vary in each one of them, giving them further aesthetic beauty. Kritis in Nata, Gowla and Arabhi start with the first beat of the tala, the varali kriti starts after the beat (half edam), and the Sri Raga kriti starts with the first finger counting of the tala.
- The use of Janata svaras, the Vadi-samvadi svaras, Svara combinations, range of stayis (Octaves) are aptly used in all the kritis with remarkable effect.

The beauty is that all these appear so simple that even a

lay listener can fully enjoy them, without any need whatsoever, to understand their intricacies.

In the next section, a very brief description of the highlights of each Kriti is given to signify their special and salient features.

To give a few general aspects of the kritis, Tyagaraja specialists observe that the Arabhi kriti was the first to be composed which reflects fully the conventional varna pattern. It was followed by Sri Raga, then the Gaula and Nata, and finally the Varali kritis. The four other kritis considerably vary from the varna pattern.

Conventionally, Jagadhanandaka starts the group singing, followed by Dudugukala, Sadinchene, Kanakaruchra respectively, ending with Endaromahanubhavulu.

Only the charanas are sung with svaras, followed by sahitya, except the last charana in all the kritis, with the exception of Jagadhanandaka

5.1. Jagadhananda karaka in Nata

To reiterate, this kriti is sung first in group singing. The lyrics are in Sanskrit and describe the glories of Lord Sri Rama. It is considered a veritable Ashtottara of 108 attributes of Sri Rama, composed in a rapturous mood in singing the great qualities of the composer's Ishta Devata. The rishaba, moving upwards, captures the rapturous mood, embellishing the kriti admirably.

The kriti has ten charanas, of which seven were composed first and the last three were added subsequently carrying the name (mudra) of the composer in all of them.

The sahitya and the svara combinations are superbly fused, demonstrating the admirable skill of the composer. For example, in the 9th charana, the flight from madyama (middle octave) 'Sa' to tara (Upper octave) 'Sa' with a sweeping graceful melody is a grand echo of the sound effect, to be in tune with spiritual concept of *Omkara.* In fact, the emotional admiration of the Lord with fascinating music invests this composition with a beauty, charm and great dignity.

The rhythmic structure of this kriti is exquisitely fused with both the lyrics and music. The majestic sarva laghu style of the kriti going hand-in-hand with the rhythm, with its medium tempo reflects the excellence of the kriti.

5.2. Dudugala in Gaula

This kriti, sung second in group singing, is in contrast with the rapturous mood of Jadadhanandakaraka. It appears it was composed in a state of depressed and desolate mood of the composer, pained by human failings all around. The composer attributes all these human failings to himself and pleads with the Lord if he would pardon him for all these and save him from disgrace. This is in conformity with the tradition of bhaktas (ardent devotees) who always chide themselves for the devilish behaviour of human beings and pray to save them from disaster. Sadagopan in his book, points out such outpourings by saiva nayanmars, vsishnava alvars and others.

In keeping with the depressed mood of the composer, the kriti is in Gaula whose Rishaba (Ri) vividly reflects the depressing mood. The Rishabha always descends to the adara shadja, identifying as the exclusive Gaula Ri, of this raga.

The kriti has ten charanas and the last one is sung without the svaras.

The svara combinations, sarva laghu and other features of the structure are as appealing as the others.

5.3. Sadinschene in Arabhi

The Arabhi kriti recaptures the general devotional mood of the composer set to the vigour of the raga. The Arabhi

Rishabha (Ri) is lively and the gamakas of the svara are beautiful and blends dexterously with the other svaras, both in the ascending and descending scale. Arabhi with melodic sharp svaras of the ascending and descending scale and with colorful gamaka prayogas, has an instant appeal. It depicts valour, heroism and dynamism.

The theme of this kriti is Ninda stuthi, chiding Lord Krishna with double standards in His behaviour. 'Samayaniki tagumata ladane' (expressing words that suits the occasion) starts the charana, indicting Lord Krishna reverentially for flouting the standards he himself had set for human behaviour. But when in the later charanas, he looks at Lord Krishna as Lord Rama, he showers praises on both for their grace for their devotees.

The kriti is composed typically in the tanavarna mode and moves beautifully with all the svara combinations and permutations, fusing lyrics and music with the rhythm.

5.4. Kanakana Ruchira in Varali

This kriti is in vilamba kala (slow tempo), describing in detail the grandeur of Lord Rama's personality and qualities. Sri Tyagaraja perceives Sri Rama as a child, as Kausalya and Dasaratha would fondle the Child Rama, as a young prince, as a romantic youth as Sita would see him and as a benevolent Chakrvarthi.

Varali in its leisurely gamakas eminently fits with the theme of the kriti, starting with an offbeat of the Adi Tala. The slow tempo adds to the beauty of the kriti. As noted earlier the Rishabha (Ri) beautifully reaches the higher flat ghandhara and gives a pleasing effect.

The other features of the rhythmic structure of the kriti are well delineated with the typical sarva laghu and svara combinations, all in the slow tempo.

5.5. Endaromahanobhavulu in Sri Raga

In this kriti Sri Tyagaraja pays his homage to great personalities who are revered not only for their musical and spiritual accomplishments but also for their greatness in every sense of the word.

The Sri Raga aptly fits the theme. The raga personifies luster, radiance, splendour, glory, beauty, grace and wealth. It stands for all that is sweet, noble, culture and refinement.

The Rishbaha (Ri) of Sri Raga is steady without any oscillation, symbolizing the concept of absolute silence. As observed by Raghavendra Rao and John Barlow, "Sri Ragam raises the Rishabham again from the shadow of the powerful Ghandharam, where it rested in the case of Varali. The Rishabham of Sri Ragam ascends to its natural position and is present in its simplest, purest form, an unvaried tone freed from the curves and the implied directionality, which it carries in Nattai, Gowla, Arabhi and Varali. This total purity is the melodic correlate of the silence of Nirvikalpa Samadhi and the Anandam that is associated with it." (Sadagopan, 259p).

The rhythmic beauty is as set as in all the other four kritis with all the grandeur and beauty.

6. SUMMARY

To recapitulate the main features of the Pancharanta kritis:

The five gems are set to Ghana ragas Nata, Gaula, Arabg, Varali and Sri, which form a group, with their intrinsic relationship of Rishabha.

The kritis are set in Tana Varna mode, which has a special significance both from the point of practice and also for its spiritual approach.

The kritis are composed in svara-sahitya pattern, which

is unique and gives a fine effect in group singing.

The rhythmic structure of the kritis is simple but highly effective, blending beautifully with the lyrics and music

In conclusion, the primary purpose of this rather cursory write-up is to provide some background information to interested listeners of the pancharatna kritis. This background may possibly enhance their enjoyment and appreciation of the five gems when they happen to them.

There are many audiocassettes and CDs, recording the rendering of the pancharatna kritis by front line artists. The recordings of Sri Balamurali Krishna are excellent, particularly, for the best rendering of the Telugu compositions, in terms of correct pronunciation of the text and also apt and appropriate breaking of words and phrases, helping listeners, to understand and appreciate the lyrics.

The recordings of Sri Maharajapuram Santhanam can be listened to for the conventional style (sampradaya) he presents pleasingly.

7. NOTES

Varna (Extracts from Sambamurthy: South Indian Music, p.128-127)

Varnas arc scholarly compositions. They are elaborate melodies replete with raga bhava. A Varna contains within it not only the nuances of a raga but also several rare and special svara combinations.

The sahitya (lyrics) of a varna is comparatively short and insignificant and may relate to either bhakti (devotion) or sringara (love) or it may be in praise of a patron or be descriptive of the particular varna.

It requires great skill, technical capacity, creative faculty of a high order and detailed knowledge of the lakshana of ragas to compose varnas. Composers of varnas are very few as against hundreds of composers of kritis and kirtanas. The number of all varnas does not exceed a few hundreds, as compared to thousands of kritis, kirtanas and other forms.

The practice of varnas considerably helps learners in the artistic, polished and stylish rendering of them. The paucity of words and the consequent profusion of vowels in the sahitya of the varnas and their even distribution make them ideal pieces for the training of the voice.

The practice of tanavarnas in three tempos (kalas) strengthen the laya jnanam. (Knowledge of rhythm)

8. REFERENCES

1. Chinna Satyanarayana, N. A Monograph on Sri Tyagaraja Swamy's Ghana Raga Panchratna Keerthanas; a detailed commentary on the literary and musical excellence of Pancharatna compositions. Secunderabad, The Author, 1995. 137p.
2. Raghavan, V: An introductory theses—Tyagaraja, *in* The Spiritual Heritage of Tyagaraja by C. Ramanujachari. Chennai, Sri Ramakrishna Mission Students' HOME, 1957. 206p.
3. Raghavan, V: Tyagaraja. New Delhi, Sahitya Akademi, 1983. (Makers of India Series). 78p.
4. Sadagopan, V: Sri Satguruvin Ghana Raga Pancharatna kritigal. (Tamil). Madras, the Author, 1991. 336p.
5. Sambamurthy, P: Great Masters. Book II Tyagaraja. 2nd ed enlarged and revised. Madras, the Indian Music Publishing House, 1970. 364p. Appendix.
6. Sambamurthy, P: South Indian Music Book 3. 10th ed. Madras, the Indian Music Publishing House, 1994. 472p.
7. Tara Balagopal: Pancha Ratna Kritis of Saint Tyagaraja. New Delhi, Harman Publishing House, 1998. 174p.

यो नित्यमच्युत पदाम्बुज युग्म रुक्मा
व्यामोहतस्तदितराणि त्रणाय मेने
अस्मद्गुरोर्भगवतोस्स्स दयैक सिंधो
श्री पार्थसारथस्य्य चरणं शरणं प्रपद्यो

... quote provided by Dr. M. A. Gopinath

20

THE ASSIDUOUS *MAMA* AS KNOWN TO RANGANATHAN YOGESHWAR

R. Yogeshwar[1]

Prof. S. Parthasarathy completed "four score and ten" years of life in 2007. This Festschrift has been brought out by his many friends as a sign of their appreciation of the person and his contributions to the profession of Library and Information Science. I am a non-professional, with only the inevitable exposure to the profession as the son of S. R. Ranganathan.

When Prof. K. S. Raghavan invited me to write an article for the Festschrift, I felt diffident. Upon reflection, by the fact that I had known him as a private person longer than most of the others, I decided to give it a try.

To be born as the first (and only) child of a father about to turn 40, was quite an event. My father's first wife had died in 1928, childless. His friends and colleagues had "bulldozed" him to marry a second time - my mother Vangal Lakshmana Sarada in 1929.

1 Retired industrial consultant, **Contact**. 39 rue deL'Ecole, L-9184, Schrondweiler (Grand Duchy) Luxembourg. E-mail: chriyog@pt.lu

By the time I was 3 or 4 and could assess the environment, it became obvious that I was not "an only child", nor my mother his second wife, but the third! Normally, an only child would become "the" important focus in the family. There were many others who got a lot of attention from my father, like his nephews and nieces, particularly when they came to live with us from time to time. But they had not been a constant or serious competition.

Matters were very different when it came to his "second" wife and the family, which came along with her to take centre stage at our home. Her name evolved from "Library" through "Librarianship" and "Library Movement" to "Library Science". This remained so till my father died in 1972. The children that she produced through father have been numerous and non-human: Five Laws of Library Science, et al.

This wife had also brought along a large number of human persons of her family. They became my "uncles", "cousins", etc. One such was a young man – S. Parthasarathy. He used to be at our home in Sami Pillai Street almost every morning, working in the office room upstairs, while I was just waking up in the hall adjacent.

When I joined primary school in the later 1930s and had started to learn writing, I was impressed by the neat and precisc script of Parthasarathy Mama. It is an asset when writing classification numbers and catalogue entries, as well as in engineering drafting (which I did later in life).

Parthasarathy Mama was probably pushed into the Library field by Alagu Mama. M. O Alasingarachari was one of the earliest members of the Madras Library Association, founded in 1928. Apart from its main object of promoting Library Movement, it also started the first Course in Librarianship in the Madras Presidency. This was later taken over by the Madras University.

Alagu Mama remained a close friend and very active associate of my father right through his life.

For us children, he was the elder brother of our cricket hero M. O. Srinivasan, wicket keeper of the Madras Cricket Club.

Whether Parthasarathy Mama got his first exposure to Library Science by helping my father at the office in our home or by attending the university course in librarianship is something I am unable to judge. In any case, it had been in the very early years of the development of the new discipline of Library Science.

The Madras University Library changed from a hardly utilised book storage depot to a dynamic centre for information after it moved to the Senate House on the Madras Marina in 1928. The new premises were still in "borrowed quarters", adapted as far as possible to suit the new purpose.

The Senate House (photo taken in 1999)

The Reading Room, Catalogue Room, Service Counter, offices, etc. shared one hall. The Stack Room was in the basement of the building.

The powers-that-were had noticed the success and importance of the University Library and it got a brand new building specifically designed for its purpose and moved over in 1936.

Spacious and with custom designed furniture, fittings, lighting, etc., the well-laid out Library departments were welcoming and efficient. Every reader even had a "private cubicle".

S. Parthasarathy, then hardly "one score" years old, had

entered a profession in which he would stay for the next 7 decades.

In those days all systems and routines in the "information supermarket" (which the Madras University Library had become) were manually operated with elaborate paperwork like cards, manuals, registers, diaries, etc. The only mechanised device was the turnstile at the issue counter and operated by pedal by the counter personnel!

I lost contact with Parthasarathy Mama when my parents moved to Benares in 1945. For that matter, my exposure to library affairs and professionals were limited to the times when I used to come home from the boarding school. Between 1947 and early 1951, when I stayed at the parents' home in Delhi University, I could get a few odd moments of personal contact with my father, invariably with the implicit accompaniment of his professional family. Parthasarathy Mama was not around then.

After finishing my degree at Delhi University, I had spent several months in South India doing apprenticeships in factories. In 1951, my father had written to me in August: "Mr S. Parthasarathy has joined (the Department of Library Science, Delhi University) as teacher. The M.Lib.Sc. classes are held at home. Lectures are from 8.30 to 9.45 and tutorials are from 12 to 1. The diploma courses are at the Library from 4 to 6. Work in the mornings is progressing with 5 of us co-operating like a choir."

Department of Library Science, Delhi University. From left to right: S. Ramabhadran, S. R. Ranganathan, S. Parthasarathy, and P. K. Garde

The team at the Department were seriously engaged in research work, partly triggered by my father's observations abroad during his many visits. He had found that "research" was missing and the team were making much headway.

New terminologies were devised: Depth Classification, Facets, Phases, etc. Their findings were regularly published in the *Abgila* of the Indian Library Association and in the *Annals of Library Science.*

The team had also pondered over Machinery Search and the demands placed on systems of classification and catalogue coding for the purpose. Machinery Search has now become Electronic Search using computer technology. Present day Search Engines on the Internet still are based on inadequate scientific infrastructure in terms of classification and coding, leaving them far from user-friendly.

When I returned to Delhi in 1952, Parthsarathy Mama was back on my scene, this time with his wife and son.

"Martyred" spouses of Library Scientists. From left to right: Mrs Parthasarathy with son, Mrs Ramabhadran with daughter, Mrs Ranganathan, and unidentified lady

It was in the early 1950s that a decision was taken to establish INSDOC (Indian National Scientific Documentation Centre) with assistance from UNESCO. It was located at the National Physical Laboratory. Parthsarathy Mama was appointed its Head.

The people who created INSDOC
S. R. Ranganathan is at the centre, flanked by Dr K. S. Krishnan and Prof. M. S. Thacker. S. Parthasarathy is next to Prof. Thacker.

While on a short visit to Delhi in 1955 (I was then studying in Zurich), I had visited Parthsarathy Mama at INSDOC. His was an uphill job in that there were not many items of documentation published in India in those years and the bulk of available material came by postal mail from abroad. The Indian scientific community had also not yet realised the important role of an institution like INSDOC.

All the same, one thing had impressed me during the visit. There was an electrical gadget on Mama's desk to neatly open envelopes! He said it was very useful in dealing with the large amount of mail being received!!

Almost two decades were to pass before we again met each other. My father had died in 1972 and my mother was inclined to move to our home in Luxembourg. Parthasarathy Mama had kindly agreed to her staying with his family in Delhi prior to leaving India. I escorted her to Delhi, but had to leave almost immediately due to my work. Mother had brought along the family's silverware and such of the jewels, which she did not wear on her person. I was to take them with me.

Export rules regarding precious items being complex, it was decided that I should take them along in my suitcase and face the situation if the customs officer were to raise questions. Parthasarathy Mama had offered to come with me to the airport and be prepared to take back the material if there would be a refusal. Flights out of India are always at unearthly hours!

As it happened, the customs officer let me through without questions and without making me open the bag. I waved out good-bye to Mama with sincere gratitude that he had taken all this trouble at his age.

It is only since the late 1990s that Parthasarathy Mama and I re-established contact, this time as co-trustees of Sarada Ranganathan Endowment for Library Science (SRELS). We have attended together several meetings of the Trustees, sometimes with differing points of view with regard to financial management and conformity with prevailing rules and regulations concerning charitable institutions.

In the professional areas he has kept himself updated on many modern developments such as information kiosks. It is my hope that the newer and younger trustees will be able to benefit from his experience and help SRELS to break out of the closed shell of "pure scientific professionalism" and to reach out to the "universe of information users" and their needs.

I wish Mama good health and happiness in the years to come.

MORE PICTURES OF S. PARTHASARATHY

In the USA with S. R. Ranganathan

21

THE INCOMPARABLE PROF. S. PARTHASARATHY

K.S. Deshpande[1]

1. A NOBLE MAN

Five years senior to me in age, but fifty times more important for the field of Library and Information Science, Prof. Parthasarathy's contributions are indeed great, as compared with the prevailing standards. And as if these achievements were not enough to achieve a niche in the field of library science, God, almighty, in his infinite mercy has blessed him with another virtue rare among human beings, viz. the zeal to rush to other's help, setting aside his own needs and compulsions. Bhirtrhari, the eminent poet of 6th Century AD, designates such persons as satpurushah - Noblemen –who stand above and .... from the common crowd. He declares:

"Yete Satpurushah Parathaghataka Swartham Parityajya Ye"

(Those really are supermen who rush to rescue others abandoning their own self-interest).

1 Professor and University Librarian (Retd.), Karnatak University, Dharward. Ph. : 0836-2790763

2. AGE OF SUPER LIBRARIANS

Both of us, probably Prof. Parthasarathy a few years earlier than me, six decades ago, launched upon the adventure of library profession, when the profession as such was still in its infancy, in the making. It did not enjoy the status of the medical the legal, or the engineering professions.

But yet again God's endless grace had endowed the profession with a galaxy of great academicians who also were giants in the field of librarianship, who in fact built up the image of the profession, and elevated it to the status of a rival of other established professions.

Their names are a legion, but a few must be mentioned here. The cluster of giants of the profession starts with Dr. S.R. Ranganathan, hailed as the Father of the Library Science, followed by other dignitaries like Prof. B.S. Kesavan, Prof. D.N. Marshall, Dr. P.M. Joshi, Dr. S. Bashiruddin, Dr. B.V.R. Rao, Prof. S. Das Gupta, et al.

3. PROF. PARTHASARATHY'S GOD FATHER

Prof. Parthasarathy and quite a few others were indeed privileged and blessed in being the direct disciples and co-workers of the Father-the Master of the Library Movement, Dr. Ranganathan. Such glorious opportunities cross the paths of the chosen of the Gods. As one leading in the favoured group, Prof. Parthasarathy, like those lucky disciples of the Upanishadic times, sat at the feet of the master and literally drank straight from the fountain of knowledge gushing forth form the mouth of the master.

In fact the mantle of the Master adorns the strong, sagacious shoulders of Prof. Parthasarathy. He has all along been a fluent, lucid, clear exponent of complicated issues, which confront our profession from time to time.

4. A FRIENDSHIP WHICH IS SIX DECADES OLD

There are a few people meeting whom is a great joy, conversation with whom is enlivening, elevating and educative. I had the privilege of and pleasure of meeting Prof. Parthasarathy, on a number of occasions. The first time I listened to him was in the early sixties of the last century. He was the main speaker at a workshop, probably the last of the series of five workshops organized jointly by the UGC and the Wheat Loan Programme sponsored by the U.S. Government. in New Delhi. As Chairman of the Joint Action Committee of the workshops, I had the privilege of presiding over his address, and I was carried away by his choice of words, mastery over the subject and absolutely clear headed thinking.

A little later in the same decade I had the privilege of being his honoured guest at his Delhi residence on the INSDOC campus, for 3 days and the entire family showered love and affection on me. We were participating in a seminar jointly sponsored by the CSIR and the UGC to formulate standards for the various day-to-day jobs in the university and special libraries including governmental libraries. We presided over the university and special libraries sessions respectively. It was his privilege to preside over the committee set up to draft the report of the seminar, particularly its recommendations to be sent to the UGC, the CSIR, and the Ministry of Education, Government of India. Needless to mention here that I marveled at the precision of the language he used and the telling way in which the sentences were constructed.

At about this time a rare opportunity came in my way of observing the working of the INSDOC, at the behest of the University of Mysore where I was heading and reorganizing the university library and helping the newly founded Dept. of Library Science in its teaching programme. This time I was the chosen guest of Prof. B.S. Kesavan, who headed the INSDOC. During the lunch breaks at the INSDOC, Prof. Parthasarathy and one or two other senior officers used to have lunch together, with Prof. Kesavan presiding over the luncheon table. Problems facing the various sections of the organization used to come up for discussions and it was a heart warming experience for me to see how Prof. Kesavan held Prof. Parthasarathy in high esteem and permitted himself to be guided, even goaded by the mature advice tendered by him.

Came 1976 and the IASLIC requested me to host its annual Seminar at Dharwad, with the full approval of my Vice-Chancellor, Dr. R. C. Hirematt, I extended invitation, to Dr. P.C. Patil, Vice-Chancellor of Shivaji University to inaugurate the conference and Prof. Parthasarathy to delver the Keynote Address, which was hailed by all, particularly by the two Vice-Chancellors.

Prof. Parthasarathy and I worked together on a subcommittee constituted by the Indian Standards Institution to formulate the principles on which the titles of Indian periodicals needed to be abbreviated.

The crowning part of my association with this saintly person come off about a decade back, when Prof. Neelameghan and others asked me to go over to Bangalore and preside over a function to felicitate Prof. Parthasarathy on his 80th birthday.

Tom Winningham, a member of the British Parliament paying tribute to Jawaharlal Nehru on his 60th birthday (1949-50) remarked that even if Nehru had not been involved in Indian's Freedom Struggle and later become its first Prime Minister, he would still have gone down in world history as a great man because he gave to the world "Better History and Better English". I may voice similar sentiments in respect of Prof. Parthasarathy and gleefully declare that he has given to us better draft and through them better librarianship.

"Vidya Vinayena Shobhate" declares an eminent Sanskrit poet and here is a learned man whose hallmark is "modesty". Tumbida koda tulukuvadilla" – A full vessel does not spill, declares a Kannada seer of the past. And, Prof Parthasarathy is a Tumbida koda of Library and Information Science.

Here in Prof. Parthasarathy we have a Library Scientist who combines in himself not merely the brilliance of mind and the splendour of the heart, but also what is a desperate desideratum of our current corrupt times, with the effulgence of ethics.

May Prof Parthasarathy, live waxing through a hundred springs and autumn is all that I wish and pray for!

22

OUR PROFESSOR, THE GRANDMASTER OF INFORMATION SCIENCE

B. Garudadwajan[1]

श्रीपार्थसारथिचिन्तामणि

अहो तिष्ठति ज्ञानार्चिः
वाग्पतिरिव शोभितः।
बोधयन् पञ्चसूत्राणि
ग्रन्थशास्त्रविधानि नः॥

अस्मदाचर्यो श्रीपार्थ
सारथिसुमहोदयः ।
तनोति ज्ञानमध्यापि
ग्रन्थवेदं सुसौरभम्॥

ग्रन्थसेवाश्रिते कार्ये
यत्र स्थापना न क्षमा।
तत्र भूत्वा गुरुवर्यो
दीर्धदर्शी सभेषजः॥

अस्मद्प्रार्थना देवाय.
चिरायुर्भूत्वा सद्गुरुः।
दर्शयन् मार्गं सर्वेषाम्
ग्रन्थमेरुपितामहः॥

1 Head (retd.), Information Centre for Aeronautics, National Aerospace Laboratories, Bangalore 560 017

When I think of Śhrimān Prāthasārathi, I cannot resist likening him to the great sage Vaśishta, the preceptor of the entire Ikshvāku race. Our Master stands like a colossus overlooking the whole universe of information: its generation, processing, dissemination, retrieval and service. I still remember the days when, as a student of library Science, I was privileged to listen to his illuminating lectures encompassing the whole vista of documentation, highlighting its role in the context of the continuously expanding knowledge base, and the need for the information back-up to a researcher working in a laboratory or a university. His lectures were as simple as they were lucid, emphasizing the systems approach to any proposition, however complex: divide a subject, however complex, into its simple constituent elements, and discuss each element and its role in information. He used to emphasize the holistic nature of information and its concomitant functions. I have always seen in his lectures a constant effort to lend accent to making an increasing use of the modern tools to process knowledge and disseminate it to the information-hungry.

This aspect of the need for an information scientist, or librarian, to constantly improve his methods of serving his clientele by improving his techniques and devising his information machine to meet the requirements of the specialist, has been the keynote of the professor's lectures; and I was greatly inspired by it. This kind of magnetic attraction has made him a keenly sought-after doyen, whenever he was available. If the problem was of eliciting user's requirements, or of analyzing user studies drawing upon the library resources and providing services to meet those requirements, the Professor was at hand to open his treasure chest of priceless suggestions. No part of information infrastructure is too modern or sophisticated for the Professor. He is as much at home with information management in the ambience of a traditional set-up as in a computerized one with a larger library budget. We have read, and heard, of the Parabrahman of the Indian philosophy as "अणोरणीयान् महतो महीयान्" It is this supreme ability in him to go down to the most elementary, or to soar to the highest regions of the esoteric in mobilizing the information machine, that has made the grandsire a highly respectable and timely advisor in showing the library ills the door.

"Familiar, but not coarse; elegant, but not ostentatious".

That was how Dr. Johnson described the prose style of Addison, both belonging to England of the eighteenth century. Our Professor, beaming history of science with special reference to information science, casts such a spell on his students that they return informed and enlightened by the simple, yet elegant and structured, exposition that cracks the most profound concepts that become no more than "gooseberry on one's palm" . (करतलामलक)

That is the poser of induction from the person of a dedicated thinker such as this professor with pearls of wisdom lying deep under the ocean of knowledge.

The Professor is not just a professor of library and information science. He is also a management expert to see beforehand the shape of things to come, and how the library has to re-orient and reinforce itself to meet the burgeoning advances in science and technology. At a time when the West was making spectacular advances in computerizing information and its services, it was inescapable for the R&D establishments in our country to take advantage of this progress and improve their information services. The idea of "information online" was to pick up, and the need was there to instantly access digitized databases already generated abroad, and to create our own machine-readable databases in science and technology. When National Aerospace Laboratories (NAL) had launched, thanks to relentless efforts of Shri.

M.N. Seetharaman, then Head, ICA (NAL), during the eighties of the last century, an experimental project to create this awareness and utilize the contemporary developments in the telecommunication gadgetry in fulfilling the information needs of R&D centers in the country, the professor's views were encouraging, prophetic and supportive. The experimental project, indeed, ran its course with reasonable success.

The Professor, I understand, is 90+. Age has neither dimmed his vision as a teacher nor blunted his zeal in transforming houses of knowledge into powerhouses of information. As I have known, he has never allowed his age to overtake his enthusiasm to actively encourage and promote information. It is a daunting exercise to capture the Pitāmaha in all his aspects of glory and excellence. The fruits of his association with information are immense and unstoppable. So says the Bhagavatgita:

यत्र योगेश्वरः कृष्णो यत्र पार्थो धनुर्धरः ।
तत्र श्रीर्विजयो भूतिर्ध्रुवा नीतिर्मतिर्मम ॥

May the Professor live for many, many more years and make more fruitful strides for the good and glory of this country in the years to come!

23

S. PARTHASARATHY : A TRIBUTE ON HIS 92nd BIRTHDAY FROM A FRIEND AND FORMER COLLEAGUE

P.K. Garde[1]

The object of this article is far from making an erudite assessment of Parthasarathy's laudable contribution to the field of Library and Information Science. The galaxy of other contributors to this festschrift, I feel sure, will do full justice to that aspect. This article attempts, rather, to recapture memories of the times we spent together – first in Madras as students and then in Delhi as colleagues.

This occasion has inevitably put me in a reminiscing mood, prompting me to take a stroll down memory lane. The year was 1940, I had just acquired my Bachelor's degree with Honours in Economics, and was planning to do post-graduate work in the same subject at the Bombay University School of Economics (Bombay was not Mumbai yet). But instead, by a quirk of fate, I found myself at the School of Librarianship at the University of Madras (Madras was not Chennai yet). That happened

1 Head (Retd.), Library & Documentation, United Nations, New York. **Contact**: SUMANGAL APARTMENT No. 301, 2291 B, Modibaug, Pune 411016

at the instance of a Professor of mine who suggested that I should rather go in for "training" in librarianship. He was a far-sighted person, and believed that the time had come when there would be a demand, at least at the college and university levels, for librarians who were academically well qualified and had additionally acquired training in librarianship. He believed that I was proper material for that newly emerging profession. At that time (1940), there were only two places in India where training for librarianship was given. One was Lahore (India had not been partitioned at that time) and the other was Madras. I opted for Madras where the university had recently instituted a post-graduate diploma course in librarianship (Dip. Lib.). It was there that I met Parthasarathy. There were only five students in the class, and only two teachers. One of them was Dr. S.R. Ranganathan who was the University Librarian, and the other was Dr. Thomas who was the Assistant University Librarian. Anybody who ran into them could sense the difference between their perceptions of the library profession. Dr. Ranganathan had a passionate belief in the role of libraries as vehicles of universal education and social change. For Dr. Thomas, by contrast, libraries were just books and shelves, and the librarian was their guardian. As the number of students was very small, there was no need for a separate spacious classroom, and Dr. Ranganathan and Dr. Thomas delivered their lectures in their own offices. Dr. Ranganathan had devised a new classification scheme (the Colon Classification, CC) for the University Library's collection, and had earned a place for himself as a classificationist. Considering the transformation, which CC has undergone over the years, it was in a rudimentary stage when I learnt it as a student. But even in its elementary form it was a scheme, which laid the foundation of analytico-synthetic classification. I enjoyed Dr. Ranganathan's lectures on classification – they were intellectually most stimulating[1].

Our annual examination was held in March/April, and the result was declared in May. Both Parthasarathy and I had obtained the Diploma with distinction. I returned to Pune, and was lucky to get a job almost immediately as librarian of the newly established R.A. Podar College of Commerce and Economics in Bombay. I worked there from 1942 to 1945. In 1945, I moved to Delhi where Sir Maurice Gwyer had assumed the post of Vice Chancellor after retiring as Chief Justice of India. He had initiated an ambitious programme for expansion and reform, and as part of that programme desired a complete reorganization of the University Library. He had great regard for Dr. Ranganathan, and it was therefore natural that he was invited to prepare a plan for creating a library befitting the country's capital. In addition, Sir Maurice had given complete freedom to Dr. Ranganathan to recruit appropriate staff for implementing the plan. The two names Dr. Ranganathan immediately suggested were Parthasarathy's and mine. I resigned my job in Bombay and went to Delhi in September 1945 and Parthasarathy followed soon afterward. I was at the Delhi University Library till March 1950 when, thanks to Dr. Ranganathan's recommendation, I got into the service of United Nations and went to Bangkok as Chief Librarian of the Economic Commission for Asia and the Far East (ECAFE). That ended my association with Parthasarathy. In the same year (1950), Parthasarathy also left Delhi and went to United States to pursue higher studies in Library Science at the University of Chicago. Parthasarathy returned to

1 One of Phase Relations of CC- the Influence Phase Relation - is denoted by the symbol 'g' (the Garde Phase Relation named after Mr. Garde who suggested the Relation)

India and joined the Indian National Scientific Documentation Centre (INSDOC) as a scientist. Scholars and research workers in scientific fields welcomed INSDOC's service with open arms, as documentation (i.e. a subject-wise listing of articles in scientific periodicals) saved them their precious time which they had to spend in searching relevant literature scattered in a plethora of periodicals. That INSDOC's fame spread beyond Indian shores is, in my opinion, Parthasarathy's greatest achievement. He had indeed made India great in the documentation field.

I am happier than I can say to felicitate Parthasarathy on his birthday, and I wish him many, many more years of good health and happiness.

24

PROFILE OF PROF. S. PARTHASARATHY EXCERPTS FROM AN INTERVIEW SESSION

Dr. Samyukta Ravi[1]

Dr. Samyukta Ravi (SR) : Good morning Professor. It is my privilege and honour that I have the chance which nobody else has had, to interview you and get some amazing facts which many people do not know and we are going to put it on record so that people for years to come will get to know about what existed in our professional field and what a great personality you are. I would like to cull out a lot of information from you and I request you that you share whatever you can for the following few queries that I would pose to you.

First one would be that we hear that we do not know much about your childhood. So can you please briefly tell us about your childhood, and school and college education?

Prof. S. Parthasarathy (SP) : I was born in Pondicherry on 23rd August 1917 to S. Srirangammal and S.

1 Librarian, Pandichery University Library, Puducherry. E-mail: samravi007@yahoo.co.in

Srinivasachariyar at 10, Duplex Street, Pondicherry. That is what the municipal record states. As described by Charles Dickens in describing the French revolution the atmosphere in Pondicherry was in its best and worst of times. My parents were involved in the freedom movement. They were publishing journals in Tamil which had to be closed down on account of British pressure. My father and his friends who were settled in Pondicherry were called swadeshis and there was a French influence on these people admiring their freedom and their freedom struggle. Therefore we had an atmosphere of swadeshi movement at home. Then we had also the spiritual atmosphere. through our association with Shri Aurobindo who was there in Pondicherry. We used to meet daily and discuss things. Also there was a religious atmosphere at home. Our family was highly religious and all these forces must have had an effect on me and I did not know how it would affect in the future.

Bharathi [Subramanya Bharati] used to come daily and sing at our home. I do not remember any of them but those forces must have acted on me in my younger days. We moved over to India after the War was over, under amnesty; my father was under an arrest warrant for his political movement. My father, Bharathi and Aiyar they all moved and lived closely together as a joint family. They moved over to Madras after amnesty. Bharathi was anxious to go to Madras earlier and before amnesty was declared but he was arrested and kept in jail for a short time and released later on. Therefore, we had an atmosphere of literature, culture, religion, and philosophy. These were the factors that influenced my early years. When I came over to Madras also as I was the last son of the family, a lot of affection was showered on me.

I have always been playful, playing games. Whatever I learnt was from my sister and others at home. I was admitted to school after I was eight years old. Till then I was playing all the local games, gilli, goali, kite, uppu kandaam, etc.

SR: Do you recall all those memories anytime?

SP: In the early days, I spent time largely playing games. I was not interested as much in studies. I did my schooling mostly in Madras and then went over to Visakhapatnam where my father was working as Professor in French in the Andhra University in 1930s. I studied in the Hindu High School one of the premier schools there; then I studied in the AVN College, Andhra University, where Sir C.V. Raman also studied. His father was Principal of the college at that time. Even there I continued my cricket. I was captain of the cricket and hockey teams of the college. I represented the Andhra University in the Rorington Baria Inter-University Tournaments.

SR: Probably that is the spirit you still walking, not getting into any vehicle.

SP: For the first time we played against Nagpur and lost. I was playing for a club also at that time. I was not very serious with my studies even then. When I came back to Presidency College I was more serious. People were serious, teachers were eminent professors. Later on I went to Delhi University.

SR: What prompted you to pursue Library and Information Science as a career?

SP: When I was studying Intermediate I had French as my second language. There was no teacher but my father knew French. Therefore, I said I would study on my own. At that time educated unemployment was rampant! An M.A. student would get only Rs. 25 [a month] with great difficulty for a job. At that time I saw an advertisement in *The Hindu* for the post of a Librarian of the Indian [Tata] Institute of Science with knowledge of a language would give Rs. 250/- as a starting salary. I thought this was an opening which was better than struggling in the highly competitive world. I took French in B.A. at the Presidency College only for this purpose. After graduation joined the Library Science course, where Dr. S.R. Ranganathan was teacher

SR: How was the graduate Library Science Programme different from what they are today?

SP: Those days graduate programmes in Library Science were designed by Dr. S.R. Ranganathan based upon his Five Laws of Library Science, where the reader was the king, what you get in modern days the concept of business and everything should be done to please him and all tools should be developed for that; tools were not important, but service was important, that the way the entire course was planned and the course was such every time Indian library science moved on due to our contributions, they were all included in our courses. It was not a frozen syllabus, everything would be the latest.

Dr. S.R. Ranganathan himself was a very inspiring speaker. It was a pleasure to work with him. He used to give a lot assignments. After graduating with Diploma in Library Science I did 3 months apprenticeship under him.

SR: What was your basic degree Professor?

SP: B.A. Economics

SR: So what made you take Library Science?

SP: The advertisement of the Indian Institute of Science gave me the idea to do Library Science. We were a very good class of 6 people each one high talented in his own field. We were all seriously involved. I was the only person taken from outside the programme. All the others had to have a professional background for joining the course. I was the only one taken without that library science qualification.

SR: Do you remember all those 6 classmates, Professor?

SP: Yes, One was P.K. Garde. We worked togcthcr

throughout in Delhi University. I went on a Rockefeller fellowship abroad and he went on a UN assignment to Thailand. He was the Chief Reference Librarian at the UN Dag Hammarskjöld Library. Now retired and is in Pune at present. We are almost of the same age.

SR: Do you keep in touch with him?

SP: I have not contacted him for a couple of years. Whenever I go to Pune I make it a point to meet him.

SR : What about the rest of the batch mates?

SP: Yes, one was Sivaraman, who was also one of my colleagues. He joined Medical Library at Vellore. His mother was a nurse there. He came over to Federation of Indian Chamber of Commerce in Delhi. He was a Librarian there till he passed away.

SR: So I think probably out of the six the two of you were close.

SP: Me and Ramabhadran were at Delhi working together and were almost called brothers.

SR: Could you tell us about your early professional life or career experiences in the beginning. How you graduated and how you started in your profession?

SP: Soon after I graduated I worked with Dr.S.R. Ranganathan in the Library, he used to ask me to apply for a number of posts, before he would recommend my name. He asked the Hindu School to take me. Therefore I joined the Hindu High School. At that time he was writing about School Library also.

SR: Could we say that you were a pet student of Prof. Ranganathan?

SP: Yes, I was a pet student of Ranganathan at that time. He used to even type the application form and make me sign it.

I also got an offer from the Delhi Secretariat, D.M. Sen

who was Under-Secretary saying 'you have been recommended." At that time it was Rs. 60. I was also offered a post at the Connemara Library. The Library after evaluating my cataloguing, my handwriting being so good asked me to join. I classified the collection in the Hindu High School using Colon Classification. I had some problem on classification of Oratory. Ranganathan made me write a paper on that. It was published in the *South Indian Teacher*. It was a very good original paper.

SR: Please tell us about your association with Prof. Ranganathan during his Madras University days?

SP: I joined the course at Madras University in the beginning, then went to Delhi and continued to have association with him writing papers along with him for a number of Conferences.

SR: Does it mean that you were working in the Madras University Library with SRR?

SP: No, I was working at the Hindu High School; I was working with him in terms of paper, meet him in the morning and evening. Go with him for morning walks with a number of people - C.V.Raman's brother, V. Raghavan, Accountant General and other older people. I was the youngest. He used to praise about me to all of them. He used to take me all along and write notes, essays and revisions at his home. He used to have oil bath at 7 or 8 am and I will be write up. I had a close association with him and his family members.

SR: Please tell us about your association with the University of Delhi and INSDOC?

SP: I went to the University of Delhi in 1946. Before that I was working in the Inspectorate of Military Explosives [in Kirkee near Pune] as a Supervisor in the information side. I got a lot of experience there in serving scientists.

SR: How did Dr. Ranganathan let you go from his

clutches? You were at Madras at that time?

SP: I studied in the Hindu High School, then worked there; when I applied my school did not let me go as I was on contract (oral commitment). They dismissed all due to war but not me. I got the same offer the following year at Kirkee, Pune. I went over there. It was a research laboratory authority for all explosives and supervises the products. Being an inspectorate we commanded a lot of respect. Even there I used to play cricket and volleyball for the organisation.

SR: When was this Prof., roughly around which year?

SP: 1944 – 46 I was there. I had an offer from the Delhi University without any interview. I was getting Rs. 150 here. I wanted more. Librarian's grade was only about Rs. 250. I did not know the scales. They appointed Ramabhadran from Madras University for the post offered to me. Again next year they offered me and I went there. Garde was already there.

SR: Was Mr. Ramabhadran a Library Science qualified person?

SP: Yes. Mr. Ramabhadran was a library assistant during my service at the Madras University Library.

SR: So you became colleagues there?

SP: I met Dasgupta [the Librarian of the Delhi University] who was a student at Madras University. Also met Palmer who was a Air Force Officer studying Colon Classification from Ranganathan at Madras. I was there before the partition, suffered all the pains of pre-partition, civil war, Hindu Muslim riots.

SR: When did you move on to INSDOC?

SP: I joined INSDOC in 1952 when it was started. I knew about the coming up of INSDOC. I was doing a project with Prof. Ranganathan [about INSDOC]; he was then in the Government of India committee and when it was started I was asked to apply and got a post.

SR: May be we can say that you were the Architect of INSDOC?

SP: Yes, I was there from the first day. I was the only specialist in documentation. All the others were in ancillary services like reprography and translation, which when requests were received were done. I was involved in all the planning.

Dr. Scheele was my boss at that time. He had bibliographical experience. He was doing atomic abstracts for BARC. Very good scientist and organiser. He involved me in all programmes. I was in the technical committee of INSDOC.

SR: How long was your tenure at INSDOC?

SP: I was there till the end. Headed for 25 years. After I succeeded Scheele, in 1963 I was head of INSDOC for 5 years, and then Mr. Kesavan was brought in as Director; I knew him even before he was selected as National Librarian. I was with him for 5 years and we had a happy time.

SR: You were a close associate of late Prof. Kesavan. What sort of a person was he, what was your experience working with him?

SP: He was largely an able administrator very good speaker and writer. He was employed as Secretary for compilation and English revision of *Wealth of India* text. Of course the relationship had to be established. He had taken away my position. In six months I was involved in all the planning of projects. I continued to do whatever I was doing. He found that I was not opposing what he did. He was a very dynamic person had connections with people in high positions both cultural and literary. He knew Sanskrit and other languages, could speak Bengali too.

SR: Just out of curiosity, do you still speak French Professor? You said that you studied French in your early days.

SP: No, I did not have opportunity to use. I would be able to understand when I read.

SR: I understand you served on the sub-committee of the Indian Standards Institution, now the Bureau of Indian Standards. Could you tell us about it?

SP: Dr Ranganathan was connected with ISI as soon it was established. ISI subscribed to ISOTC46 which was on documentation and information. The drafts used to be sent to Ranganathan in 1940s, 48, 49 to comment upon. I was also involved in it. Prof. Ranganathan used to come home and we used to read, write our viewpoints. Our comments were very well received abroad particularly in Hungary. Varman who was the Director of ISI said we will start a sub-committee; so ECII sub-committee was started for documentation. It was one of the earliest committees to be established by ISI in 1948. The first one was for our National Flag. I was then at the Delhi University. I was a member of the sub-committee from the first year. It had a number of sub-committees for building and furniture, layout of periodicals, bibliography, colon classification. I was the Chairman of that sub-committee also after I returned from USA.

SR: Prof, please tell us about the work of the UGC as a member of the review committee? I think you were there?

SP: I was in the committee from 1949-59. UGC established a committee with Prof. Ranganathan as Chairman and I was at INSDOC at that time. I was made a member of the committee representing documentation. We had others such as Kesavan, Prof. Hinghway, Department of Library Science, Pune University were all members. We were asked to recommend and visit places and give a scheme for development of University libraries.

SR: As early as the 1950s ?

SP: In 1949, we went to different places - Calcutta, Baroda, Vallabhai Patel University near Anand and gave a detailed report how to setting up of courses and curriculum for training of person and so that Librarians grades were equivalent to academic staff grades. All the grades should be available to Librarians. Of course there were groups opposing, like Kesavan. We got the reports passed, approved and implemented. There was a question of UGC funding for purchase of books. There was a problem of lapsing of funds. Therefore we said it cannot lapse, it can be kept for a couple of years as running account. Some procedures for book selection were also given in another report. I visited BHU to advise them for development library as a member of a UGC team. Again I also went to Calcutta to set up the National Library section with one Prof. Malhotra as Chairman.

SR: All these years you have been instrumental in establishing and guiding those Universities and institutions of high learning to establish their libraries and train their personnel. Through these decades how do you see the growth; do you think there has been a lot of development or have the standards come down from the vision you had?

SP: Suggestions that were made in the reports by Dr. Ranganathan we are very good that period in terms of development. Computes had not yet come, every thing was done manually. For example, his three-card system for serials management was the best then compared to any business or commercial tools. The thing was that status quo was maintained in the libraries; no innovation was absorbed or introduced. They thought as if that was the last judgment which should not be crossed. That was on the part on profession not of the UGC. It was a felt need by the UGC and their fore it was done. After wards

UGC was only giving grants to libraries, and there was no question of improving library education. It took many years, 30 to 40 years before anything new could be introduced in the library curriculum. That is why when in the early 60s we found that there was stagnation in the education and training programmes in library science in the universities we stated the DRTC as an advanced course in keeping with the requirement of the changing times. And immediately thereafter we started another one at INSDOC.

SR: But why is it that you could not be instrumental in upgrading the education curriculum at the Universities rather than starting another organisation?

SP: We started it because it was easier to develop in this manner. Many of the leading librarians have been produced by these two institutions have produced without even any recognition by the universities; but later on they themselves recognized the course, the Government of India recognized it and UGC recognized the post graduate programmes of these institutions as equivalent to the M.Lib. Sc degree.

SR: But was it started just because it was very difficult to implement these sort of courses in the University?

SP: No, there was no initiative locally, it's not a question of implementing.

SR: That was an impediment for you?

SP: There was no initiative although people were occupying positions, but their mentality was only what was existing earlier. The entire object was they found that this was the pattern, they followed pattern of examination papers, it was all set easy.

SR: So that led to this?

SP: Many of the special libraries took people turned out by industry, took people turned out by DRTC and

INSDOC, earlier we wanted to do it at INSDOC itself a training course but I prevented them from doing it because we are not an academic body to authorize the thing:. This one was started here. Later on when Kesavan said we also wanted to have in INSDOC, we started one there.

SR: You have been on several missions of UN organizations to various countries, what has been your experience, any particular experience or incidents or events that you would like to tell us about, Professor.

SP: When I was in INSDOC, INSDOC was the local centre for representing India on the International Federation for Documentation (FID). From the beginning in 1952, when it was established it had connection with the FID. We had a contact with them from the beginning. And Dr. Ranganathan used to attend all the FID conferences on behalf of India, representing INSDOC for a number of years; in earlier years he attended many of them and his contributions had lot of impact on the international field. And we had also one issue the INSDOC was started with 3 UNDP experts and our own staff Indian staff who were very qualified staff in the earlier in all divisions.: we just took them for advise the running was entirely ours it was not so in other organizations. We were one of the two to do it, we said we don't want more than 3 people .: we had from the beginning all our own people were involved in the development of the systems, etc.: the 3 people who were there were only taken as advisors, we may follow it or not follow it. Pakistan and other countries, they ran the whole show and not the local people. Which was set up later on the basis of ours and then here at that time we had a UNESCO proposed a seminar for scientific documentation for Asian countries. It was organized by INSDOC, I was leading the INSDOC. I organized the entire thing. We had excellent people from all over the world not only Asia, we had Prof. MiKhailov representating

VINITI, Moscow; and the director of the CNRS Document Centre in Paris. Also a director from the John Crerar Library, Chicago; one expert from Australia who was a reprography specialist and then the heads of scientific centres in Philippines, Korea, Egypt. For people who had come for that seminar we had already prepared an entire document on how to provide documentation services, etc. Dr. Ranganathan made us do that type of work and with his guidance we brought out a manual and presented it. The UNESCO was highly pleased with it. It appeared as a document in Documentation and its Facets later on as a publication, modifying, editing and doing it with Dr. Ranganathan as editor and I as one of the collaborators. That conference impressed them very much, and I was offered a number of times posts outside the country.

SR: You did not venture to go out of India?

SP: No, but then locally Kesavan said I should be here and not to go out. We had lot of contacts with international organizations and then I was elected as the FID president's council member once for 5 years. I was attending the FID conferences and was a member of their sub committees. I was representing Government of India, Indian delegate for inter governmental conference on UNESCO's UNSIST along with Dr. Kamath. Similarly I was again representing India on the inter-governmental conference on National Technical information, NATIS information system.

SR: You were also associated with planning and implementation of NISSAT. Looking back at all these how do you feel about the progress India has made in implementing the national information infrastructure.

SP: Sri C. Subramanian had appointed about 300 and odd scientists to prepare a plan for science development, in 1972-73. He held regional meetings for various subjects in different places; when it came to Delhi I knew the organizers. I was in close contact with DST. It was done by the National Committee on Science and Technology who were advisers to the Government of India, on S&T. I asked them to include Documentation as one of the topics to be discussed. I was asked to prepare the theme paper. I prepared theme paper on NISSAT and presented in May 1973 at National Physical Laboratory, Delhi. Sri C. Subramanian presided over it. Dr. Ramachandran was the DST Secretary. Immediately after presentation C.S. asked me to give the financial implications for implementation. We had a panel also with Kamath as the chairman; the next day we discussed and recommended that the plan be accepted. Within a month it was included in the National plan. About 4 crores was asked for it in the Fifth Plan. For the first time documentation was included as an item of expenditure by the government.

SR: So, looking back at all these what do you feel? Whether they are implementing National Information Infrastructure?

SP: The main thing is we had planned very much in advance the NISSAT programme. I was also in the advisory committee. We wanted to develop manpower within NISSAT; NISSAT should have all capabilities of all modern networking, computer facilities, software development etc. All should be available centrally, NISSAT should take care of it other than creating regional centers subject centers we wanted them to develop, so that the subject centers would all be cooperating centers, joining all subject library together and providing a center to manage the network. Instead of that they started giving funds to various laboratories in various subjects and they all used the funds in developing their own libraries and not play the role of subject centre concept. Earlier we wanted Prof. Neelameghan to join as head. He could not; it went to people who were not familiar with documentation science; it became a money giving operation rather than a technique development operation.

SR: Do you feel that the national information infrastructure has not been developed in the right direction as you visualized?

SP: Yes, because all the development projects come under the management side they wanted it to be developed, they were willing to give money but, we have not had people with enough motivation to make use of the funds to provide services. The entire scenario is such that the profession is not reacting to develop the required system which the management wants to bring in.

SR: Prof; could you tell us about your activities after you returned from INSDOC, your association with MALA and RCIS?

SP: After, I returned from INSDOC, I joined DRTC as an Honorary Professor. Even before retirement I got that for one year I was there. I was in the IACODLA, an UNESCO advisory committee for 3 terms.

SR: How long was one term?

SP: Two years. Normally they do not allow more than one term. But that the Director wanted me for 3 terms was unusual. Third time, I was made the Vice Chairman.

SR: Was this after you retirement, Professor?

SP: No. I was there before retirement and had programmes for the assistants. I was offered field assignment offer asking me to advise the Ethiopian government on setting up a National Scientific and Technical Information system. They forced me to go there saying it was important. When I went there, there was an internal civil war, shooting all around, the government was not at all interested in anything except for one person working in the scientific department. : I prepared a plan for them on National Scientific Information Policy which was the only document in science policy in UNESCO reports. Later on I got an offer from UNIDO for setting up a information system in Nigeria with the Federal Institute of Industrial Organisation. I went there for one year but found no manpower to work with.

SR: Was it frustrating because of lack of manpower to support to assist you?

SP: They would ask help for books or material. They wanted technical manpower but all programme efforts in African countries were wasted because there were no counterparts to carry on the project. They again wanted me for another six months. I went again to Nigeria. I prepared a detailed report for them and they said they would implement that one.

SP: For a two year period. I was the Leader of UNIDO delegation, organized several Industrial Information Conferences. I invited experts such as Peter Lazar (hundary) to take care of technical information.

SR: What was your Association with MALA and RCIS?

SP: Dr. Ranganathan was there in the 1940s, when I joined the course. Later I became a member of MALA; others were eminent people in Madras. We used have an annual meeting, when Ranganathan would release a book. First time he released Reference source and bibliography volume 1. It was held in Bar Council premises. K.V. Krishnaswmy lyerr was also there at that time. Annual report was presented and included in the Memoirs [of the Madras Library Association] which had technical articles .It carried articles on many subjects and many facets discussed by many, I also wrote one on Economics.. By 1945 technical activities had gone down. For sometime the pattern continued.

SR: Did you take up as a successor of Ranganathan any official position through which you carry any social activities.

SP: When Dr. Ranganathan left Madras, he prevailed on Mrs. Suseela Kumar and Mr. Kumar to take up MALA. Kumar used to take it as an order from Dr. Ranganathan to carry out and was deeply involved in the development.

SR: How was your association with RCIS?

SP: After retirement, started a Institute of Information Studies in 1984 as part of the Sarada Ranganathan Endowment for Library science and there I did a number of workshops on CDS ISIS is a number of places with Neelamegham as the resource person. The introduction of computerization in libraries in South India largely depended upon the people trained who implemented it [software). The Department of Library Science was one of the earliest to take up training at the Madras University.

SR: I even recall your asking us to collect data for MEDLARS or Medical Information System

SP: Under the Institute I was asked to do for NIC to help them propagate and disseminate MEDLARS information. Several seminars for medical librarians we organized; the impact was less because we were dealing with librarians who had no power in implementation. Therefore the last one due at Delhi, invited all doctors who were heading various medical institutions, who were decision makers It had the greatest impact.

SR: How did RCIS come into the picture after the Institute of Information Studies?

SP: After the death of Ranganathan I had started all this. Then came the birth centenary of Ranganathan. The Institute had also a branch in Bangalore, which had all the manpower, equipment etc. After the centenary celebrations we gave up the Institute and started RCIS. We brought out a video film on Ranganathan, we celebrated on a grand scale, released a stamp, first day cover. We had an elite group C. Subramanian,

M.S.swaminathan, Anandkrishnan, we formed a committee, of senior librarians .... Kumars, Gopinath, Raghavan. It had a blazing start, a t rail of major events which had impact later on the development of information systems.

SR: Professor, would you tell us about your current areas of interest?

SP: I am also in touch with education. I am a committee member of Hindu educational organisation which has 3 major school libraries. I am also secretary of MOP Charities which jointly started the MOP Vaishanav College for Womens. I am on its Board of Governors. It is one of the leading colleges in the country. Therefore I am involved the development of students. Also involved with a school for the poor scheduled caste.

I am involved with religions - Vedic society, a very old one. I am a member of The Vedavedanta vardhini, Saraswathi Bandaram Committee which has a temple at Ayodhya, South Indian style, my own mutt,. Mandayam Srivaishnava Yadugiri Ethiraja Mutt. In social field also I have been a President for 10 years of the Bharathi Paasarai which is a society for promotion of ideals of Bharathi.

SR: Do you think the time is sufficient for you to do all these activities.

SP: Yes, it keeps me busy. I read widely, go to British Council, American Consulate libraries; my object of learning is to pass it on to others. That is how I am able to suggest this to the college to do to others. It is not for enlarging my knowledge at this age. It has no use in terms of it. But I do read because it is interesting and useful to society at large.

SR: I have always seen you as an enthusiastic, active, smiling mentor all through my career for the last three decades. I never seen you say 'I am tried' or 'I cannot come' or I never heard a 'No' from you. What is the secret of this?

SP: I am accustomed to walking from early days. I am intellectually active. If one is intellectually active, health behaves itself. And of course God's grace.

SR: That's a really good statement.

SP: All these are not planned or organised. I travel a lot. I travel by bus. I enjoy mixing with crowd.

SR: You never felt age as an impediment.

SP: No, I am not tired in terms of it.

SR: It must be the positive attitude.

SP: Yes I have a positive outlook.

SR: It is been a great pleasure talking to you for last few minutes. Professor, you have been a guiding spirit to all of us in our profession, not only in our Profession, I think but any one who has met with you and who is in touch with you, they would really get more spirited talking to you or first by are even thinking about you, suppose we take it as an example and point and say "Look at Prof. this is how he is, you learn from him". It has been a great honour and indeed a great pleasure talking to you Prof. We need your blessings, and we wish you good health and prosperity for years to come. Thank you very much Professor.

SP: Thank you.

25

BIO-DATA OF PROF. S. PARTHASARATHY

BIRTH

Born in Pondicherry (now Puducherry) on 23rd August 1917

EDUCATION

- BA Degree (Econamics), Madras University
- Diploma in Library Science, Madras University 1940-41, (studied under Dr. S. R. Ranganathan).
- Research Courses at the Graduate Library School, University of Chicago, USA.1950-51 (with Guide Dr. Jesse H. Shera) on a Rockefeller Foundation Fellowship. Also site-visited various technical libraries in USA.
- During 1951, he visited London for 10 days to study in the working of technical libraries.

PROFESSIONAL EXPERIENCE

- Worked as Librarian, Hindu High School, Madras 1941-44

- Senior Technical Assistant, Inspectorate of Military Explosives, Kirkee, Poona, 1944-46
- Senior Technical Assistant, Delhi University Library, 1946-52
- Lecturer in Library Science, University of Delhi, 1951-53
- Junior Documentation Officer, INSDOC, 1952-56
- Senior Documentation Officer, INSDOC, 1956-61
- Head, INSDOC, 1961-63
- Assistant Director, INSDOC, 1963-69
- Scientist-in-Charge, INSDOC, 1969-1977

CONTRIBUTIONS TO S&T INFORMATION SYSTEMS

He joined the Indian National Scientific Documentation Centre (INSDOC) in 1952 when the organization was started. He was associated in the planning and organization of a range of Documentation services for the scientists in India. Location of articles required by scientists, compilation of bibliographies on different topics, provision of translation services for various languages, preparation of a current awareness services of articles appearing in various scientific journals, building up of a library of scientific journals, supplementing with existing collections available in libraries in India. He was the Head of INSDOC from 1959 to the beginning of 1963 and was responsible for the planning organisation and development of the Centre during that period. He organised and conducted the UNESCO Seminar on Scientific Documentation for Asia at INSDOC in 1961. He also organised the Seminar on Scientific Translation in 1962. He prepared the Third Five Year Plan for INSDOC.

Since the beginning of 1963, he had participated in the

preparation of the following plans and projects for INSDOC:

Development of INSDOC Regional Centre at Bangalore: Training course in Scientific Documentation and Reprography: Organisation of Project Information Files and Technical Assessment of CSIR Libraries: National Science Library: Information Retrieval Project: Plan for an Intensive Translation Programme in collaboration with the National Science Foundation, USA; and the Fourth Five Year Plan for INSDOC.

- Member of the Working Group set up for the preparation of a plan for establishing a Data Library and Documentation Centre for ICSSR, 1970.
- Member, Panels of the National Committee on Science and Technology (NCST) relating to the development of information systems for (1) Marine Data; and (2) Civil Engineering. 1975
- Member, Advisory Committee for the National Information System for Science and Technology (NISSAT) of the Department of Science and Technology of the Government of India. 1976
- Member of the Committee to advice R&D BHEL, Hyderabad for setting up of an Information dissemination network for their organizations.
- Member of a committee to advice SAIL, Ranchi for setting up an R&D Information system for steel industry in their organisation.
- Member, Indo-US Meet on Scientific and Technical Information organised by the Department of Science and Technology of the Government of India, 1977.
- Member, Advisory Committee of the National Information Centre for Leather and Allied Industries (NICLAI), CLRI, Madras, 1984.

Member, Advisory Committee of the National Information Centre for Food Sciences NICFOS), CFTRI, Mysore, 1988.

Organised two UNESCO projects in INSDOC:

1. A project for providing SDI services for two years to scientists in South Asia region using Chemical Abstract database. INSDOC organized and ran this service using CAN-SDI software on the IBM 370 computer available at IIT Chennai for matching and retrieval based upon user profiles. (1974)
2. Accessing information at global distances – providing access to online databases available at ESRIN, Frascati, Rome. On-line demonstration was arranged for one week at TFIR, Bombay for the benefits of the scientists. More than 500 scientists participated in this programme and retrieved information on their specific topics. First demonstration in India. This project was supported by the Department of Science and Technology, 1976.

Projects and Directories:

1. Directory of scientific institutions in India, **(Unesco project)** 1972.
2. Information facilities and requirements in India relating to new and renewable energy sources: A preliminary report. **(Unesco project).** 198O.
3. Current research projects in the fields of metallurgy, corrosion and mineral engineering. (Prepared for the Council of Scientific and Industrial Research, New Delhi) 1981.
4. Compilation of a Directory of Scientific Societies in India for the Department of Science and Technology of the Governaent of India,
5. Projects for the MEDLARS Programme of the

National Informatics Centre, New Delhi

a) Compilation of data on medical libraries in India

b) Seminars on Biomedical Library and Information Network, (Organised 5 Seminars at Bangalore, Calcutta, Lucknow, Bombay, and New Delhi)

c) Identification of Nodal Centres for MEDLARS Services.

d) Compilation of a Union Catalogue of Biomedical Periodicals.

6. Development of a software for an integrated information system for FOSTIS, CFTRI, Mysore.

PROFESIONAL VISITS ABROAD

Visited Honolulu, Tokyo, Manila, Hong Kong in Aug.-Sep., 1961 to participate in the Scientific Information Session of the Tenth Pacific Science Congress at Honolulu, 1961, at the special invitation of the National Academy of Sciences, USA, and to visit the Documentation Centres in South East Asia.

Visited Cairo Mar-April 1963, to conduct the UNESCO Regional Training Course in Scientific Documentation, Cairo, as UNESCO Expert.

Visited Tokyo, Japan to attend the First General Meeting of the Commission for Asia and Oceania of the FID from 12th-16th, April 1970.

Visited Hong Kong to site-visit the organisations and agencies specialising in Chinese Scientific Literature, for the period of 19th - 22nd April, 1970

Visited Brussels (Belgium) to attend the meeting of the Council of FID for 12th-13th February 1971 and joint meeting of FID & IFLA for 15th -16th February, 1971.

Deputed to Ottawa and Paris for three months to attend the:

i) FID meeting on 30th September,1971 in Paris.

ii) Third Session of the International Advisory Committee on Documentation, Libraries and Archives (as a member) held in Paris from 13 to 16 October 1971. The Committee considered the recommendations of the UNISIST with special reference to providing adequate documentation facilities for developing countries.

iii) Ottawa Conference on Conceptual basis of Classification of Knowledge from 1st - 5th October 1971.

iv) Hungarian Central Technical Library and Documentation Centre and other libraries in Budapest from 29.8.72 – 16.9.72.

INTERNATIONAL COOPERATION

Visited German Democratic Republic (GDR) to finalise an agreement on direct cooperation for promoting the exchange of information between the Central Institute of Information and Documentation (ZILD) of the GDR and INSDOC, from 16th to 21st September 1972 .

Deputed to attend the Fourth Session of the International Advisory Committee on Documentation, Libraries and Archives (as a member) of UNESCO, held in Paris from 18 to 21 September 1973. Programmes relating to training of personnel at all levels, development of computerised documentation services, preparation of working documents for the Intergovernmental Conference on Planning national overall documentation, libraries and archives infrastructures, assistance to developing countries for creation and development of documentation services etc. were recommended as areas requiring UNESCO support during 1974-80.

- To participate, as a Consultant, in the meeting of the Working Group held in Paris from 2 to 4 May 1973 to consider the problem of copyright and photographic reproduction - in response to an invitation from the Director-General. World Intellectual Property Organisation (WIPO).
- To study the organisation and working of computerised information services in the field of science and technology in U.K.
- To attend the meeting of the Council of the FID from 14 to 16 May 1973 at the Hague.
- To attend the meeting of the Bureau of the International Advisory Committee on Documentation, Libraries and Archives of UNESCO (as Vice-Chairman of the Bureau) held in Paris from 11 to 13 March 1974, 24th-26th June, 1974 and 23rd -27th September, 1974
- Visited Russia for the period of two weeks from 24th July, 1974 for the Indo-Soviet Agreement on Applied Sciences and Technology under the Project "Continuation of Cooperation in setting up and development of Scientific and technical Information System in India. Member of the Department of Science and Technology delegation consisting of Prof H. Mahabala, Dr Ashok Khosla, and S. Parthasarathy to visit USSR for studying the state of library automation in that country.
- Deputed to visit Paris, Brussels, Luxemburg, FRG and UK for the period of 10th June - 9th July, 1975. Also visited France and Netherland for the Period of 25th April, 1976 to 30th April 1976. Member of the Department of Science and Technology delegation consisting of Dr V.A. Kamath, Prof A.

Neelameghan, and S. Parthasarathy to visit the EEC countries for exploring the possibility of cooperation within the EEC countries in the areas of scientific information and automation.

TECHNICAL ASSISTANCE MISSIONS

- Expert Member in Documentation with Industrial Development Centre for Arab States, Cairo under the Indian Technical and Economic Cooperation Programmes, 1971.
- Worked as a UNESCO senior expert in scientific information in Ethiopia to help in the formulation of a national science information policy for that country. Sept to Dec 1978.
- Worked as a UNIDO senior expert in industrial information at the Federal Industrial Research Institute, Lagos, Nigeria, to prepare a five-year plan to UNIDO for developing industrial information system for Nigeria. (1979-81 for 18 months)

LIBRARY AND INFORMATION SCIENCE EDUCATION

He taught courses leading to the Diploma in Library Science and Master in Library Science of the University of Delhi during 1951-1953. He delivered lectures on documentation in the UNESCO Training Course in Scientific Documentation for South Asia held at INSDOC in 1956, the UNESCO Regional Training Course in Scientific Documentation for Asia held at INSDOC in 1956, the UNESCO Regional Training Course in Scientific Documentation for Middle East held at Cairo in March-April 1963, and the UNESCO Regional Training Course in Scientific Documentation for Asia held at INSDOC in October-November 1963. He taught in the Training Course in Documentation and Reprography conducted by INSDOC from 1964 onwards.

- On his retirement from INSDOC in 1977 he accepted an invitation from the Indian Statistical Institute to be Hon. Visiting Professor at the DRTC, Bangalore.
- Member. Faculty of Arts of the University of Delhi, as an expert member in Library Science, 1952-1977.
- Member, Committee on Libraries of the University Grants Commission, 1958,
- Expert member of the University Grants Commission for reviewing the development plans of the Banaras Hindu University Library, 1962.
- Member, Board of Studies, Documentation Research and Training Centre, Bangalore, 1962.
- Member, Board of Studies, Training Course in Documentation and Reprography, INSDOC, from 1964-1977.
- Member, Board of Studies, Department of Library Science, University of Delhi, 1962.
- Member, Board of Studies, Department of Library Science, University of Rajasthan, 1962.

LIBRARY AND INFORMATION SCIENCE STANDARDS

- Member, Library Buildings Fittings and Furniture Sectional Committee, Indian Standards Institution, from 1960-1977
- Member, EC-2 sub committee on Documentation Sectional Committee, Indian Standards Institution, from 1949-1977. Chairman of the committee 1974-1977.

CONTRIBUTIONS TO PROFESIONAL ORGANIZATIONS

- Sarada Ranganathan Endowment for Library Science (SRELS), Bangalore

- Member, Board of Trustees (1996-). On the Advisory Board of the *SRELS Journal of Information Management.*
- Organised Workshops on CDS/ISIS Ver 2 +. (7 workshops) under the auspices of the Institute of Information Studies (1984-1992), a division of the SRELS
- Ranganathan Centre for Information Studies (RCIS), Chennai (1993 -)
- As a founder member, involved in the formulation of policies and activities and conducting of workshops, lectures and conferences on various topics.
- On the Advisory Board of the *Information Studies* an organ of the Centre.
- MALIBNET, Chennai

MEMBERSHIP IN OTHER PROFESSIONAL BODIES

- Life Member, Madras Library Association, 1944-
- Life Member, Indian Library Association, 1946-
- Member, Library Research Circle, Delhi, 1952
- Member, Delhi Library Association, 1956
- Life Member, IASLIC, 1958-
- Founder Member and Vice President Indian Scientific Translators Association, 1961
- Founder Member and Vice President Institute of Scientific Information, 1976
- Council Member, International Federation of Documentation, 1970-75
- Member, FID Committee on Developing Countries, 1970-75

- Member, FID Committee on Classification Research, 1974-77
- Member, FID Commission for Asia and Oceana, 1970-75

CONFERENCES, SEMINARS AND WORKSHOPS

International

1. Annual Conferences, Special Library Association (USA) 1950
2. Annual Conferences, American Medical Library Association, 1950
3. Annual Conferences, American Library Association, 1950
4. Seminar on Bibliographic Organisation, Graduate Library School, University of Chicago, 1950
5. Scientific Information Session, 10th Pacific Science Congress, Honolulu, 1961 (at Special Academy of Sciences, Washington)
6. Ottawa Conference on Conceptional basis Classification of Knowledge, 1-5 Oct. 1971 (as a special invitee)
7. International Seminar on Organisation of Information Services in Less Developed Countries, Brussels, 1971 (sponsored by UNESCO)
8. Inter-Governmental Conference on UNISIST , Oct. 1971 (as a delegate of the Government of India)
9. 36th FID Conference and Congress, Budapest, 1972.
10. IFLA Conference, New Delhi, 1992.
11. UNESCO Inter-Governmental Conference on National Information System, 1974. (as a delegate from India: was elected as the Vice-President of the Conference).

12. UNESCO Meeting for Reviewing the Information Infrastructure, resulting in the setting of General Information Programme (PGI), (attended the meeting as representative of IACODLA)

National

Organized, conducted and participated in large number of national level conferences and workshops, including the Seminar on Library Automation and Information Retrieval: Challenges and Opportunities in collaboration with the Indian Institute of Science, Bangalore.

SPECIAL LECTURES

1. Das Gupta Memorial Lecture organised by the Delhi Library Association, 1971
2. Sarada Ranganathan Lectures, Sarada Ranganathan Endowment, Bangalore, 1974
3. Ranganathan Memorial Lecture, Vikram University, Ujjain, 1977
4. Presidential Address, IASLIC Conference, Bangalore, 1986
5. Presidential Address, Indian Library Conference, Calcutta, 1990

PUBLICATIONS

Editorial and Advisory Work

- *INSDOC List of Current Scientific Literature* (1954-63);
- *Bibliography of Scientific Publications of South and South East Asia* (1955-63);
- *Annals of Library Science* (1955-63) as Joint Editor;
- *Annals of Library Science and Documentation* (1964),

- *Library Science with a slant to Documentation* (quarterly) 1980 onwards; and
- *Information Studies* (quarterly), RCIS, 1993 onwards.

Books, Reports and Papers

1. INSDOC and its regional activities. American Documentation 1962, 13, 334-37. (Paper presented at the *Scientific Information Session of the Tenth Pacific Science Congress,* Honolulu, 1961).
2. Scientific and technological documentation, including the problems of language and terminology. (Paper submitted to the United Nations Conference on the *Applications of Science and Technology for the Benefit of the Less Developed Areas,* 1963).
3. *Documentation and its facets* (a symposium of papers). Asia publishing House, (in collaboration with Dr. S.R. Ranganathan and others).

   Titles of the papers by Prof. SP included in the volume

   - *Emergence of documentation*
   - *International Federation for Documentation*
   - *Post-War National Documentation Centres*
   - *Growth of documentation in India*
   - *Development of INSDOC*
   - *Organisation of INSDOC*
   - *Problem of personnel*
   - *Standard for bibliographical reference*
   - *Future of documentation in India* (in collaboration with Ranganathan S.R.)
   - *Future of international documentation* (in

collaboration with Ranganathan S.R.)

4. *Project oriented documentation: an INSDOC-NML Project* (in collaboration with the project team)
5. Field documentation. *Annals of Library Science and Documentation* 1964, 11. 17-22. Classification
6. Oratory and its place in classification. *South Indian Teacher* 1942,15, 291-96.
7. Economics in Decimal and Colon Classification. *Proceedings of the Sixth All India Library Conference,* 1944, pp.88-91
8. Form division of the Universal Decimal Classification. *Abgila* 1950, 1, 165-67
9. Optional facets in library classification: Systems of physics and special physics. *Abgila* 1952, 2, 265-67.
10. Optional facets: Diffuse treatment of systems and specials. *Abgila* 1953, 3, 7-10.
11. Role of octave. **In**: *Depth Classification and reference Service.* 1953. pp 53-61.
12. Anterior common subdivisions, **In** *Depth classification and reference service.* 1953.pp.134-39
13. Facet formula for institutions, **In** *Depth classification and reference service.* 1953. pp. 150-60
14. Depth classification. 16. Packet notation. *Annals of Library Science and Documentation* 1955, 2109-11
15. Colon classification in retrospect. *Annals of Library Science and Documentation* 1957, 4, 13-18
16. A grammar of depth classification. *Annals of Library Science and Documentation* 1958, 5, 122-31
17. Second International Study Conference of Classification Research: a review. *Annals of Library Science and Documentation* 1965, 12, 151-53

19. Faceted classification as an approach to machine coding, **In** *Advance in Documentation and Library Science*. V.3. Pt.1.1960 Inter science. pp.289-94. Conference organized by Dr Shera at the Western Reserve University, Cleveland.

20. Cataloguing of associated books. *Abgila* 1949, 1, 64-69. (in collaboration with P.K.Garde).

21. Union Catalogue of Learned Periodical Publication in South Asia. Vol. Physical and Biological Sciences. 1953. *Indian Library Association* (in collaboration with Ranganathan and others).

22. Union Catalogue of Periodical Publications. *Annals of Library Science and Documentation* 1954, 1 99-108.

23. Studies in cataloguing. *Annals of Library Science and Documentation* 1955, 2, 58-64.

24. Persian Names. *Annals of Library Science and Documentation* 1959, 6, 63-64.

25. Make-up of learned periodicals. *Library Herald* 1958, 1, 84-89.

26. Limitations to standard on indexing. *Annals of Library Science and Documentation* 1960, 7, 31-32.

27. Training of library personnel in India, *Library science in India*. 1953. Madras Library Association. pp. 158-62.

28. Industrial development: An assessment. 1965. pp. 26. (compilation of current) literature of Indian industries). A theme paper submitted to *CSIR for consideration at the Directors Conference.*

29. National Information System for Science and Technology. (Paper presented at the *Seminar on the Approach Paper on the Science and Technology Plan,* organised by the National Committee on

Science and Technology of the Government of India, Mew Delhi, 21-23 May 1973. This provided a blue-print for the development of NISSAT)

30. Modern trends in information processing. (Paper presented at the *Seminar on Access to Bibliographic Data Bases*, Bombay, 18 Sep 1976)
31. Libraries and the challenge of education, (paper presented at the Seminar organised by the Madras Library Association, 12 Dec 1985)
32. Guidelines for choosing a system. (Paper presented at the *Seminar on Library Automation and Information Retrieval*, Bangalore, Oct. 1985
33. Edited Computer application to libraries, IR and networking, Sarada Ranganathan Endowment for Library Science, Bangalore. 1986
34. Areas of library automation. (Paper presented at the *Semimr on Library Automation* organised by the Madras Library Association, 19-20 June 1986)
35. Information communication barriers, (Paper presented at the *National Conference on Scientific Information for Defence* organised by DESIDOC, New Delhi, 25-26 Peb 1986)
36. Features of a public library network for Tamil Nadu. (Paper presented at the *Seminar on Public Library Services and Information Networks* organised by the Madras Library Association, 4-6 Jan 1988)
37. Curriculum development in information studies with special reference to information technology. (Paper presented at the *Seminar on Curriculum Development for Information Technology* organised by the Madras Library Association, 20-22 Peb 1990), Written in collaboration with Prof A, Neelameghan.

SUPPORT TO SOCIAL AND RELIGIOUS ORGANIZATIONS

1. Member of the Hindu Educational Organisation (Management of one Higher Secondary School set up 150 years back, and two CBSE schools). 1984 –
2. Trustee, MOP Charities, management of one primary school, and MOP Vaishnava College for Women (in collaboration with Vallabh Vidya Sabha) 1993 –
3. Sri Saraswati Bhandaram Committee – propogation of Sri Vishnava literatures and running of Sri Ramaswami Temple at Ayodhya 1987-
4. Veda Vedanta Vardini for promotion of Vedas 1995–
5. Yadugiri Ammal Trust for providing assistance to the needy 1990 –
6. Pradhan Tirumalrao Trust for providing assistance to temple services. 1990 –
7. Bharati Pasarai for popularizing Bharati's thoughts. 1985 – 1995. (Served as its President)
8. Madras Book Club 1995 –
9. Parthasarathy Swami Sabha for promotion of classical music, dance and drama, and lectures by eminent personalities. 1978 – 1985.

HONOURS AND AWARDS

1. Rockefeller Foundation Fellowship for pursuing advance studies in Library science and for observing scientific and industrial libraries in the USA, Awarded for 1950-51
2. Fellow of the Indian Standards Institution for services rendered in the field of Documentation Standards. Elected in 1974.

3. Honorary Fellow of the Indian Library Association in recognition of a long and distinguished career in the field of Library and Information Science. Awarded in 1984.
4. Fellow of the Society for Information Science, 1984.
5. Scroll of Honour presented by ILA, IASLIC, IATLIS, and GILA on the occasion of the Joint Library Education Centenary celebrations, in recognition of distinguished service to the cause of Education for Library and Information Science in India, 1987.
6. Certificate of Honour, IASLIC, Golden Jubliee (1955-2005) 2006.
7. Awarded Life Membership, MALA, 2006.

CONTRIBUTING AUTHROS

ABBAS GILVARI

Deputy of Research & Development, Agricultural Scientific Information and Documentation Center (ASDIC), Agricultural Research and Training Organization, Tehran, Iran

AMBA, S

Deputy Director (Retd.), Central Leather Research Institute, Adyar, Chennai 600 020. Contact: No. 225, III Street, Ramnagar North, Velachery, Chennai – 600042

AMUDHAVALLI, A

Professor & Head, Dept. of Information Science, University of Madras, Chennai

ANUP KUMAR DAS

Centre for Studies in Science Policy, School of Social Sciences, Jawaharlal Nehru University, New Delhi - 110067, India. E-mail: anupdas2072@hotmail.com

BIBHUTI BHUSAN SAHOO

Central Library, Indian Institute of Technology, Delhi 110 016. E-mail: bibhuti.sahoo@gmail.com

DESHPANDE, K S

Professor and University Librarian (Retd.), Karnatak University, Dharwad Ph: 0836-2790763

GARDE, P K

Head (Retd.), Library & Documentation, United Nations, New York

Contact: SUMANGAL APARTMENT No. 301, 2291 B, Modibaug, Pune 411016

GARUDADWAJAN

Head (retd.), Information Centre for Aeronautics, National Aerospace Laboratories, Bangalore 560 017

GHOSH, S B

Former Professor, Indira Gandhi National Open University, XY-72, Sarojini Nagar, New Delhi – 110023, India. E-mail: sbghosh@hotmail.com

HARAVU, L J

Trustee, Kesavan Institute of Information and Knowledge Management, Hyderabad.

E-mail: haravu@newgenlib.com

JACQUES TOCATLIAN

Director (Retd.), General Information Programm, UNESCO, Paris, France

NARAYANA G J

Scientist (Retd.), Aeronautical Development Establishment, DRDO, Bangalore 560 017.

Cont. #1270, MRHB Colony, Govindaraja Nagar, Bangalore 560 079. Ph. 23303598

E-mail: gjnarayana@gmail.com

NEELAMEGHAN, A

Hon. Visiting Professor, DRTC/ISI, Bangalore-560059. **Contact**: 216, 16th Cross, 4th Main, Banglore 560055; E-mail: anm2002@vsnl.net

PRASAD, K N

Executive Officer, Sarada Ranganathan Endowment for Library Science, 702, 42nd Cross, 3rd Block, Rajajinagar, Bangalore 560 010. Ph: (080) 23305109; E-mail: srels@dataone.in

RAGHAVAN, K S

Professor, Documentation Research and Training Centre, Indian Statistical Institute, Mysore Road, 8th Mile, Bangalore 560059. E-mail: raghavan@drtc.isibang.ac.in; ksragav@hotmail.com

RAJAN, T N

C-343, East-end Apts. Mayurvihar Ph. 1 Ext. Delhi 110 096; Ph.011- 22742362

RATNAKAR, A

O 13, 'Niveditakunj', Sector X, R K Puram, New Delhi 110022, India. E-mail: aspari_r@hotmail.com

RAVICHANDRA RAO, I K

Professor and Head, Documentation Research and Training Centre, Indian statistical Institute, 8th Mile, Mysore Road, Bangalore 560 059.

E-mail: ikrrao@hotmail.com

SANKARAIAH, K

Regional Librarian, British Council Libraries, South India (Retd.) Chennai

Contact: 'Padmalaya', 58, Fathima Nagar, 3, Kurinji Street, Valasaravakkam, Chennai - 600 087. Tel: 044 - 2486 1240, E-mail : sankariahk@dataone.in

SATYANARAYANA, R

Professor & Head (Retd.). Faculty of Library & Information Science, Indira Gandhi National Open University, New Delhi

SEETHARAMA, S

Professor & Head (Retd.), DRTC, Indian Statistical Institute, Bangalore 560 059

Contact: 17, Vardarajulu Naidu Street, Egmore, Chennai 600 008

SEETHARAMAN, M N

Consultant, Information Systems & Services, 502, 3rd Cross, 7th Main, HAL II Stage, Bangalore 560 008 E-mail: mns27@hotmail.com Ph: 080-25285837

SEN, B K

Scientist & Head (Retd.), Training Division, National Institute for Science Communication & Information Resources (CSIR), New Delhi

Contact: 80 Shivalik Apartments, Alaknanda, New Delhi - 110019. Email: bksen@airtelmail.in

VIVEK PATKAR

Independent Research Scholar. Contact details: D-1, Anita Cooperative Housing Society, Plot No.612, Sector 6, Charkop, Kandivali (West), Mumbai – 400 067. e-mail: vnpatkar2004@yahoo.co.in

YOGESHWAR, R

Retired industrial consultant, **Contact**. 39 rue deL'Ecole, L-9184, Schrondweiler (Grand Duchy) Luxembourg.

E-mail: chriyog@pt.lu